Penelope Green was born in _____ ____ ____
journalist around Australia fo__ __.__ade before moving to
Rome in 2002. Her first book, the bestselling *When in
Rome* (2005), won the Grollo Ruzzene Foundation Prize
in the Victorian Premier's Literary Awards. *See Naples and
Die* was shortlisted for the same award. Penelope writes
for various publications including *Australian Gourmet
Traveller*, *Madison* and *Marie Claire*, and now lives on
Procida, an island off the Campania coast near Naples.

Also by Penelope Green
When in Rome

SEE NAPLES AND DIE

Penelope Green

HACHETTE AUSTRALIA

To Pa, Dad and Alfonso

HACHETTE AUSTRALIA

This edition published in 2008

First published in Australia and New Zealand in 2007
by Hachette Australia
(An imprint of Hachette Livre Australia Pty Limited)
Level 17, 207 Kent Street, Sydney NSW 2000
Website: www.hachette.com.au

Reprinted 2007 (twice)

National Library of Australia
Cataloguing-in-Publication data

Green, Penelope.

See Naples and die : The crimes and passions of
Italy's darkest jewel

ISBN 978 0 7336 2289 2 (pbk.).

1. Green, Penelope. 2. Women journalists - Italy - Naples -
Biography. 3. Minority journalists - Italy - Naples -
Biography. 4. Australians - Employment - Italy - Naples -
Biography. 5. Naples (Italy) - Social life and customs. I.
Title.

070.4332092

Front and inside cover design by Christabella Designs
Cover photograph of Penelope Green by Fabio Cuttica
All other photos by Penelope Green
Text design by Bookhouse and Christabella Designs
Digital production by Bookhouse
Printed in Australia by Griffin Press, Adelaide

Hachette Australia would like to thank the following for their kind permission to
reproduce copyrighted material in this book: Tullio Pironti Editore for extracts
from Matilde Andolfo's *Il Diario di Annalisa*, I.B. Tauris & Co. Ltd for
extracts from Tom Behan's *See Naples and Die: The Camorra and Organised
Crime*. All correspondence has been reproduced with the permission of the authors.

'Fill You In' words and music by Josh Pyke © Mushroom Music.
All rights reserved. International copyright protected. Reproduced with permission.

Vide Napule e po muore

NEAPOLITAN

See Naples and then die

Rome, December, 2004. It was the headline that made me stop at the newsstand. It was just before Christmas and I was in my local inner-city piazza, where a couple of urchins were booting around a soccer ball to the general amusement of passers-by.

'Napoli e sangue. Naples and blood' screamed the headline in fat white text rendered even more conspicuous by the bleak background hues. Then the subtitle:

'Piu di 120 morti in un anno. Un fatturato di 25 miliardi di euro. La Camorra controlla la città e nessuno riesce a fermarla. More than 120 deaths in one year. A turnover of 25 billion euro. The Camorra controls the city and no one can stop it.'

Naples, I knew, was the headquarters of the Camorra, the criminal clans that operate in the Campania region in Italy's south. Above the cover headline of *Internazionale*, a weekly Italian-language magazine, was an ominous photograph of Naples' skyline at dusk. The city's derelict apartment buildings looked forbidding amid the gloom. In the blue-grey background loomed Mount Vesuvius, its two humps resembling unevenly shaped breasts of a gigantic bust, cast, as if by chance, on the shores of the Gulf of Naples.

As I bought the magazine I thought of the morbid collection of magazine and newspaper articles stored among the hurriedly packed boxes I had left with my parents in Australia. That was before I quit my life in Sydney and moved to Italy in 2002 on a whim and a prayer.

I'd collected magazines splashed with the chilling image of Sydney road worker Ivan Milat, the so-called 'Backpacker Killer', who kidnapped seven young travellers unlucky enough to hitch a lift with him on a lonely stretch of a New South Wales highway, only to end up murdered in the depths of a thick forest. Every Sydney newspaper the day after Diana, Princess of Wales, died was also in the pile, including an ill-timed magazine with a cover story of Diana's 'new life' that had gone to print hours before news of her sudden demise reverberated around the world. Books on grisly topics, including *Mindhunter: Inside the FBI's Elite Serial Crime Unit*, were stacked high, full of gory details about the world's most evil assassins.

Serial killers, in particular, fascinated me. While I had been a reporter for *The Australian* newspaper in Perth, three young women were murdered by someone who remains at large. I was working on the Sunday the body of one of the victims was found in a paddock on the outskirts of the city, and I caught a taxi to the crime scene. Later I was interviewed by detectives who, at the time, suspected that a person driving a taxi might be behind the crimes, which explained how the young women had seemingly disappeared into thin air. Well-versed in the fact that serial killers often can't resist returning to the scene of a crime – to relive the thrill of their heinous acts – my blood ran cold. Had I hailed a taxi driven by a serial killer moonlighting as a cabbie?

I absorbed *Internazionale* magazine's cover story. Naples was in the grip of a bloody Camorra turf war, where rival clans were clamouring for the biggest chunk of a billion-dollar drugs market. In particular, the destitute outlying neighbourhoods, or *quartieri*, of Scampia and Secondigliano were attracting headlines. Not content with slaying each other, members of the Camorra had abandoned their unwritten code, and were now killing friends and family members of rivals, including the innocent.

In one of the most chilling cases, fourteen-year-old Annalisa Durante was gunned down metres from her front door, her only crime being that she was in the wrong place at the wrong time. The schoolgirl, with long blonde tresses and a melting smile, was struck by one of a hail of bullets fired when two hired killers, or *sicari* (as they are known to locals), riding motorbikes attempted to assassinate the son of a local Camorra boss – who saved his own skin by dragging Annalisa across his body as a human shield.

Having satisfied my morbid curiosity, I stowed the magazine among the meagre possessions in my rented room and promptly forgot about Naples, whose woes seemed remote from life in the Eternal City.

A year passed before I had reason to dwell on Naples again. Back in Rome after a holiday in Australia, I was becoming increasingly frustrated about my future in Italy. Almost three years had passed since I had fled Australia in a pre-turning-thirty crisis and now I had half a mind to return to my homeland. Until now, I had been content chasing *la dolce vita*, waitressing and working in a wine bar as I learnt the language that would, I hoped, enable me to eke out an existence as a freelance journalist. But the insecurity of being a roving reporter was starting to weigh down as much as my sporadic restaurant shifts – no matter how good the idea, magazine editors never have generous budgets.

The novelty of being *una straniera* – a foreigner – in Rome was also wearing thin. I yearned for a real job to help me determine if I was capable of developing a career in Italy and, more importantly, if I wanted to stay put for life. In short, unless I found the job of my dreams, or the love of my life, I couldn't justify hanging around.

Finding an Italian stallion seemed improbable. A string of romances, while entertaining at first, had left me with the overwhelming impression that although Italian men were more than happy to date an exotic foreigner, they would never see me as real potential, as if scared I would pack up my bags at any minute and move on. Italian men, it seemed, liked to settle down with their own, as the saying goes, *moglie e buoi dei paesi tuoi*, or 'wives and oxen from your own country'.

Love conquers all. What piffle. If in Australia I had dated a legion of men who were lifelong members of the No Commitment Party, in Italy I had yet to date *un ragazzo* who wasn't attached to his mother's apron strings. Cupid, I was convinced, would not find me in Italy, where ninety per cent of the Italian men I knew were *mammoni* – mummy's boys who still lived with their parents and slept in single beds. My only two Anglo girlfriends with Italian boyfriends had met their partners outside Italy, and would swallow thumb tacks to avoid a rendezvous with their betrothed's suffocating *famiglia*.

The cultural divide can crumple the most promising of blossoming rapports. If on the one hand I dreamt of meeting Romeo to give substance to my Italian life, on the other, I loathed the idea that I was waiting for a man to complete my existence. Half the reason I'd moved to Rome was because I was fed up waiting for Mr Right. Patience is not one of my virtues. I had wanted to take charge of my life.

And I couldn't complain about the results. In Italy, I had managed to change the course of my life. I was realising my dream of living in a country I had always adored and learning the language; and, I was enjoying work, indeed life, once again.

But what now? It's all good flying by the seat of your pants when your hips ease into tight jeans, but my love handles were growing and, to my surprise, I had caught myself thinking that children might be more than scary little monsters best hidden from public view.

Then suddenly the distraction I so desperately needed just fell into my lap. Through a contact, I landed a permanent job in Naples. The day I found out, a frisson swept through me as my mind flashed to my souvenired copy of *Internazionale*.

Naples, bloody Naples.

Like many tourists, I had passed briefly through Naples, en route to the picturesque Amalfi Coast, a playground for the rich and famous with private moorings in the postcard villages of Positano and Amalfi. But now I would be *living* in Naples, working as editor on the English website of ANSA*med*, a news agency about the Mediterranean created by ANSA, Italy's oldest news organisation.

And so, within a week of moving back to Italy and settling happily into a new share house in Rome, I found myself preparing to relocate to Naples: another new city to adapt to, with no friends at hand and no home to speak of.

The position that awaited me, I was told, would be relatively dull at first, editing largely economic content for the website. Numbers and I had never added up: I studied the lowest level of maths in high school, 'vegie' maths, and leave my tax return to an accountant each year. But the position, I was assured, would become more interesting as the website grew to include more feature articles and stories on the arts, music, culture and religion. And there would be other benefits. For the first time in four years I wouldn't have the stress of trying to extend or change my visa, or worse, living illegally in Italy. Better still, I would have a decent, fixed wage. When I first arrived in Rome I was earning 480 euro a month for six days work a week as a waitress and paying 360 euro in rent. While I never wanted for anything, the idea of having cash to splash on a few luxuries was appealing.

Then there was the ocean. My trips to the sea near Rome had always left me yearning for home, where waves crash mercilessly onto yellow sand, and bodysurfing in cappuccino froth is a basic human right. Naples was right on the sea and close to idyllic destinations like Capri and Sicily, one of my favourite Italian destinations. All I needed to do was make the right contacts and my summers could be spent flitting from port to island on a handsome yacht.

But if I'm honest, I must confess that my motives for wanting to move south were built on more sinister foundations. When I fished out the copy of *Internazionale* to examine the inside photograph of a massive police raid to capture one of the Camorra kingpins, I could almost smell the gunpowder.

The adventurer in me was reawakened.

In my last frantic days in Rome, I began to read up on Naples and the Camorra. I knew Naples is one of the biggest cities in Italy today, but I didn't know it was once the third largest in Europe, and the glorious capital of the Kingdom of the Two Sicilies under a Spanish Bourbon monarchy in the sixteenth century. Some say the term 'Camorra' comes from the jacket worn by Spanish bandits known as *gamurri*, others claim it hails from the secret Spanish criminal society Garduna, operating in the late Middle Ages before arriving in Spanish-occupied Naples. Or maybe, as others purported, it simply comes from the Spanish word *morra*, whose various meanings include 'to fight or brawl'.

I learnt that the Camorra began decades before the Mafia, but many – including me, at least until now – err in placing the two bad eggs in the same criminal basket. While Sicily's Mafia is a relatively organised, pyramid system of power with one kingpin at the top, the Camorra is made up of groups that vary in structure according to their territorial influence, organisation, economic strength and modus operandi. Thus, the Camorra is far more volatile than the Mafia, with frequent outbreaks of violence like the *faida*, or feud, I read about in *Internazionale* magazine.

The more I read, the more my curiosity grew, and the night before I left Rome, I sat chatting at the dinner table with two of my flatmates, both of whom were born and bred in Naples. Adriano and Massimilliano (Massi for short) left because they found it too chaotic, with too few employment opportunities. Determined to remain positive about the challenge ahead, I nonetheless grilled them for information as they attempted to teach me phrases in the Neapolitan dialect. And just when I was starting to feel confident in Italian!

'*La prima cosa che si impara a Napoli…*' Adriano began, telling me that the first thing you learn in Naples is to flatten yourself against walls and turn around every time you hear a motorbike behind you.

'It's a habit I haven't lost,' admitted Adriano, who chose Rome over Naples seven years earlier. 'People can rob you or simply annoy you, who knows…hit you with a long tube of cardboard, like they did for a few months every time I was walking near my house in the Spanish Quarter. Naples is not a tranquil city, but you learn to live with this.'

'After being terrorised,' continued Adriano, taking a swig of his red wine as if he was only just warming up, 'I would tell you to hang in the piazza, because Naples is the city of bumping into people in the street, of spontaneous invitations, of days passed with people you don't know but you follow them, to their houses, to their parties.'

One of the reasons I left Sydney was because I'd grown tired of the rat race, of having to make appointments a week in advance to pin down even the dearest of friends. My hopes rose as I imagined myself gaily tailing locals around Naples, like one of the mice scurrying at the heels of the Pied Piper.

'Then,' he continued, shredding my fairytale, 'you will learn that Naples is a city of appointments that are made but never respected, of telephone numbers exchanged but never used – because the classic idea is "in Naples you will bump into so and so" – so there is no need to make an effort.

'You will go crazy, sometimes, when someone tells you "I'll call you, naturally we'll hear from each other, let's make a time to meet" – and then you never hear from anyone. Why don't they call? I don't know – in Naples you just don't.'

Listening intently, I asked Adriano and Massi how the average Neapolitan was different to the average Italian. Massi was the first to offer his opinion.

'Neapolitans are inherently relaxed towards life and seek to run from effort wherever possible,' he said simply.

Fine by me, I thought, conscious of the fact that the Italian lifestyle – famous for its indulgence of food, free time and general pleasure – had already made me three times calmer, if not disorganised, than the stressed robot I had resembled in Sydney.

'Naples is a city that has suffered continuous dominations and invasions and this has rendered it – more than anything – tolerant

8

towards and curious about diverse cultures, races and customs,' concluded Massi.

For Adriano, who admitted he left the city not just for a new job in Rome but because he felt suffocated by 'everything and everyone', the hallmark of a Neapolitan is the absolute absence of faith in the rules of coexistence, and in the institutions that should guarantee order and respect in a community.

'Even Sicily, with the Mafia, has an order of power, but Naples hasn't – the Camorra is about absolute anarchy,' said Adriano. 'They organise themselves alone, in their own groups, look to concrete objectives and are more cunning.'

On that note, Massi cut in. 'Never, ever, *ever* wear anything valuable or carry anything precious with you,' he warned, his playful disposition hardening suddenly before returning in a flash. 'More than anything, keep your eyes wide open and don't take everything that you hear seriously.'

I rubbed my thumb over the delicate, white-gold and ruby ring on my right ring finger. It had belonged to my late grand-mother and in the fifteen years since she had died, I'd only taken it off once, on a previous overseas trip. During that time, my mother had worn it, twisting it on her finger every day, she later confessed, as her way of keeping me safe from harm.

Returning to my room after dinner, I slid the ring off my finger with reluctance and put it in a small jewellery purse for safekeeping, telling myself I was sensible enough to play by the rules in a city infamous for petty street crime. Still, I couldn't help but feel naked. It was as if I had relinquished my guardian angel, my grandmother Oriel.

See Naples and then die, said the German scholar Johann Goethe after visiting the city in the late eighteenth century.

But would I leave Naples in one piece?

Fatte l'amice 'ntiempo e pace ca te servono 'nteimpo e guerra

Make friends in tranquil times, because they can help you in difficult moments

As the Naples-bound 7.25 am Intercity Plus train edges away from Rome's Termini station, I scan the headlines of the Italian newspaper in my hand. Savvy travellers know ye who holds a *Lonely Planet* guide or map is asking for trouble. Ride a bike in Amsterdam, brandish a baguette in France: whatever helps you to blend into the landscape.

I examine my fellow passengers on the sly. A couple in their fifties are leafing through a telltale *Rick Steves* guidebook, the bible of many American tourists. Thin and pale, the woman has a worn expression and a peace tattoo on her lily-white left ankle. The man sitting in the window seat beside her occasionally looks up from the guidebook to watch the scenery flashing by. Opposite him a bespectacled Italian man, old enough to be on the pension, attempts English now and then with the tourists. Across from me is his wife, overdressed Italian-style in designer jeans, a sequinned top, and large, tinted sunglasses covering her face.

The Americans seem somewhat preoccupied.

Content with my newspaper and jittery about what faces me in Naples, I've decided not to show my hand, knowing the minute I give away my nationality I'll have to face a string of questions I don't really feel like answering.

But something is bothering me: the tourists both wear rings and watches.

Days earlier Naples had made international headlines when the local council announced a new scheme aimed at protecting tourists from the city's notorious *scippo*, or bag snatch, typically performed by young hoodlums on motorbikes. Tourism officials had earmarked 40,000 euro to fund a plan to give visitors cheap plastic watches, in a bid to encourage them to leave their Rolexes in hotel safes when sightseeing. The plastic watches, adorned with a picture of one of the city's two most famous images – the Gulf of Naples backed by Mount Vesuvius, or a pizza Margherita, invented in Naples – would be accompanied by a brochure with tips on how to stay out of trouble.

Perhaps it's that the Americans are my parents' age that eventually forces me to pipe up.

'Without wanting to sound alarmist, it might be a good idea to remove anything valuable…like your wedding rings,' I tell the couple, following it up with what I'd heard about the tourist initiative.

Thanking me for my concern, the man then asks me a few general questions about the city. As I attempt to answer, the Italian woman, sitting opposite me, interrupts.

'Sarebbe una buona idea di dirgli di non portare oggetti di valore cosí in evidenza…'

'I've already told them,' I say, glad to have my instincts justified. But as I start to chat to the Italian lady, I can't help but notice she is Bulgari personified, flashing four rings on each hand, shiny bracelets and a necklace worthy of Ivana Trump.

'Pardon me for being so frank,' I say, 'but why are *you* wearing so much jewellery if Naples is, as you say, dangerous?'

'This stuff?' the woman says with a throaty laugh. 'It's worth nothing – I bought it at a street stall.'

Suzy and Delfo are Neapolitans returning from a weekend trip to Pisa. I act as translator in the three-way conversation that ensues and discover that, far from heading to Positano or Pompeii on a whirlwind holiday, the Americans are set to stay in Naples for six months. Suffering cancer, the woman has booked herself into a local hospital that offers treatment unavailable in the United States.

Dismayed at this revelation, Delfo urges me to translate an important message to the Americans. 'Stazione Centrale, the train station in Naples, is not nice for tourists, and these people are already traumatised,' he says. 'Tell them that we'll take them to the taxi stand…and they must pretend they're good friends of ours. That way the taxi driver will treat them better, because we're locals.'

'It's embarrassing for us to say,' adds Suzy, 'but as much as we love our city, it can be dangerous…Sometimes we're not proud to be Neapolitan.'

When I translate their message, tears well in the eyes of the Americans. Touching his chest in a gesture of affection, the man stutters *grazie* and urges me to thank the locals.

We are strangers on a train, but Suzy and Delfo's solicitude seems to verify the reputation Neapolitans have in Italy for being *simpaticissimi* – extremely friendly. As the train nudges into stazione Centrale, I swap numbers with the locals, who also insist on giving their contact details to the tourists, and I offer to translate for them if they need me to.

Suzy works for the local *metropolitana*, the railway authority, and I readily accept her offer to meet for a coffee one day at the station, curious about the transport hub, which has the worst reputation in Italy, if not in the First World, as a magnet for all things noxious.

As I walk along the platform my thoughts fill with emails from friends about their experiences of arriving in Naples by train. Backpacking around Europe, a girlfriend on a budget found herself killing time in the station's waiting room overnight before boarding an early morning train. Unable to sleep on a plastic chair, she lay down on a piece of cardboard on the floor, only to wake up to find two women seated on the chairs above her head.

'More girls than women, these dark-eyed females had fiercely patrolled the heated waiting room with their well-laden trolleys in the earlier hours of the night,' my friend had written to me. 'I remember how the ugliness of their voices – loud, strident and self-assured – seemed wrong given their youth. And I think about how they looked out of place in that waiting room, like well-fed high school girls on an expedition to sneer at the witless and lost.'

Then there was a British friend who stepped into Piazza Garibaldi, the large concrete piazza at the front of the station where taxis and buses converge. 'I didn't hear a thing, but all of a sudden I felt something yanking on my shoulder,' she said of the motorbike bandit who whistled past to claim handbag booty including well-padded wallet, air ticket and mobile phone.

An Australian acquaintance alighting from a train was approached by a man flogging a video camera for 100 euro. Warned by his friend that it was a sham, he ignored the tout and headed to Capri for a day trip. Arriving back on land in Naples, however, he couldn't resist the second approach of another street hawker.

The strapping Brisbane lad carefully examined the goods, complete with cables and batteries and packaging, before handing over a single, green euro bank note, still crisp from the ATM machine. He was almost at the train station when, smug about his bargain purchase, he peeked into the box. Inside was a large rock and shreds of newspaper.

Furious, he nonetheless had to give full points to the *furbizia*, or cleverness, of the vendor, recalling the moment when his eyes had strayed from the merchandise during the haggling.

Perhaps my favourite Naples arrival story, though, belongs to a colleague of an Italian friend who alighted at Piazza Garibaldi one steamy summer day to attend a global architects' summit. Shocked and dismayed by the absolute chaos erupting around him, he went back inside the station and leapt on the next ride to Rome. By the time the summit organisers called him, worried about his late arrival, he was already enjoying a stroll near the Pantheon.

I arrive at the end of the platform and notice a gaggle of Polish women with gold-plated teeth gathering on concrete seats. They chatter and, take-away coffee in hand, nibble on sweets that bear no resemblance to *cornetti*, the traditional Italian breakfast pastry.

I dodge a few drunk or drugged itinerants before emerging into sunlight at Piazza Garibaldi. Beneath a clutch of palm trees, fifteen taxis queue. On the pavement beside them sit groups of down-and-outs, sipping beer and smoking as if in their own lounge rooms.

In the face of all things Neapolitan, the chaotic Eternal City suddenly seems like Zurich.

The aural assault comes first: shouting from the rowdy loiterers and street marketeers, the screech and roar of brakes and throttles of motorbikes and cars and honking public buses, the incessant beeping and ringing of mobile phones.

Having already examined a map on the train, I make my way to Corso Umberto I, the main thoroughfare that leads to the city centre. Accustomed to Italian traffic (or so I think), I walk out onto the zebra crossing in a bid to force the cars to stop. Instead, they just swerve. Road rage engulfs me.

Along the corso, scores of NBL-tall African men sell fake handbags by Gucci, Prada and Dior, which they display on conspicuously white sheets used to cover the filthy street. Their eyes keenly survey the territory around them, their limbs at the ready to bundle up their stash and take flight if the authorities even look like they're on the approach.

A few bars, or cafes, have small stalls outside selling *sfogliatelle*, which I learn is the famous local pastry filled with ricotta, a few bits of candied fruit and a dash of lemon. They come in two forms: *riccia,* made of a rippled, filo-like pastry and shaped in a shell; and the scone-shaped *frolla,* made of a more standard dough.

Rubbish is everywhere. Bags overflow from street bins and accumulate in crude stacks in the rabbit warren of streets leading off the main drag. Has the city got a garbage disposal system? It seems not.

Within twenty minutes I arrive at the office of ANSA*med.*

I'm in Naples for a quick meet and greet before moving to the city within a week. Stepping into the elevator I realise I can't go anywhere until I put a five cent coin in the slot of a small box. The doorman tells me the money is collected for the maintenance of the building. In my three years in Italy I've never seen such a contraption, but it's a good way to get rid of all the brown coins at the bottom of my purse.

In the office I shake hands with a group of people who will be my colleagues, but I forget their names within seconds. Predominantly in their early thirties, like me, they seem pleasant enough. My two older bosses, Mario and Enrico, take me out to lunch at a nearby trattoria. I find myself lost for words, which often happens when I'm nervous and want to speak decent Italian. Flustered, I try to engage them in conversation, telling them I'm looking forward to developing the website, but I get as much interest as I would when trying to talk to my dad when the Wallabies are playing.

I escape happily to go for a stroll before heading back to the station. Walking along via Toledo, the main shopping strip of Naples, I come to the roundabout of the beautiful Piazza Trieste e Trento, where I sneak a look at my guidebook to read about the impressive church of San Francesco di Paolo, a mini-version of the Pantheon. A small pang of Rome-sickness tugs at my chest.

I stop in at nearby Gambrinus, the frescoed, chandeliered cafe where tourists pay three times the usual amount for a cappuccino, simply so they can sit down on the plush furniture in the elegant salon. Electing to stand at the bar, I order an espresso and am reminded of one of the small joys of my new home. Apart from having what most Italians agree is the best coffee in the nation (rivalled only by Sicily), in Naples customers typically receive a complimentary glass of mineral water before the coffee is served. It amuses me that Naples, up to its neck in poverty, gives away what you must pay for in other Italian cities.

I use the time it takes for the barista to crank the coffee machine into action to check out the others standing at the bar. Eye candy, zero. But the gesticulations of the two men talking beside me keep me entertained. I try to eavesdrop, but the southern dialect is almost impossible to decipher, with a heavy accent on the letter 's'. *Aspetta*, meaning 'wait' in Italian, for example, becomes a slurred *aspett*, pronounced 'ashpet' in Neapolitan. Accustomed to the guttural Roman lilt, to me the Neapolitans sound sloshed.

The barman puts an espresso before me and, in my rush for caffeine, I narrowly avoid third degree burns to my lips. I drop my gaze to see that the espresso cups sit in a tray full of boiling hot water. I learn that unless I'm keen for plastic surgery, I must wait for my cup to cool, or ask for one that is not being 'disinfected' in the simmering tray.

I leave a tip on the bar and walk out, cross the piazza and arrive at via Partenope, a section of the street that changes names as it snakes along the Gulf of Naples. Following it back towards the station, I try to shut my left nostril to the smog of the afternoon traffic snarl and breathe in the salty gust of the Tyrrhenian Sea to my right, while trying not to pine for the peaceful coastal walks I used to enjoy at Bondi.

Four days later and dusty from a farewell party in Rome, I find myself racing to Termini station again to jump on a south-bound train. This time, however, I'm heading to Naples indefinitely. I've left behind most of my belongings and carry a wardrobe to last until I find somewhere to live. My mind whirs with all the random thoughts of recent days. After three years Rome has finally started to feel like home, filled with people and places I treasure: new and old flatmates, my adopted family at Il Nolano, the wine bar where I worked for two years, and expatriate friends; streets like via Governo Vecchio and its weird and wonderful boutiques and thrift shops, the Pantheon, which I rode to on my bike at least once a day to sneak a peek at its beautiful dome and take in the energy of the piazza…Am I making a mistake?

'If you think Romans are entertaining, wait till you get to Naples!' said Betta, one of my old flatmates, two days ago over coffee in our favourite piazza in inner-city Monti. 'You'll soon find your feet, and it's not like you're abandoning Rome for good – it's not that far away!'

I know she's right, I'd always have Rome, but am I really ready for a new challenge?

In a daze I scramble onto a train with my flatmate Adriano, who is returning to his hometown to see his family. He reassures me that Roberto, his cousin in Naples, will be invaluable in helping me find new digs. For the weekend, at least, I can stay at the home of Adriano's brother, Paolo, and his young family. I'm relieved to have some company on my first weekend in a new city, especially as Adriano has promised to introduce me to his friends. Once again I'm going to be a foreigner in a new town. It took so long to form a close group of friends in Rome, and I suddenly feel tired at the thought of starting from scratch again.

I take a deep breath and close my eyes. I know Rome is dissolving outside the window, giving way to farms and villages. Excitement slowly overtakes my nerves.

An hour and a half later we alight at Mergellina, one stop before stazione Centrale. It makes sense to get off at the earlier stop, because it's closer to Paolo's home. But I suspect, too, that Adriano wants me to see the nicer side of his Naples, where instead of the stench of rubbish, urine, beer and human desperation that plagues the inner-city there is a mild sea breeze and opulent homes with million-dollar views and realty prices to match.

We walk to a nearby bar and *pasticceria* on the promenade, separated from the gulf by a stream of traffic. After pulling up chairs at an outside table, we order cappuccinos and warm *sfogliatelle* delivered by a tubby man in a white tuxedo jacket.

A horn honks and we look up to see Paolo, his wife, Francesca, and their two young daughters, Chiara and Alice, double-parked across the street.

Scooping one of the girls onto his lap, Adriano jumps in the front seat as I hop in the back. The car skirts along the ocean, past the rock sea wall and boats bobbing in small ports before we pull up on a corner and spill out of the car to buy fish from the back of a small *Ape* truck. With skin as scaly as his merchandise, the vendor chats merrily as he tosses squid and clams into a bag, throwing in a fish for free as he is ready to close.

Squashed like sardines in the car, we head further along the gulf to arrive at Posillipo, which Adriano explains is one of the most exclusive suburbs in Naples. Located in a terracotta-coloured palazzo beside an old fortress perched above sea rocks, Francesca and Paolo's elegant home reminds me of a soap opera set. By no strange coincidence, *Un Posto al Sole,* one of Italy's most successful early evening dramas, is shot in a building in the same street. Their split-level apartment is modern and light-filled, with wooden floors, open-plan living areas and at least three balconies overlooking the sea. I walk around enviously, having always dreamt of living in a house where I could wake to see the ocean from my bed.

Francesca prepares lunch, an entree of pasta with a scrumptious sauce of swordfish, tomatoes and tarragon, then a plate of various seafood she fries in a huge saucepan of bubbling oil. I make a silent note to angle for more lunch invitations in the future.

Adriano and I sleep for two hours on couches in the spare room before hopping onto a battered, blue Piaggio scooter and heading into the *centro storico,* or historic centre. As we hurtle along I notice that the majority of the *motorini* we pass are just as vintage, in varying states of decay and in beautiful colours, from fire-engine red and classic mint green to perky purple and orange. At least half the motorbike riders are not wearing helmets. It's a national law, and one of many sneezed at in the wild South, where locals created headlines when, to thwart mandatory seatbelt laws, they designed a white T-shirt with the imprint of a black slash on the front.

We park near Villa Comunale, once the royal gardens. There are plastic swings for the kids, but the caged iron fence encircling the park gives it an eerie feel that I imagine lingers from dawn to dusk.

Prada and Gucci are among the ritzy boutiques that line the street leading from the villa to Piazza dei Martiri. A few steps away, I stumble on a peculiar sight in contrast to the moneyed surrounds: jutting from a second-storey shop window is an enormous, yellow, papier-mâché dragon, its long neck stretching out a good metre so its gaping mouth can 'chew' the leaves at the top of a tree growing in the street below. In a touch of King Kong-inspired class, emerging from the monster's mouth amid the tangle of leaves are the shapely legs of a mannequin clad in black fish-net stockings and red stilettos. Written on the adjacent wall is the Freudian phrase *l'insaziabile fame dell'inconscio,* 'the insatiable hunger of the unconscious'. Near the trunk of the tree, a gypsy in a stained cardigan sits on the pavement, a plastic cup at her feet.

Adriano and I make our way along via Chiaia, one of the most exclusive streets in the suburb of the same name, where swank shops and bars blare radio-friendly tunes. At 5 pm on a Saturday we've hit the post-lunch *passegiata* hour, when locals with nothing better to do stretch their legs and window-shop. As my eyes rove I notice the graceful facades and the washing that hangs from almost every window, a reminder of domestic routine amid the commercial hubbub.

Arriving at Piazza Plebiscito, a gust of salty air arrives from the gulf. I can't wipe the smile off my face. Change, I remind myself, is good for the soul and my Piscean spirit surges: I am once again living close to the sea.

Adriano knocks on a door. We head up a long corridor with stained white walls then a flight of steps to arrive in a small gallery where his cousin Roberto is attending an art show and poetry evening. We wait for a woman to finish reading and then a slight man with woolly black hair and a joker smile approaches and gives Adriano a bear hug.

Having promised to help me find accommodation, Roberto says he has found me temporary digs at the home of Francesco and Carlo, two friends who live in the *centro storico*. I inspected a bleak serviced apartment on my last trip, so I'm more than happy to have company while I search for a new home.

In a wine bar I expect never to find again, Roberto and Adriano introduce me to one of my new flatmates, Francesco. Slightly taller than me, he has curly hair, a strange cross between a goatee and a beard, and an outfit rivalling Starsky and Hutch: slightly worn, too-tight woollen pants, a 1970s Yves Saint Laurent tie, and a corduroy jacket. A pair of Camper shoes are the only clue that he is abreast of current trends.

Francesco and I chat as he leads us towards his home and I laugh out loud as he chastises me for walking too fast. He lights a cigarette and ceremoniously announces that we have arrived at Piazza del Gesu, its cobblestoned centre dominated by a towering, spiralled obelisk topped with a statue of the Virgin Mary, or Madonna, as she is called in Italy. We continue up Spaccanapoli which, notes Francesco, literally means 'split Naples', because the street slices neatly through the centre of old Naples, before abruptly hooking right. Slipping through a palazzo door into a small courtyard, I notice there is no lift, so I follow Francesco up the stairs. I rest on the sixth floor and watch him take yet another set of narrow stairs that lead to a rooftop terrace. There, seemingly added as an afterthought, are three flats. Huffing, Francesco unlocks the middle door.

In the small entrance lounge room a red leather divan adds a touch of class to what is clearly a student house, complete with a white-painted Zincalume ceiling. Down a small step, the brown-laminated kitchen offers a bird's-eye view of the neighbourhood, including two churches and the obelisk in Piazza del Gesu.

The same mesmerising panorama is the showpiece of the boys' rooms, which are furnished with single beds. Across the hall, with a window the size of a coffee-table book, is a room as 'cosy' as the stuffy bathroom adjacent. An ugly plastic desk, small bedside table and single bed take up almost every inch of floor space. I eye them with dread.

I thank Francesco for his generosity (I can stay for free if I find myself a new home within two weeks, beyond that 'a 200 euro contribution per month is welcome'), and tell him I'll be 'home' tomorrow, as he hands me a set of spare keys.

The night descends into a bar crawl steered by Francesco, Adriano and Roberto. We start at Superfly, a hip bar a few blocks away, which has walls decorated with 1970s ties – one of Francesco's favourite haunts, perhaps by no coincidence. A DJ plays cheeky lounge tunes at the end of the bar, his face contorted in concentrated pleasure as he lovingly fingers the vinyls. We bump into a handful of friends and head to Mutiny, a nightclub celebrating, in black and white on big screens behind the DJ, the closest Hollywood got to porn in the 1950s. By the time we reach the next bar I realise I'm the only girl standing and the boys are barely managing. *Christo*. In less than forty-eight hours I start an important new job. With addled logic, I tell myself it's equally important to meet as many people as I can before Adriano heads back to Rome.

Around 4 am we somehow get back in one piece to Posillipo on the Piaggio and wake in time for another delicious lunch prepared by Francesca. After rounds of grappa and coffee, night has fallen by the time Paolo, Adriano, Alice and I hop into the family's luxury four-wheel drive and head back towards the old town. I watch the fairytale palazzo disappear in the rear-vision mirror and note the change in scenery as we move from salubrious Posillipo to be slowly engulfed by the squalor of the inner suburbs. We wind in and out of dark streets devoid of human life and pass shadowy piazzas where people loiter in clusters.

I cling to little Alice, warm against my chest, and listen to my heart drum. What is it about Naples that makes it appear so menacing at night? How much about the crime rate and the Camorra is urban myth?

Paolo pulls up around the corner from Francesco's house. I thank him for the hospitality and Adriano walks me to the front door of my new palazzo. I struggle in vain to push the lump in my throat back to where it came from. After a weekend of plush surroundings, home-cooked meals and social thrills and spills, my only link to Naples is abandoning me in a ramshackle house with strangers. Sensing my panic, Adriano pecks me on the cheek and gives me an awkward embrace before disappearing into the night.

I fumble with the keys Francesco gave me, five in total. You can never lose your keys in Italy, they're so big, but carrying them around becomes a chore. I know, at least, that the largest key, which seems as heavy and as long as a spanner, fits the keyhole to the front door. I push it open with force and lug my gear through the small entrance.

After little more than a day in Naples I'm beginning to think the locals are stumpy for a reason. A random check of front doors reveals that at least half were built for dwarves: stooping is obligatory to avoid physical injury when entering or exiting. I unlock the next steel door, which leads to a stairwell on the left. It clangs shut behind me like a prison gate as I face the first of many stairs. Finally I'm on the roof-top terrace under the Milky Way.

Francesco and Carlo's flat is dark, empty and arctic, with no central heating in the bitter heart of winter. I dump my belongings in my room and make a cup of tea, then slip under a blanket on the couch.

Soon bored with channel-surfing mindless Italian television, I make a dash to my shoebox room to retrieve some books I bought on Naples, then snuggle back beneath the blanket to satisfy my latest crime fixation...

The Camorra is said to have started in Cagliari, Sardinia, in the thirteenth century, reaching Naples in the sixteenth century during the Spanish occupation. Recognised in 1820 as *Bella Società Riformata*, or Beautiful Reformed Society, it was viewed as a local phenomenon, with its members meeting in a local city church. Its urban appeal distinguished the Camorra from Sicily's Mafia and Calabria's *Ndrangheta*, known for their rural roots.

For centuries, I read, local powers failed to shrug off the Camorra, and used it to keep the masses in check. In turn, the Camorra exploited the administrative incompetence to fill its own coffers and guarantee 'protection' to a populace that felt abandoned by governments and institutions. It became a culture, an economic system – a state in itself. Today more than two hundred Camorra clans operate in and around Naples, infiltrating public tenders, organising clandestine immigration, and drug trafficking...

At close to midnight my eyelids begin to drop and I conclude that my flatmates have retreated to the comfort of their family homes. Great. I'm living with a pair of *mammoni* who fly back to the nest at the slightest sign of discomfort. Wimps.

I find a rug in a cupboard and layer myself in a tracksuit and jumpers before hopping into bed. Dogs howl some place nearby and the wind rattles the furniture on the *terrazza*. In the middle of wondering if I've been too rash in uprooting my life again, I suddenly remember the one positive thing about sleeping in a single bed: body heat spreads fast.

A crack of lightning pierces my eardrums before rain pummels the tin roof. During my childhood in Tamworth, in rural New South Wales, my family lived for a short time in a tin shed as our new home was being built. When it rained, it seemed like Armageddon, water falling like bullets. Strangely comforted, I'm almost asleep when a text message beeps on my mobile phone. To my surprise, it's Suzy, the Neapolitan lady I met on the train.

Meeting near stazione Centrale the next day, Suzy says that she and her husband have failed to trace the American couple, who accidentally left a number missing a digit.

'*Delfo è passato in ospedale ma li non hanno voluto dargli informazione per via della legge sulla privacy*,' she says, explaining that her husband visited the hopsital, but the staff couldn't help because of patient privacy rules.

We decide to take a walk in the streets around the station, and as we weave among streets crowded with Chinese and African markets selling a strange hotchpotch of merchandise, Suzy talks openly about her thirty-three years working metres from the *stazione,* which she calls the 'black hole' of Naples.

'When I first came to work here the station was just like any other in the world – dangerous, yes, but not like today,' she says. 'It's very crowded because it's surrounded by poor areas, where people are without work, without anything.

'All of these tiny streets,' she continues, pointing around, 'are full of immigrants. Often twenty or thirty people live under the one roof in apartments they rent from Neapolitans who charge high rent and make them live like animals.'

When I venture to ask her about the Camorra, Suzy cuts to the chase. 'It directs everything… The markets here make so much, the Camorra wouldn't let an occasion slip them by.'

I scan the endless row of street stalls and the vendors with eyes as empty as their stomachs, selling goods from designer sunglasses to whitegoods, and wonder how slim their profit margin must be once the Camorra has taken its cut.

Suzy stops suddenly to point to Porta Capuana. It's one of the gates to the old city, she explains, with an impressive carved marble arch.

'Look,' she says with a huff, pointing to an ugly modern window in an apartment somehow built into the curve of the arch. 'No doubt one of the *camorristi* paid someone to build here – it's a disgrace.'

As we wind back through the fish-market, I stop beside a live octopus pushing its tentacles against the confines of a shallow bucket.

'It's not all fresh here,' Suzy warns. 'These people often freeze produce and throw it in sea water to thaw it out. When you buy *sardini*,' she adds with an air of conspiracy, 'don't buy the ones that have traces of red on them…It means they've travelled a long way to get here…'

Stopping for a coffee, Suzy is curious to know why I've moved to Naples.

'This is a final test after three years in Italy to work out if I want to stay here.'

Suzy's grey eyes flicker before she pecks me goodbye. 'I have a good feeling things will work out for you,' she says, slinging her shoulder bag over her neck. 'Stay in touch, and don't forget to call me whenever you need something…anything.'

Buoyed by my new friend's optimism, I make my way home along corso Umberto I, the main street leading from stazione Centrale.

As rain starts to fall I wait in anticipation. Sure enough, within seconds a street-seller clutching a range of coloured umbrellas appears from nowhere. Handing over a two euro coin, I turn to open my umbrella when I hear a din behind me.

Across two lanes of traffic I see the doors of a crowded orange transit bus fling open. A Chinese man, somehow juggling a wooden board to which he has tacked cheap jewellery, hesitates on the step. Blood streams from his nose and onto his grey tracksuit top. As the driver shouts for him to get off the bus, a passenger elbows her way through the crowd to hand him tissues.

The man steps onto the median strip and stands in the rain, his miserable figure attracting nothing more than a few fleeting stares. Misfortune doesn't appear to be a stranger to these parts.

I press on but can't erase the image of the man's bloodied tracksuit.

Napoli e sangue.

Fai l'arte che saie, ca si nun t'arricchisce camparraie

Do the work you know, even if it doesn't make you rich, it will help you get by

Neapolitans would sell their souls if they could get away with it.

In the sinners' paradise that is the historic centre, the locals are experts in what they refer to, with more than a pinch of pride, as *l'arte di arrangiarsi*: the art of arranging oneself, of doing whatever it takes to make ends meet.

In the fifteen-minute walk from Francesco and Carlo's home to work every morning, I navigate a path through a human circus. Metres from their front door loiters a fat, greasy haired man who holds a cardboard box on his belly, popcorn-vendor-style. Arranged neatly in it are rows of cigarette lighters. At the approach of a potential customer or a passer-by, the man grabs one of the lighters and flicks a flame that he watches with such enthusiasm you would swear it was the first time he'd seen fire.

Minutes later I pass another tubby chap pushing an over-loaded shopping trolley. Apparently comfortable with his niche market, he sells nothing but pile upon pile of tape measures, neatly rolled and fastened with rubber bands.

And if I have time for a quick walk before work, the free *spettacolo* continues…

On via Toledo, a colourful and intricately detailed painting is chalked on the concrete pavement by a bearded man, who looks more bikie than an artist. The subject is always religious, from a pensive *Gesu* to a serene Madonna with child. And at night the man covers his work with a plastic sheet that he fastens to the ground with masking tape. During the day, though, he is rarely there, yet miraculously, in a city known for its destruction or theft of anything of value, no one ever tries to ruin the chalk paintings, which range in size from a large poster to a sheet. I never hang around long enough to know how much time the paintings take to finish.

A metre from the enormous entrance to the Galleria Umberto – a domed, steel-and-glass arcade whose 127-year-old elegance is often compromised by loitering riffraff – a small, neatly dressed man pegs out his territory at seven-thirty sharp each morning. Through Coke-bottle glasses, he watches the commuter flow as if his life depended on it. Armed with a stool, a wood and brass box full of polish, and a rag, the man does his darnedest to cajole the owners of the feet that pass him to stop for a buff and shoeshine. When a customer appears, he dons white felt gloves and orders the client to raise their leg and place their shoe on a little ledge. When he sets to work, buffing here and buffing there, it's with a deft yet purposeful stroke of his hand, and all the rhythm of an orchesta conductor.

Within view of the shoeshine stall, another man sets up camp on a street off via Toledo, just before it hits Piazza Trieste e Trento. He puffs his chest out like a penguin and slips a cloth duck puppet onto his hand. Moving his fingers to open and close the orange beak, he alternately cheeps and blows a whistle with all his might in a bid to sell other puppets just like it.

Halfway along the Riviera di Chiaia, separated from the Gulf of Naples by Villa Comunale public gardens, I've become accustomed to the sight of a dumpy woman selling underwear. Amid the glamour of the *riviera*, she stands out like a bosom escaping a bikini. Dressed in a floral cotton frock that bargain-hunting *casalinghe*, housewives, buy off the rack at markets, she sits on a chair on the pavement with no other competition in sight and a bored expression on her face. Beside her is a square cart piled high with boxes of underwear that seem to have been on special for two decades, judging from the dusty wrapping. The fact that the woman is selling daggy knickers less than two steps from some of the richest real estate in Naples adds a strange, incongruous charm to the mix.

And just when I think I've decided upon my favourite hawker, balloon man emerges. He pulls a tyre pump from a dirty bag at his feet, blows up a bunch of balloons and then ties them to string. With his fist pumping the balloons to attract attention, he bursts into song for added effect. I've only once seen him actually sell a balloon.

If in Rome I had grown accustomed to the surprise and delight of locals who were impressed that I hark from an exotic, untamed slice of paradise, in Naples I soon learn just how unique I am. Not only am I from Down Under, but a good job has led me to a city battling one of the worst unemployment rates in the nation. In 2002 the Campania region (of which Naples is the capital) was dealing with twenty-one per cent unemployment, compared to the national average of nine per cent. And youth unemployment figures were even grimmer at almost sixty per cent, compared to twenty-seven per cent on a national level. After a few confrontations that leave me feeling guilty about my good fortune, I decide to tell the odd white lie if I suspect I'm not going to cross paths with my interrogator again – I'll say that I'm in town to study the language.

After two years juggling writing and waitressing jobs, full-time work comes as a shock. Notwithstanding my desire to use the journalistic skills I spent a decade honing in Australia, sitting hours on end in an office is nothing short of suffocating. In Rome, I might have lived off the smell of an oily rag, but there was a hefty upside: working freelance had given me the freedom to roam the streets, make appointments at my leisure and have lunch at home – followed by a powernap. On my walk to work during my first few weeks in Naples, I fight a sense of dread that seeps invisibly from the pavement and into my bones.

ANSA*med*'s headquarters is on the seventh floor of a building made up of offices and apartments. The first person to greet me when I walk into the 1970s-style, timber-panelled entrance at 10.30 am is the moustachioed doorman, standing with a cigarette in his mouth.

The office is one large space with white walls covered here and there with newspaper clippings. There are microwave-style computer terminals, a whiteboard, printer, two mounted televisions and a wall of windows and sliding doors leading out to a balcony stretching the length of the office. The balcony faces the apartments opposite; the residents hang their washing on the concrete railings and stand outside to smoke and ponder their lot. From the street below comes the babel of honking traffic, loud locals and the occasional car accidents that prompt us to rush to the balcony to watch the ensuing ballyhoo.

Although my bosses, Enrico and Mario, raise their eyebrows at me, I elect to work a nine-hour day, just as I would at home. The rest of my colleagues work an average eight hours, but my

Anglo–Aussie work ethic keeps me there. Given the circumstances, I'm also keen to show that I'm dedicated to the task at hand.

ANSA*med*, as the marketing spiel goes, is a news agency about the Mediterranean, *for* the Mediterranean, created by ANSA – *L'Agenzia Nazionale Stampa Associata*, or the National Associated Press Agency – a news agency founded by Italy's leading newspapers in 1945.

With partner news agencies from eighteen countries in the region, ANSA*med* has correspondents and collaborators in Lebanon, Morocco, Algeria, Turkey and Greece, among others, who file stories in English and Italian for us to edit and send live to the news wire in Italian, English and Arabic.

The Italian and English news desks occupy the large office space where I work, and the Arab desk is in a smaller room that adjoins our office. There, Iraq-born Mahmud takes a toke of a cigar alongside youthful Khalid, a Moroccan raised in Italy.

Until the site expands to include more feature articles and photos, it's all about trying to put some sizzle into a stream of largely dry economic stories. And as the new kid on the block and *capofila*, leader, of the English site, I find I have to tread carefully. It's not that my colleagues aren't friendly. On the contrary. But until I arrived they had collectively worked hard to do my job. I just want to do what I've been hired for, but it seems that my presence has put a few noses out of joint. Or maybe I'm just nervous, or paranoid, or both. In any case, I soon realise that I'm going to have to deal with something I've not had to face for three years: office politics.

One evening, noting my gloomy disposition, stormier after the eight-flight stair hike to our freezing student cave, Francesco lights the lone gas heater, pats his hand on the red leather divan and orders me to explain what's going on at work.

'Practically none of them is Neapolitan and none of them wants to be in Naples!' I spit out in frustration.

As *una straniera* I know I'll always see the charm in things that Italians take for granted. And my parents always encouraged me to make the best of what was at hand. So even though Naples often shocks me with its wretched poverty during the day, and scares me witless with its Wild West lawlessness at night, I'm trying to keep an open mind. But the prevailing attitude to Naples at work is bugging me. Eight out of my eleven colleagues were not born in the city and most seem to resent or regret their secondment, despite the fact that home for them is just a brief train ride or cheap plane ticket away. Half their luck!

Bureau boss Enrico is a fit-looking Roman with a smart-casual wardrobe; his leather moccasins always make me think of the luxury boat owner I have yet to meet. Driven to distraction by correspondents who don't pull their weight to file stories then spring into action only to send drivel, Enrico yells with rage from his office and steps onto the balcony to scream at the chaos below.

Chief-of-staff Mario, a snow-haired, sleepy eyed journalist with thirty years experience as a correspondent across the globe, is six months away from retirement. Every Friday he boards a fast train back to his family in Rome, returning on Monday just before noon, indifference etched on his face.

Benedetta, a feisty, opinionated thirty year old, seems to be the only one who embraces the city for better and worse, despite returning home to Rome every few weeks. A hard worker who dresses streetwise-hip and puffs Gauloise reds on the balcony, she is the colleague I identify with most, though her abrupt manner has me walking on eggshells.

Hailing from the region of Puglia, Annalisa is a slim girl with a sharp news sense, a wicked sense of humour and a Holly Golightly wardrobe. When I arrive at work she's often still hiding behind oversized 1960s sunglasses, which she sometimes leaves on until midday. She speaks a reasonably fluent, plummy English, thanks to the fact that her diplomat father moved the family to London when she was young.

Tania, short for Gaetana, is a vertically challenged, cheery Italian who was born in Toronto. Her Sicilian parents moved the family back to Italy when she was nine. She's no-nonsense and tenacious and I warm to her immediately; we work as a team on the English desk, and I appreciate her enthusiasm. A baker's daughter, she's always munching on a stash of goodies she keeps in her desk drawer (which I often raid), and has an endearing habit of ending points of conversation with *Tu immagini?* – 'Can you imagine?' She worked on a newspaper in Canada with Annalisa for a few years and tunes in to a Canadian radio station every week to listen to 'Funky Friday' hits.

Arriving a few weeks after me is Marco, a Neapolitan who has returned home after four years in Paris. Full of energy but easily distracted, he tells me early on that he's determined to view Naples anew in a bid to rediscover the streets he knows so well. With this outlook, he sets himself apart from the others in the office.

Naples-born Nando is a journalist cum computer whiz who solves all our technical problems with self-effacing cheer. Noting that I almost never leave the office for lunch – we're too busy, so I usually pack my own – Nando often kindly pulls me aside to check that I'm coping.

Another welcome face is Francesco, a cuddly local who works part-time on both the Italian and English desks. An unlit cigarette dangles continuously from his lips, and his razor-sharp wit often has everyone in hysterics, defusing office tensions he doesn't have to deal with full-time.

Alfonso is a tall, bespectacled, German-looking Italian from Salerno, about an hour's train ride away, though he rents a room in the same apartment block as Annalisa. After high school, he travelled to London on a whim and stayed for thirteen years, training as a journalist and working in the field. He's keen for a chat with anyone about current affairs, and his humour brightens the monotony of the daily grind.

In a bid to improve the standard of English on the site I gain Enrico's approval for a working system by which my colleagues, who alternate between the Italian and English news desks, give their edited stories to me for checking. I make any necessary corrections before we send the story live. My intention is to boost the general level of English in the office, so that when I'm not around the standard of writing on the site stays more or less the same.

Tania agrees at once, and within weeks I notice that she is polishing her already good English by tweaking the emphasis of stories to reveal buried leads, and stripping out propaganda that may have previously slipped through the editing process. To begin with I'm a bit timid about jumping into the new role because I've never been an editor before and I'm working in a totally foreign environment. While my colleagues seem genuinely helpful and interested in improving their English, at times I sense a slight antagonism in the office; it's like they're suspicious an outsider has suddenly been pulled in to monitor things that previously escaped surveillance.

So for the first few weeks I keep a low profile. If it takes me longer to learn the ropes it's because I sense resistance everywhere. But all I want to do is what I've been hired to do.

I want to fit in at work, but I decide to limit the amount I socialise with my colleagues outside the office. It's not only because they don't seem keen to connect with me, but like a wounded animal, I feel the need to retreat and protect my privacy.

The only person I trust instinctively is Carlo, the vice director of ANSA and the man who hired me. Full of can-do enthusiasm, he occasionally pops up from his office on the floor below to see his staff, crack a joke and monitor office morale. Intermittently I email him my thoughts for improving the English site, knowing he has more important things to worry about, but certain that he is listening.

'I have a feeling you're going to stay in Naples forever,' he says when I visit him in his office. 'But we need to find you a good pizza maker.' He winks at me and sinks his teeth into a cigar.

I'm not sure if he is right, but as the first few weeks roll past, I pester my colleagues for their thoughts on Naples, and learn that at least Enrico, Mario, Benedetta, Annalisa and Tania could be justified in their prejudice against it.

In May 2004, barely a month after they had each arrived in Naples to start their new jobs with ANSA*med*, the five went to a restaurant in the Quartieri Spagnoli, or Spanish Quarters, recommended to Benedetta by a Neapolitan friend.

'The dinner was really lovely, a relaxed atmosphere,' recalls Benedetta. 'It was the first time the five of us had gone out together after work.'

They left the restaurant just after eleven and Enrico and Mario led the group in Indian file down the narrow street, close to the wall to shelter from the rain and to avoid a garbage truck that had suddenly rounded the corner.

'I was the last in line, so I couldn't see much,' Benadetta says. 'Four young guys wearing sweat tops with hoods approached Mario and Enrico. Enrico reacted and whacked one of them with his briefcase before another kid pulled out a gun and pointed it at Mario, who had slipped on the wet pavement and fallen onto the ground.

'Annalisa, the first to see everything, turned around to us and yelled, "Let's go, let's get help!" Mario, meanwhile, pulled out his wallet and gave it to one of the kids. We made it back to the restaurant and everyone came out to help us, but the kids had run away.'

It was the first time Benedetta had seen a gun.

'Maybe it was fake, maybe not, but those fucking things!' she says in harsh Roman dialect. 'It was a trauma for all of us, for months none of us told our families...It was the "baptism of fire" that changed our perception of the city. It really scared us.'

After this, the first few months were difficult for Benedetta, but she soon found that Naples was forcing its way under her skin.

'Once I decided to "go with the flow", the city's response was splendid,' she says, then takes a sip of her *caffè macchiato* freshly delivered from the bar on the street below.

A common sight in downtown Naples is the stream of young boys in black pants and white shirts delivering round trays of coffee to office workers. The squad of young men who come to ANSA*med* often have us in stitches, updating us on their love lives and playing their Walkmans full blast.

As Benedetta talks on, her list of the city's delights makes my stomach rumble. 'The scent of warm tomato and stringy mozzarella on pizza fresh out of the oven at 11 am on a Saturday, when I walk down the street, still digesting my coffee. I love the smells...sweets, sauces, detergent, the sea. And then, I love the way women here don't hide their well-rounded features – instead they flaunt them with gall, at times touching on vulgarity.'

Benedetta rattles off a string of adjectives to describe the Neapolitans: soft, generous, welcoming, garrulous, latecomers, chatterboxes, careless, vague, time wasters, verbose.

'A verb essential to understanding the inhabitants of this city is *intallarsi*, which comes from the Greek *entaurin,* meaning "to put down roots" or "to settle down",' she says. 'In the Neapolitans' case, though, it means to waste time. I mean, have you ever noticed those young things sitting in bars who "settle down" for hours? They don't move!'

With a scowl, she is quick to denounce the violence, aggression and rage that cast a shadow over Naples. 'The fact that I can't leave home with a handbag, jewellery or clothes that are too showy... that I can't walk alone at night to get home at whatever hour, like I did in Rome,' Benedetta laments. 'It's not that I *can't*, but I decide not to. When sometimes I do find myself at 1 am on via Toledo, I'm anxious and paranoid.'

Tania, too, has changed her habits to survive in Naples. And she comes from the island controlled by the Mafia.

'In Palermo, I can walk around at any hour without fear, but here I usually have to get a cab home,' she says, chewing on a plum cake from her drawer. 'Milan and Rome can be dangerous as well, but not on the same level. In Naples it is more obvious: you can see it, smell it, touch it.'

And yet there is grudging admiration for the sheer effrontery of the locals. Pointing, for example, to the comic brilliance of Toto, the stage name of famous Neapolitan actor Antonio de Curtis, Tania rates the locals as *geniali,* or ingenious.

'They are always full of fantasy and love for life. Even if they are sinking in their own problems. Their motto is "Who cares, tomorrow is another day!"'

But this is precisely what stops Naples from getting ahead, argues Alfonso, pulling absently at the collar of his crisp British-styled office shirt. 'For a city to change, it must move itself, but Neapolitan society does not move – it's pathological,' he says.

He hates the pollution, the traffic, and the flagrant disregard for the most elementary rules of civil life. 'It's like being in a jungle. Everyone does what *they* think is best. The Neapolitan, by nature, is individualistic, thinking always of personal interests and trying to extract advantage from every situation ... They put themselves first and, if they can, they'll cheat the next person – like when you get a cab from the airport or station, you have to insist repeatedly that the taxi driver turn on his meter.'

He's right. The one time I hailed a cab in Naples, fresh from the station with only a small backpack, I got charged extra for luggage and argued with the taxi driver the whole way.

'But you can feel at home in Naples,' Nando pipes up with his usual optimism. He rates Naples over New York, Milan and Rome as a place to live, saying the humanity and tolerance in the city is second to none.

'They are incurable fatalists,' Enrico cuts in. 'Everything that happens to Neapolitans and their city is fruit of a destiny from which they cannot escape. It's like a surrender, a sense of impotence in the face of a harsh, complex reality full of human misery...'

Enrico appreciates Naples' rich artistic culture and historic heritage, as well as its natural wealth, from Vesuvius to the Gulf of Naples and the islands just offshore.

'It's a succession of postcards like no others in the world. It's a school of life and thought that's difficult for a foreigner to understand. Of all the cities in Italy, it most closely resembles "organised" anarchy – or, to use the expression of a taxi driver, "democratic" anarchy.

'Here, everyone can find their own dimension. The poor man lives in a context where poverty and misery are the rules, while the rich live each day as if they were on holidays. It's unique and must be visited.'

Francesco says that whether you are rich or poor, you are always in company in Naples.

'Even if you go to have a coffee in a bar where there are three complete strangers, there is always a conversation going on and you are always welcomed to join in,' he says.

He highlights a sense of community that I'm already appreciating: when I'm short of change, shopkeepers often just tell me to pay next time. But while Francesco loves the openness and generosity of the people in his hometown, he and his wife are nonetheless on the hunt for jobs overseas.

'I don't like the incapacity of Neapolitans to value their city and themselves,' he says. 'This city has always been governed by politicians the locals elect to cultivate their own, small interests: it's not the politicians who are corrupt, we are the ones who continue to elect them.

'I don't mind the general disorder, but I don't like the sense of self-pity…always waiting for something from above.'

Francesco contends that you can be in any city in the middle of the night and risk being robbed, but Naples has a more sinister side.

'If I decide to open a bar or if I've won a work tender, I must take into consideration that, without doubt, I'll have to pay a slice to the Camorra,' he says. 'The petty crime is a common phenomenon, but the Camorra is the second government you have to answer to every day.'

His comments remind me of my constant attempt to work out which shops in my neighbourhood are Camorra-controlled. Strolling with my flatmate Francesco one evening, he objected when I suggested grabbing a coffee at a bar in a piazza near our home, explaining that it was a dodgy operation.

'But how do you know?' I teased.

'*E' così*,' he said in hushed tones, only adding to the mystery: It is just fact.

Sipping a Campari in Piazza Bellini one steamy afternoon after work, I listen to Marco wax lyrical about the city he calls a 'big family'.

'Neapolitans are light and shadow. On the one hand they're generous and give you everything – this human dimension does not exist in any other Italian city,' he says. 'It's enough to speak a few Neapolitan words and people adopt you. This is one of the most beautiful things about Naples. On the other hand, Neapolitans have an excessive presence. There is little respect for the privacy of others. People know who you are and what you do because of the grapevine.'

With a cheeky grin, Marco likens Neapolitans to the famous local dessert *baba*: 'It's delicious and sweet, but the rum makes it strong, the cream adds lightness and the egg makes it heavy.'

Naples is renowned in the whole of Italy for the theatrics that pass as daily life, but Marco suggests that locals exaggerate for more complex reasons.

'Naples has so many problems that if you face things in a rigid way the city will just crush you…But if you can be ironic, let things go or pass over you, you will survive. This is popular wisdom here, the philosophical Neapolitan attitude of *fatalismo*.'

But Marco despairs at the traffic, smog and pollution borne of such determinism. 'People are always waiting for others to do something, the individual never takes responsibility for keeping the city clean,' he growls. 'Neapolitans throw everything in the middle of the road because they think, Oh well, the rubbish truck will pass and clean it up. They just don't care about anything – there's no respect for the rule of law. But it's fascinating,

I guess. In a way. I mean, people arrive here and say, "Where the hell am I?"'

Fortunate to have never been a victim of crime, Marco speaks of *l'arte di arrangiarsi* before warning me of the classic Neapolitan trait of trying to pull the wool over the eyes of the innocent.

'My favourite story,' he says, 'is that of a friend of mine who was in a car with her boyfriend when a motorbike on the road ahead of them had an accident.

'My friend and her partner stopped and jumped out of their car to help, and the two riders picked themselves up off the road, pulled out guns and robbed them.'

When I wonder out loud how the hell you can stay sane and safe in Naples, Marco cuts to the chase.

'If you can survive here, you can survive anywhere,' he says with enthusiasm. 'To resist everything that happens here is not easy, but you develop an inner strength...so much so that when you go to any other place, it seems like a fairytale! When you see the positive side, it allows you to move ahead, to survive, to live. *Chist 'e 'o paese d' 'o sole.*'

As I walk home I consider Marco's comment that locals adopt anyone who knows a word or two of their dialect. I'm only a little way into my Neapolitan sojourn but I'm struggling to make sense of it.

Eyes fixed to the cobblestones, I repeat Marco's closing sentiment – *Chist 'e 'o paese d' 'o sole*, 'This is the country of the sun' – and run smack-bang into the gypsy seller metres from my house. I've never bought anything from a hawker in my life, but today I have a new appreciation for *l'arte di arrangiarsi.*

I pull a euro coin from my pocket and select a cheery orange cigarette lighter before bidding the man *buona sera.*

Videla, ammirala, e nun a' tucca

Watch her, admire her, but don't touch her

Despite being a bush kid, the best part of my childhood was spent under water. Family holidays were whiled away by the sea; after long days of body surfing we would waddle back with sagging cossie crotches to our rented beach shack to peel cold prawns as red as our skin. At night, the rumble of the ocean was a welcome distraction from the scratch of sand grains between sweat-sticky sheets.

In the summer months the first thing my sisters and I did after school was flop into the backyard pool. Swimming and floating was for sissies. I just wanted to sink. Expelling the air in my lungs, I would sit cross-legged at the bottom, sipping imaginary tea and chatting with invisible water creatures; or I'd hold my breath to do underwater lengths until oxygen deprivation gave me a head spin.

Wonder Woman, who was emblazoned on my school drink flask, impressed me with her glittery hot pants and practical lasso skills. But she lost her superpowers the moment the film *Splash* hit the box office. Watching Daryl Hannah's blonde bombshell mermaid sealed my ambition to dwell beneath the sea.

It's no surprise, then, that in Naples I'm suddenly in my element: I can see the ocean when I step onto the office balcony and can reach it from home or work within five minutes. So it's natural, then, that I happily swallow the folklore that pins Naples' birth to a comely *sirena*.

Around 680 BC Greek colonists founded the original settlement of Parthenope on the tiny island of Megaris, where the majestic Castel dell'Ovo, Castle of the Egg, commands an outcrop of the Gulf of Naples today. According to legend, the settlement takes its name from a beautiful mermaid who was splashing about the coastline with her sisters, enchanting sailors with their sing-song.

Things were going swimmingly for Parthenope until the Greek warrior Ulysses passed by. Tipped off that shiploads of sailors had fallen overboard after being bewitched by the mermaids' voices, Ulysses plugged his crewmen's ears with wax and then tied himself to the mast. Heartbroken, Parthenope drowned herself and, when her body washed up on Megaris, mariners buried her there.

Thinking of the history that links both Penelope and Parthenope to Ulysses, I like to entertain the idea that it was destiny that brought me to Naples.

The original settlement was attacked by testosterone-fuelled armies and dynasties, among them the Romans, Goths, Vandals, Byzantines, Lombards, Franks, Saracens, Normans, Sicilians, Hungarians, Spaniards and Austrians. And centuries of foreign 'interest' has, as Massi, my flatmate in Rome, pointed out, instilled in the Neapolitans a great tolerance for other cultures.

But it's the feminine and fanciful touch of the mermaid that I feel lingers over Naples like an imaginary, and perhaps soiled, bridal veil. As I walk around the inner-city I sometimes think that women outnumber men by three to one. Their presence seems greater, too, because many have physiques that a kind person would call voluptuous, but others would deride as chubby, even obese. The fact that southern women are typically shorter than their northern counterparts doesn't 'weigh' in their favour.

Let's just say Neapolitan women like to let it all hang out. They wear tight hipster jeans with tank tops that leave at least one mini-tyre roll of flesh exposed. Fresh from Rome, where many women are gym junkies on low-carb diets, I'm impressed by the sudden might of my sisterhood. On the one hand I admire their nerve, on the other, their brash feminism makes me cringe.

Girl power is always around the corner in Naples. In the *centro storico,* shrines of the Madonna can be found at least every two blocks. Some are archaically beautiful, others rather tacky, some exposed to the elements, others covered by plastic or glass; but they're always surrounded by candles and fresh or plastic flowers.

'In the old days,' Francesco explains as we leave home one Saturday morning, 'the Madonnas lit the streets. Haven't you noticed how beautiful they are at night?'

We walk down two flights of stairs to buzz the apartment door on the landing. Dirt and grime cover the stairwell, but passing through the front door of Francesco's friend Gianluigi's apartment, we find a spacious, open-plan room with a mezzanine bedroom. I smile gratefully at Gianluigi and load my dirty clothes into his washing machine. For reasons I have yet to determine, Naples is devoid of coin-operated laundromats, which are everywhere in Rome. While Francesco and Carlo have offered to take my washing to their family homes, I really don't want their *mamme* folding my undies. So for the next month Gianluigi accepts my bundles, which I collect later, always insisting on leaving a small contribution, a bag of chocolates, or a sticky cake from the local *pasticceria*.

On our way to the train station, Francesco drags me into via San Gregorio Armeno for a peek. Just weeks before Christmas, there is elbow room only between impatient locals and bewildered tourists. Crammed along both sides of the sloping street are small shops selling tiny handcrafted nativity figurines by the hundreds. Why anyone would want these kitsch ornaments in their homes is one thing, but how the stallholders make a profit with so much competition is anyone's guess.

Francesco and I board the metro at stazione Centrale and alight at Ercolana. We wander through the streets to eventually find the Resina flea market, where stalls sell second-hand leatherwear, clothing and jewellery.

Francesco stands patiently and offers some advice as I prepare to haggle with a stall owner for an emerald green, cashmere jumper that has caught my eye.

'Always offer at least half of what you want to –'

'Listen, Fra,' I cut in, 'my dad sells used cars and if I don't get a cracker deal I'll be a disgrace to the family.'

I offer two euro for the jumper and the stall owner slips it into a used plastic bag.

Pleased with my purchase, I wander into another stall where two men are talking in thick dialect. Although I hear the word *Inglese*, I have no idea what they're saying. The pair eye me up and down, their body language hostile.

In my few weeks in the South, I'm starting to feel quite edgy and constrained. I try to explain my unease to Francesco, but he argues that it's safer for women in Naples, and the South in general, than it is in other regions.

'Here there is less violence against women because society dictates that you *don't harm women*,' he says. 'That doesn't mean violence doesn't exist, but if it does, it tends to happen behind closed doors.'

He points out that a number of women have led Camorra clans, and explains that Neapolitan women have always had a strong presence in their society. 'For example,' he says, 'if police go to a *quartiere* to arrest someone, women often block the streets and create chaos to try to thwart the arrest.'

One such episode occurred in January 2005, when police arrested thirty-one year old Cosimo Di Lauro, the son of Camorra kingpin Paolo. Considered by police as one of Naples' most bloodthirsty and powerful Camorra bosses, Paolo Di Lauro was the mastermind of a lucrative drug network in the city's northern suburbs. Untraceable since 1997, and a fugitive since 2002 (when he skipped court), the balding boss hardly lived up to his fearsome reputation when police, acting on a tip-off, came knocking very early one September morning in 2005. Inside, Paolo Di Lauro, known as *Ciruzzo 'o Milionario*, had been sleeping. 'I'm calm, stay calm...' he muttered as handcuffs were clicked around his wrists.

The brutal *faida* – the focus of the *Internazionale* cover story that captured my attention in Rome – had been sparked by Cosimo, who, in his attempts to shake up his absent father's dynasty, put offside *camorristi* members who formed a breakaway group dubbed the *scissionisti*, or secessionists. They began slaying each other in a bid to gain control of the drug trade.

Wanted on the suspicion of drug trafficking and a string of homicides, including the murder in broad daylight of the mother of a member of a rival group, Cosimo 'Fat Boy' Di Lauro was on home turf in the drug infested northern zone of Secondigliano when the police nabbed him. As word spread, a crowd of about four hundred, mostly women, poured onto the street to hurl abuse at the law enforcers. From the balconies of the squalid buildings in the suburb the women let loose, throwing crockery, glass bottles and whatever they could get their hands on to deter the arrest.

'Neapolitan women,' elaborates Francesco as we sit down to lunch at the quaint Vive il Re, a restaurant tucked behind the market, 'function as defenders of their husbands and relatives to state authorities. There's even a series of films that depict them in these kinds of roles.'

In one such film, *Ieri, Oggi e Domani*, or *Yesterday, Today and Tomorrow*, a voluptuous, young Sophia Loren plays the lead in three short films, set in Milan, Rome and Naples. In Naples, she's a feisty street seller of contraband cigarettes who, exploiting a legal loophole, repeatedly falls pregnant to avoid being evicted from her home. Loren is still considered the queen of Italian cinema in Naples, where she grew up, and she recently posed for the famous Pirelli calendar at the age of seventy-one.

Francesco, a newly elected councillor for the *Partito della Rifondazione Comunista*, or Communist Refoundation Party, remains hopeful that Naples' mayor, Rosa Iervolino Russo, will put some punch into her second term.

'She's a very honest woman who understands compromise, but she has limits, and this is important because the political class in this city doesn't recognise limits any more…' he says, tucking into the classic Neapolitan dish *pasta alla Genovese*, served with a sauce of onions and beef stewed in a saucepan full of olive oil.

According to Francesco, the former mayor Antonio Bassolino, now president of the Campania region, made giant strides when his leftist party came to power sixteen years ago. Kneecapped by the *tangentopoli* – bribesville – decade of the 1980s, when government mismanagement and corruption reigned, Bassolino's agenda was about bringing back a sense of civic pride, cleaning up the streets and piazzas, and outlawing the century-old street sale of cigarettes, among other measures.

In 1994, when the city snaffled the right to host the G7 Summit, the world watched news footage of majestic Vesuvius, the shimmering Gulf of Naples, and leaders like Bill Clinton strolling through the historic centre with pizza in hand. But over a decade later, Naples is still haunted by its unsavoury past, with an administration rife with cronyism and nepotism, the wives of political leaders, for example, landing plum jobs, and a general sense of personal interests prevailing over the common good.

'As far as the Camorra is concerned,' says Francesco, having found room to squeeze in a *secondo* of roast rabbit with caramelised fennel, 'there is no easy solution. It's an historic problem – the Camorra was initially the secret service for the Spanish Bourbons.' He pauses to take a sip of the fine bottle of wine slowly diminishing on the table. 'There are more than twenty thousand people affiliated with the Camorra in Naples, so it's enormously powerful. It helps the poor to earn in simple ways, so it'll never be defeated.'

I sing out to the waiter for the dessert menu, and listen closely as Francesco doesn't stop to draw breath. He thinks the *faida* between the Camorra clans from late 2004 to early 2005 is to blame for the current scourge of petty crime. With the Camorra distracted by internal conflicts, Francesco conjectures, wayward youth had more opportunity to prey on the public. Other locals have told me that during the *faida* there were so many cops on the ground that not even a leaf could rustle without suspicion. Happy not to quibble on the point, I sink my dessert spoon into the delicate *panna cotta* before me.

Summing up his theories, Francesco insists that the first step to at least trying to handicap the Camorra is job creation.

'It's a structural problem,' he says with a sigh. 'Naples is a poor city, and if the national government doesn't provide more funding, things will remain the same.'

Later on, walking in Forcella, the squalid inner-city *quartiere* less than a ten-minute stroll from Francesco's home in the historic centre, I notice the word 'Annalisa' written on a wall. Francesco confirms my suspicion that we're in the street where fourteen-year-old schoolgirl Annalisa Durante died in a Camorra ambush in 2004.

Not long after arriving in Naples I saw Annalisa's cheeky smile lighting up the cover of *Il Diario di Annalisa, The Diary of Annalisa*. The book includes interviews with her parents and friends, and details of the trial of the man charged with her murder, Salvatore Giuliano. But the most fascinating part of the book is the heart-wrenching stream of thoughts that Annalisa, the younger of Carmela and Giovanni Durante's two daughters, wrote in a diary that was found after her death.

Known as *Annalisa la bellissima* in her neighbourhood, the model student met her fate one Saturday night as she stood beneath her home in via Vicaria, chatting with two girlfriends after an afternoon playing hair and make-up.

Annalisa was approached by Salvatore Giuliano, the twenty-year-old scion of the local Camorra clan of the same name. The Giuliano clan was one of a cartel known as the *Nuova Famiglia*, or New Family, which was engaged in bitter warfare in the 1970s and 1980s against Rafaelle Cutolo's *Nuova Camorra Organizzata*, or New Organised Camorra (NCO). The death toll in the recent *faida* between the two clans was horrific, but small in comparison to the bloodshed between the NCO and New Family in the 1980s. Between 1980 and 1981, around four hundred *camorristi* were murdered before the two cartels died out to make way for other groups.

Salvatore Giuliano, known as *Sasa' 'o Russo* for his red hair, had never stopped to chat to Annalisa before, but the two had exchanged a *buongiorno* or *buona sera*, obligatory for anyone in an Italian community.

That night, however, Giuliano asked Annalisa to buy him some cigarettes that were sold illegally from a nearby flat. She ran the errand on the back of a motorbike driven by Giuliano's brother, Antonio.

After giving Salvatore his cigarettes she was again standing outside her home when the usually rowdy street suddenly emptied.

Antonio Giuliano was the first to notice a *motorino* approaching with two riders wearing helmets. Since barely anyone, at least in poor areas, wears protective headgear, locals instinctively know that riders wearing helmets could well be *sicari*, hired killers.

Annalisa's friends ran for cover, but somehow she got stuck in the middle. Salvatore Giuliano grabbed Annalisa by her hair and dragged her across his body for cover.

He escaped without a graze, but Annalisa was rushed to hospital with a bullet wedged in her neck. She survived for a few days before her life-support system was turned off.

Annalisa's death made international headlines because the world could see that the Camorra now seemed willing to sacrifice the lives of innocent civilians. The fact that she was so young and so photogenic wasn't lost on news editors, either.

Reading *The Diary of Annalisa* makes me want to speak to the Durante family and learn more about her, not least because she had, at once, youthful innocence and a profound maturity born of having to survive in a rough neighbourhood.

While expressing her desire to own a new motorbike, as well as the other things Italian teenagers typically pine for, Annalisa also wrote about religion, about life lessons learnt at school, and her intention to always see the good in others, because that meant, she thought, there was also good 'inside of me'.

Annalisa's closest friend recalls that the schoolgirl was preoccupied with a sense of mortality in the days before the Camorra robbed her of her life.

'I'm alive and I'm happy to live, even if my life is not what I would have hoped for,' she wrote, before adding of her hope that her young, noncommittal boyfriend would return her ardent affections. 'I know that a part of me will be immortal. And I will go to heaven soon.'

Thoughts about Annalisa Durante and conflicting impressions of Neapolitan women are still revolving around my head when I bump into Manola on Christmas Eve.

Manola is the partner of Roberto, who helped me find my temporary home with Francesco and Carlo. She is an educational psychologist who works with disadvantaged children in a destitute suburb on Naples' periphery. With cat-like, emerald-green eyes, olive skin and long, wavy hair, Manola is one of those people whose words often fall on deaf ears, her audience distracted by her natural *bellezza*, beauty.

I accompany her on a walk to her mother's home, and recount Francesco's version of Neapolitan women having a strong influence in the community, but being the weaker sex behind closed doors.

'Naples is a matriarchal city, a mother who cuddles her young and doesn't see their defects,' begins Manola with careful consideration, sucking back one of her trademark Winston blues. 'That's why men lack independence here – because their mothers fuss over them until they're in their thirties and forties, especially in high society.'

Manola is speaking from experience. Madly in love with Roberto, she nonetheless despairs at the fact that he has no burning desire to find a job and lives off the largesse of his mother, who often pops in to the couple's inner-city love nest with food parcels, or pays for domestic help. Manola works long hours while the well-read, gregarious, lovable Roberto is busy being a free spirit.

As we stop to have a cocktail at Superfly, where I'm already on cheek-kissing terms with the fetching barman, Antonello, I notice how the majority of people around me are dressed down to the extreme. A tomboy at heart, in Rome I learnt to get in touch with my feminine side, having been shamed into taking greater care of my appearance to get better treatment from the image-obsessed Romans.

In Naples, with each passing day I'm embracing shabbiness, because my theory – supported by most of my acquaintances here – is that the poorer you look, the easier it is to blend into the landscape and avoid being a target of crime. My work uniform is jeans and sneakers, which I swap for nicer heels at the office, where I might also put on some earrings that I keep in a drawer. I don't usually carry a handbag, but I always have fifty euro in my pocket ready to throw at a thief should I get confronted on the street at night.

An SMS arrives and, hearing the familiar beep, I instinctively reach to respond before realising that it isn't my phone. Well, it was until Manola fell victim to a classic *scippo*. Standing on the street chatting on her *cellulare*, she was left talking to thin air when a motorbike passed close enough for the passenger to snatch it from her hand. Since a friend had just given me a new phone, I gave Manola my old one.

Manola laughs as she tells me about another time her phone was stolen.

'I was sitting at a table in Piazza Bellini having an *aperitivo* when all of a sudden I saw a hand emerge from the hedge beside us and snatch my bag, which had my phone, house keys, everything…' she says. 'When I screamed, the "boss" of the piazza suddenly arrived and was pissed off when he realised the thief wasn't local, and had trespassed on his turf.

'The boss called the thief on my telephone and they started arguing, and then I ended up talking to him, too, but he refused to give me back my phone and claimed he couldn't remember where he had thrown my bag. It was *bizzarro*…'

Sipping her beer, Manola maintains that she's not frightened of the Camorra or the young hoodlums on the street.

'Neapolitans are born into this environment, they learn to live with it,' she says with resignation. 'It's just that when bad things happen continually, you have to ask yourself whether it's normal to live like this…'

I'm constantly asked by locals where I'm from as soon as I open my mouth, and I ask Manola why someone like me, who is easily recognisable as a foreigner, hasn't run into trouble.

'Because you're arsy,' she says simply. 'If I stopped to count how many times I've suffered small abuses…You either adapt and find an equilibrium, or you leave the house with a shield. Maybe nothing will happen to you, but if you're on a bus, in a crowded place, anywhere…be careful. I do whatever it takes – carry my bag over my neck or under my jacket in winter. I look around because the moment you're distracted, you get done over.'

As Manola prepares to head to her mother's house for dinner, I ask her what it takes to survive Naples.

'You need a stroke of luck, Penny,' she says, a glint of sadness in her eyes. 'Because honestly, sometimes you have what it takes, you have energy and will…but sometimes you just can't face it.'

Night has fallen as I walk home across Piazza del Gesu, past groups of dreadlocked youths wearing hipster jeans, drinking from beer bottles and stroking mongrel dogs. I imagine myself leaving for work tomorrow dressed in knight's armour, complete with shield and dagger.

I stand nervously near the entrance to my office building, waiting for a woman I've only spoken to by phone.

Rosaria is a journalist who works at the local ANSA bureau, writing about *calcio*, soccer, and *cronaca nera*, which translates literally as 'black news' but means crime. She was born, and still lives, in Forcella, Annalisa Durante's neighbourhood. Given her role as a *cronista*, or crime reporter, she has a strong connection to the case. She knows Father Luigi Merola, the local priest in Forcella and outspoken critic of the Camorra, which is strangling his parish.

Hearing my name, I turn to see a stocky woman sitting on a powerful motorbike that has just pulled up on the corner. Dressed in tight jeans, jacket and cowgirl boots with a fake Gucci bag slipped over one shoulder, Rosaria firmly shakes my outstretched hand.

'*Sali*,' she says, then orders me to get on her bike without offering me a helmet. I swing a leg over the seat and have barely grasped the handrail behind me before we're zigzagging in and out of traffic towards Forcella.

Rosaria mounts the kerb and parks her bike outside a church and tells me to follow her inside. We find a group of people waiting patiently for Father Merola, so Rosaria bosses me outside again, and before long we're on her *moto* and a compulsory tour of her neighbourhood.

As we pass along the street where Annalisa lived, Rosaria bellows out hellos to the locals, and speaks to me in hushed tones so as not to attract attention. Small children wander the street near a fruit shop stacked with produce that looks like it has seen better days. A few young girls about Annalisa's age mill outside a video-game shop.

'That's where she was shot,' says Rosaria, nodding quickly towards a palazzo door. 'And see that man sitting on the chair there? That's Annalisa's dad.'

I barely have time to look at the short, grey-haired man before Rosaria hoons on, talking with a lisp that makes her dialect even harder to understand. I remember reading in Annalisa's diary that Giovanni Durante sold contraband cigarettes and souvenirs, and whatever he could to feed his family.

Carmela Durante, says Rosaria, is a destroyed woman who has dressed in black since the day her daughter died. Giovanni Durante has spoken to the media, but only on the recommendation of Father Merola, who knew Annalisa. Hours before she died, he bumped into her on the street and reminded her not to miss mass the next day.

Rosaria parks again in front of the church. Moments later a silver Mercedes with tinted windows and a blue police light on its roof pulls up. Father Merola has had a police security escort for two years, ever since his campaign to clean up his neighbourhood rankled the Camorra.

I know Father Merola is the same age as me, but I'm still surprised when a tanned, boyishly handsome man wearing designer spectacles emerges from the car with a smile. He looks more like an athlete than a member of the God squad. At the same time a beefy man wearing white jeans and black sunglasses steps from the car and wastes no time in lighting a cigarette.

Holding his white priest collar in his hand, Father Merola approaches the church, saying hello to a few of his flock before Rosaria catches up and asks if I can speak with him. He ushers me into a side office of the church and I explain how I've come to Naples, and my curiosity about the city and the Camorra.

Our conversation lasts barely two minutes. Father Merola checks his diary and tells me to come back in a month.

'You can talk to Annalisa's dad, I'll arrange a meeting for you. I'll call as soon as I know.' He pushes back his chair and pulls something from his jacket pocket. 'Look,' he says with excitement to Rosaria. In his hand is the latest CD of an Italian singer I've never heard of.

Being a 'lapsed' Anglican and now agnostic I've never been close enough to the Catholic Church to form an impression of a priest as an individual. But in the few times I have been to mass, the men leading the congregation have been either balding or grey-haired and have notched up at least half a century of devotion to God. Father Merola seems like an impostor. Not that religion is uncool, but he's almost too hip to be holed up in church all day.

I shake Father Merola's hand, follow Rosaria out of the church, and accept a ride home. As I slide off the motorbike, she cheek kisses me and urges me to call her for any favour before *vrooming* off, still without a helmet and chatting on her mobile.

Manola's warning about keeping a low profile rings in my ears as I withdraw a chunk of cash at an ATM machine. I quickly stuff it down my bra when no one is looking. I marvel at how some Neapolitan women, like Rosaria, are all flash with no fear.

As I walk home along the Spaccanapoli, I realise that setting foot in the church today has, as usual, provoked me to question my sketchy beliefs which seem flimsy next to the deep-seated faith of Annalisa Durante.

'*L'amore di Dio è al centro della mia vita,*' she wrote in her diary: 'The love of God is at the centre of my life…'

Today at school the religion professor asked me who the idols are of a girl my age. Soccer players, singers, my boyfriend, motorbikes, cars...I realised that there was something in me I had to change. My life has become different since I started to pray. For me to pray is like talking with God, to pray for the people who are at war, to feel my family close.

I want a happy world. I don't like it when people die. The other day an uncle died and I saw Mum cry...And so I decided to dedicate myself to make her happy...I put on a pair of Dad's jeans, just to see the reaction of Mum and [sister] Manu.

I walked downstairs and I said to them, 'How do they look?' The jeans were too long and the waist was falling almost halfway down my legs. Mum started to laugh and said, 'Annalisa, don't you see they're too big for you?' Then Dad arrived and said, 'What are you doing wearing my jeans?' It was ridiculous. We all collapsed with laughter.

I want a life without bad things and sickness. God, please protect Mum, Dad and Manu.

I stop two blocks from home and take a closer look at one of the city's shrines to the Madonna. I focus on the details of the small oil painting surrounded by candles, and block out the noise of pedestrians and motorbikes.

Thank God for the Madonna. If stepping inside a church often makes me feel tense, she never fails to calm me.

Morte e marito, nun aspetta maie quanno veneno

Death and a husband, don't wait for them: decide your destiny

'Neapolitans, *Napoletani*,' opines my colleague Alfonso with a snigger, *'sono nati fidanzati*, are born engaged.'

In the late afternoon, young couples barely in their teens join at the hips and lips in Naples' city centre, gathering en masse in via Toledo, near the intersection of Piazza Trieste e Trento. They smooch and mooch beside their colourful Vespas and falling apart Piaggos – or hotted up motorbikes, if they're in cahoots with the Camorra.

I've discovered through office gossip that beauty treatments in Naples are half the price of those in Rome, and I meet one of the *giovani fidanzati*, young engaged, as I treat myself to a pedicure at a hair salon near work. Baby-faced beautician Filomena takes me under her charge, ordering me to sit and place my feet in a tub of warm water. Around me a gaggle of Italian women boss their hairdressers about and eye each other without discretion.

Filomena – dressed in trendy black tracksuit pants and a cropped top popular with the young Italian *ragazze* who dream to be as good as the dancers who vie for fame in *Dancing with the Stars*–type shows that clog Italian television – grabs one of my weary feet and begins her work. As she busies herself with my cuticles, she explains that she started training as a beauty therapist when she was still at school. I look at her eyebrows with amusement. Plucked to perfection, heavier on the inside to thin out for effect, she must think my never-been-touched numbers are prehistoric.

When I ask her if she has a boyfriend she nods her head and smiles. '*Sono fidanzata da sette anni.* I've had a boyfriend for seven years,' she says, adding that it has been a beautiful relationship.

Filomena is obviously begging to reveal her story, and I can't resist asking. A hopeless romantic in every sense, I'm more than happy to get lost in mindless beauty salon chitchat.

Filomena was thirteen when she spied Pino, short for Giuseppe, when she was walking around town one Saturday afternoon along via Toledo.

'Pino was beautiful, sunny, kind – the type of boy every girl dreamt of having,' she says, carefully placing my first buffed foot in a fluffy pink slipper, then ordering me to raise the second out of the tub of warm water.

Sixteen-year-old Pino, training to be a pastry chef, also noticed Filomena and asked after her when he bumped into her friends a few days later. After a few casual and inconsequential meetings between their respective groups of friends, the two hooked up again when Pino threw a party for his seventeenth birthday at the home of his parents, who were away for the weekend. Finally finding themselves alone, the two young lovers locked lips.

'Do you know how long that kiss lasted?' Filomena says, leaning forward abruptly, her dark eyes boring holes in mine. 'Two hours!'

'What, you didn't come up for air?' I tease, taking immense pleasure in her Neapolitan candour.

'No, I mean we kissed each other continuously for that whole time,' she says, painting me an image of two young teenagers with swollen lips and throbbing body parts.

The two were then inseparable, she says, opening a drawer of her beauty trolley to show me a range of nail polishes. But young lust can be intoxicating. She wanted to go out with her friends; he just wanted her to himself. After two weeks she ditched him.

'I was too young,' says Filomena, now all of twenty-one, with a grown-up's seriousness.

But after a week, around the time that he began casually dating her friends, she realised her mistake. Back together, the two travelled abroad and grew together, and their parents watched their *bambini* blossom.

But after three years they split up again. At the time, Pino was finishing his apprenticeship and Filomena, having finished high school, was studying beauty therapy and frequently travelling around Italy to work in fashion shows.

Six months later the pair were back in each other's pockets, and last year things got even more serious. After a friend's wedding outside Naples, they returned to their hotel room, where Pino whipped out a bottle of champagne and a heart-shaped chocolate cake he had baked then iced in white and pink.

'It was the day before my birthday, so I jokingly asked if he'd made it to avoid having to give me a present,' says Filomena, with flushing cheeks. 'Then he just said, "Sweetie, I want to marry you."'

Filomena repeats his words '*Chicca, ti voglio sposare*', lost for a moment as she brushes some clear polish over my toenails.

'Pino's uncle has a wedding-dress shop in Miami and I've already started sending him ideas for my gown,' she says, placing a wad of tissue between my toes to prevent smudging. 'The villa where we're having the reception is beautiful, and we'll marry in our local church...I want to arrive in a white carriage with two white horses, then when we come out of the church we'll release white doves...'

Trying not to laugh, but loving the theatrics, I ask Filomena if she isn't curious to play the field. Marrying the first and only person you've ever kissed strikes me as a bit trigger-happy.

'You know,' Filomena says simply, 'maybe it's like...when you find the right person you don't want to know anyone else.'

She gives my leg a friendly pat, a sign that my afternoon of pampering has come to an end, and I reluctantly stand up. My first Neapolitan pedicure, amid the snip of scissors and the chitchat of perfumed ladies, has been more fun than I imagined. Filomena walks me to the front of the shop and offers me a kiss on both cheeks before disappearing back into the hubbub of the salon. As I stand at the counter to pay, I look down at my newly scrubbed and painted toes. I feel like a princess.

Stepping outside, I can't help but smile at Filomena's innocent and enviable view of *amore*. But within weeks of arriving in Naples the pessimist in me has decided that I've chosen the wrong place to shack up. With job possibilities scarce, those with any sense or ambition – like my flatmates in Rome, Adriano and Massi – appear to have fled town. The remaining trickle of talent seem to be entwined in relationships that last longer than the average modern-day marriage.

My friend Gigi, a Neapolitan I met when working in a wine bar in Campo de' Fiori in Rome, is a case in point. He met his girlfriend, Paola, because she lives on the floor above his parents' house, where he still lives at the age of thirty-seven. That was eleven years ago. Then there's Massimo, a friend of my flatmate Carlo, who quite takes my fancy. He's a writer and publicist for the Communist Refoundation Party and, I later learn, he has been *fidanzato* for a decade.

According to my workmate Marco, born and bred in Naples, Neapolitan men are *sciupafemmine,* or womanisers. The verb *sciupare* means 'to spoil', while *femmine* is 'female'.

'They are very charming, they have charisma and great success with women,' he tells me one day, then admits that a phone call he received from a woman moments earlier was not his French *fidanzata*.

'When I was living in Paris, the Italians I knew had a reputation for being philanderers, but a Roman girl I knew always said to them, pointing at me, "Okay, but *he* is Neapolitan."'

My first encounter with a *sciupafemmina* arrives during a visit to the post office in the historic centre, minutes from work. After waiting half an hour in queue, as is custom, I walk with purpose to the counter to send a package to Australia.

Noting the address on the package, the teller, with a name tag 'Fausto', asks me why I'm in Naples. I answer him politely while glancing at my watch in a vain attempt to convey that I'm in a hurry to get to work, but Fausto continues his inquisition.

'*Hai un fidanzato?* Do you have a boyfriend?'

'*Ma quando mai, non ho tempo per nessuno.* I have no time for a man in my life,' I joke, noticing the marriage ring on Fausto's finger.

'*Posso prendere il tuo numero?* Can I have your telephone number?' he asks, then suggests a coffee.

Apart from the fact that he's older than my father, Fausto seems to have forgotten that he is *married.* I stifle rising anger and give him my office number because I'm worried he'll sabotage my mail. Thank Christ I didn't put my home address on the package.

Arriving at work, I let off steam to Tania and Alfonso: '*Sono stanca morta di 'sti provoloni!*' They burst into laughter at my weariness of *provolone,* a cheese made from cow's milk, but in Roman slang – drawn from the verb *provare,* 'to try' – it means a man who 'tries it on'.

There and then I decide on a strategy that I put into action on my next trip to the post office, when I'm served by a man slightly younger than my previous antagonist. He asks me what brought me to Naples.

'*Amore,*' I say, giving him a faraway look.

The man is quiet for a moment and I cheer silently, until he follows up with another question. He wants to know my boyfriend's occupation.

'*Lui ha un'azienda di construzione.* He owns a construction business.'

My interrogator's smile disappears, and as I walk back to the office I suddenly wish that I did have a beefy lad to ward off the wedded wolves.

The lack of heating in Francesco and Carlo's flat pushes me to start househunting. But when I receive an email from a friend who lived in Naples for two years, I'm hardly inspired.

'The areas to avoid are near the train station, Piazza Garibaldi, Santa Lucia, Quartieri Spagnoli, Piazza Marina and Beverello, as well as high-risk areas like Secondigliano, Soccavo, Cardarelli, Piscinola and Scampia,' she says.

The few places that make the list are the highly bourgeois Mergellina, Posillipo and Vomero, all of which are too far away and too soulless for my tastes.

After buying the local newspaper *Bric a Brac* and contacting a rental agency, I look at a string of small apartments in the city centre and discover nightmare design features like the all-in-one kitchen and bathroom. I realise that an unfurnished flat also means no whitegoods, which doesn't suit me, yet those that are furnished are cluttered with the ugly bits and pieces of long since parted relatives. And then I'm introduced to the *basso*, the traditional Neapolitan ground-floor flat of cramped dimensions. In just one step from the street, a visitor finds the kitchen, lounge and bedroom in the main front room, with a pokey bathroom tacked on the back. Most owners leave their front door and window wide open, lest they develop claustrophobia, giving passers-by an uncensored view into their lives.

Inspecting what turns out to be a dim *basso* in Chiaia one day, the landlord looks at me with disappointment when I tell him that I want a place with more light. 'My mother, Maria, was born here and gave birth to me here…I liked the idea of a young, independent woman being here,' he says, and I make a hurried exit, imagining midnight conversations with ghosts.

Francesco and Carlo have made me increasingly superstitious, claiming that Naples is full of *munacielli*. Meaning 'little monks' in Neapolitan, *munacielli* are child spirits who apparently get around in smocks and shoes with silver buckles. Some of their gestures are amusing, like leaving money or lotto clues, some not so friendly, like hiding things and breaking plates, and others border on flirtatious, like softly brushing past people. My flatmates naturally blame our *munaciello* for the mysterious interruption of our hot water system. And when the lights black out in our centuries-old palazzo, short-circuiting doesn't enter the equation for Francesco, who refuses to position his bed in the most logical way in his room, with the legs facing the door, because it brings bad luck.

One afternoon I have an appointment to see a flat in the notorious Quartieri Spagnoli – the rabbit warren that spreads west, up hill, from the wide thoroughfare via Toledo. Created in the early sixteenth century by the Spanish viceroy Don Pedro di Toledo, the hilly zone takes its name not because it's inhabited by a Spanish community, but because it was built to house troops of the Spanish occupation.

Poorly planned from the start, the poverty-ridden area is covered in dust and rubbish but is full of colour, large families and stunted elderly folk who live very public lives in their *bassi*, occasionally stepping outside to do some grocery shopping or to sit on a rotting chair for an hour or two to see if the day will bring them something new. Groups of men gather around small tables playing *tombala*, while clusters of spongy women with flaps of underarm you could peg to a washing line play the card game indoors, perhaps to stay closer to the kitchen, where something is always in the oven or on the stove.

In the narrow grid of streets decorated with strings adorned with small Italian flags, the smells of pizza, sweets and *fritture*, fried foods, waft from windows and collect in tiny spaces which rarely attract fresh air or natural light at any time of the day. Sheets hang from windows high above the exhaust fumes from the scooters ridden by helmetless urchins. These youths seem to do nothing but hoon along looking for action despite the fact that little ever seems to happen. Until now, I haven't been game enough to walk through the *quartieri*, even in the middle of the day.

A little daunted, I have asked Manola to accompany me to the flat, but my heart still beats faster as we wind our way up through the streets from via Toledo. Scooters whir past and I rest my hand instinctively over my bag, hung across my chest, thinking of my old flatmate Adriano telling me that one soon learns in Naples to be wary of the sound of *motorini*.

I press a buzzer and wait. A woman's voice instructs us to come to the top floor. We duck to step through the dwarf-sized door and inside I notice a pokey tailor's shop at the back of the square courtyard, before we hook right to take the steps. There is an elevator out of order and I count five flights of stairs before we arrive at the last landing. At the top of a final flight of stairs waits a small, pigeon-chested woman. When I reach her she ushers us into what is obviously her home. We sit down on one of the plush, green velvet divans and she offers us coffee and a cigarette. I accept both, despite the fact that I just want to see the flat. Here, I'm learning more than ever that you have to go with the flow. In Rome, people have a sense of time. In Naples, lunchtime can mean four in the afternoon, while dinner is commonly enjoyed after ten.

Introducing herself as Nicola, but instructing me to call her Nicoletta, the woman observes me through chic blue eyeglasses that slip down her nose as she tells me a little about herself: she is chief architect at the Ministry for Culture, a divorcee who has lived here for twelve years.

'*Venite*. Come,' she says, leading us through her small, neat kitchen and onto a pretty, pot-planted *terrazza*. I take in the view and note the dome of Galleria Umberto, the San Martino monastery high on the hill, Vesuvius and the roof terraces of homes in the quarter.

We cross the terrace to an iron door painted brown, which Nicoletta opens to reveal pastel-green tiling. Inside is a short corridor that leads to a small living area with a table and chairs. The windows of the room face across the palazzo's central courtyard to Nicoletta's apartment, while those in the adjoining kitchen offer views of the city, Vesuvius and, if I strain my neck, the sea. Light streams into every room of the apartment. The bathroom is small but modern and the bedroom isn't bad, notwithstanding the frilly, girly curtains, it's a good size and has ample wardrobe space. I ask her what's behind the locked door just on the right after entering the apartment.

67

'I store some belongings in there, but I rarely go in and if I need to, I'll ask permission first,' she says.

In a few places I've looked at, the owner has had a room in the flat and it's something that bugs me, for lack of complete privacy. Nicoletta walks back to her apartment, giving me some time to look around on my own.

'It used to be a bed and breakfast,' I tell Manola as we stand in the kitchen. 'The agency told me she wants 800 euro.'

'Try and bargain her down a little, but I think you should take it – it's full of light, really modern and in a good suburb,' she says, adding that the street below is wider than most of the alleys in the area.

Within days I've accepted the apartment for a slightly lower price, and late one Friday night Adriano arrives from Rome with the twelve boxes that represent my life. We eyeball the broken elevator. It takes a good half hour to lug the boxes up the flights of stairs, and I tell Adriano that I have a big debt to repay him before he disappears to have dinner with his *fidanzata*.

The next day I'm keen to begin unpacking, but Nicoletta insists on showing me a few things in the flat first. It's only when I'm in the kitchen that I realise there's no oven. How did I overlook something so obvious? Nicoletta points to a small electric oven on a shelf and says it works well. I hope she's right; despite my limited culinary skills, I still like to experiment. She disappears after promising to deliver the washing machine next week, and telling me to ring her buzzer if I feel like sharing a bite to eat with her at lunch.

I dust and unpack for a few hours, wasting time idly staring at the rows of VHS films on the bookshelves in the living room, and the vinyls stashed in an unused record player. I find Grace Jones' *Nightclubbing* and put the album cover out on display: a striking image of the singer armed with a sexy, confident stare, white cigarette hanging from glossy lips that contrast against her smooth, black skin.

When midday rolls around I don't feel like disturbing Nicoletta. While I appreciate her offer, I'm still coming to grips with the idea of being chummy with my landlady. What if something goes wrong in my flat? Won't it make it harder to negotiate? I make do with what's in the kitchen: spaghetti, capers and chilli left by the last bed and breakfast guests. Happily, I find a bottle of *limoncello* liqueur in the fridge.

Dusk fades and I see no signs of life from Nicoletta's flat. Having stocked up on food supplies I cook a mini-roast and discover with delight that the oven is a winner. I watch a DVD of *Picnic at Hanging Rock,* perhaps pining for the Australian bush, and flick off the light beside my makeshift double bed – two single beds squashed together, Italian-style.

I listen to the sounds on the street six floors below: the random roars of a scooter and the screeches of women I hope are having fun, and not being assailed.

I'm just dozing off when an almighty boom erupts from some place nearby. A second shot rings out. I jump out of bed and open my blind to look out over the barely lit *quartieri*.

BOOM, BOOM. Fireworks shoot high into the sky, their explosions echoing slightly. I watch, enthralled, until the last one fizzes out leaving a spiral of smoke. It's a presage of what is to come: six nights out of seven, fireworks ring out across the sky.

'When there are fireworks,' explains Nicoletta late one Sunday morning, 'it often means that one of the Camorra has been let out of jail.'

I later read that the fireworks are the latest method used by the Neapolitan underworld gangs to send a message to rivals: the bigger the fireworks, the greater the power.

I sit on the kitchen step and watch my landlady in action. Won over by her friendliness, I gave up trying to play 'distant neighbour' when she promised to teach me the secrets of Neapolitan cuisine. Today I'm all ears as she makes lasagna.

'This classic hails from Bologna,' Nicoletta says as she rolls dough on a wooden board.

The ingredients of the northern version are *ragù*, minced meat, white sauce and pasta made with eggs. But despite not having egg in the pasta, Neapolitan lasagne is much richer, layered with ricotta, sausage, boiled eggs, the usual tomato-based *sugo*, or sauce, and meatballs.

'They are a pain to make,' says Nicoletta, rolling the last tiny meatball by hand. She fries the meatballs in oil and then I watch closely as she cuts squares of fresh pasta and drops them in boiling water. After three minutes, she takes them out and places them on a wet tea towel. She dollops *sugo* on the base of a glass baking dish and covers it with a thin sheet of pasta, then sprinkles *parmigiano*, a little ricotta, another layer of pasta, slices of the fried sausage, another layer of pasta, then more ricotta, a few meatballs, and so on.

It's still too chilly to dine on the *terrazza* so we sit inside. I will soon learn that Sunday lunch is one rare occasion when Nicoletta does not have the television switched on. On any night of the week she eats dinner watching the soap *Al Posto al Sole*, or the political talk-back show *Ballarò*.

Glad to have her undivided attention, I settle in for what I know will be an entertaining lunch. The more time I spend with Nicoletta, who, at fifty-five, is the same age as my mother, the more I warm to her affectionate and passionate spirit, and consider her a friend and confidante instead of a landlady. Judging her as an intelligent, articulate and independent woman who doesn't settle for second best, I'm curious about why she hasn't met her soul mate. But I'm also impressed that she doesn't waste time worrying about it, preferring to *prendersi in giro*, take the micky out of herself, and playfully mock the male of the species. I sometimes wonder if I will share her destiny.

When I turn the conversation back to the fireworks, Nicoletta stabs her lasagna and looks up at me. 'The Camorra is not a political problem but a cultural one, and the idea it exists because of the poverty is just not true,' she says with an exasperated sigh. 'If you look at the poorest areas in the South, where there are almost no opportunities for youth, not everyone becomes a delinquent. The Camorra is an organic, cultural beast that brings protection and advantages.'

Nicoletta argues that economic development can help deal a deathblow to the Camorra. She points to Bagnoli, an industrial, seaside wasteland, which has been awaiting grand development since the early 1980s when the major steelworks closed down.

'The Camorra stayed away because the steelworks were an important institution, and Bagnoli was a workers' quarter where three generations of families had toiled. It was the factory that educated that community…' she says.

'As soon as it closed, in comes the Camorra, which hates school and education because it doesn't make money. The only education that members of the Camorra have is consumerism. They dress in the latest trends, know fashion labels by sight, and yet many can't read or write.'

According to Nicoletta, plans to build a university in Scampia, the lawless suburb in northern Naples notorious for its rampant drugs market and underworld gang wars, is at least one step forward. Announced by Antonio Bassolino, President of Campania, in April 2006, the twenty-two million euro medicine and surgery faculty is due for completion by the end of 2008.

'It seems total madness to build a university when there are so many shootings and deaths, but the problem can be solved by breaking this homogeneity, this mass that clings together. To break up the mob you have to install "clean" things,' Nicoletta says. She gets up from the table to retrieve the salt shaker from the kitchen and check something in the oven. 'If you bring in and establish these sorts of things, slowly they begin to take shape and the cultural DNA of the Camorra is isolated and destroyed.

'At Scampia, at the start, the university students won't be that happy, but then small communities will develop, and instead of going into an alley to shoot up, kids will go to a bar and have a beer. All kids do in Scampia is get high because there is nothing else to do.'

My curiosity to go and have a look at Scampia amplifies, but my Neapolitan friends have warned me not to go alone.

Having cleared our plates Nicoletta carries grilled zucchini with breadcrumbs and *parmigiano* to the table and tells me that economic development is not enough to wipe out the Camorra.

'There is a saying that goes "*piatto ricco, mi ci ficco*". Literally, "rich plate, I grab from it",' she says, dishing me out some vegetables. 'Bringing in welfare won't beat them because they'll just wheedle their way inside. Where there is money, there is Camorra.'

Naples, Nicoletta argues, needs extra assistance.

'Going to school here is not like going to school in Milan, because here there is high truancy, here people die,' she says with a shake of her hands. 'From the moment a child is born in this city it needs special attention, to be monitored, to be raised in a healthy way…Maybe if we do this we can beat the Camorra.'

Rubbing my belly, swollen by all things richly Neapolitan, Nicoletta's next remark makes me feel even heavier.

'The thing I hate most about this city is when Neapolitans say, "Oh well, we'll see." It's not like, "Today I'll do this and I'll do it well because then in the future I'll have prospects." This loser's fatalism is soul-destroying.'

I shift in my seat. Recently I've been trying to understand why I'm already feeling more at home in Naples than I ever did in Rome. Maybe the novelty of being in a new city hasn't worn off. But why am I searching so hard to see the positive side of a city renowned for its wretched desperation, a city which so many are quick to condemn, or abandon?

'Well there must be something good in this town if you're still here,' I say.

'It knows how to surprise me,' says Nicoletta simply. 'If you go out you always find something new…Light one day will bring out particular colours of Vesuvius, or you'll discover a little bit of history…This crumbling splendour always has something to tell you.'

I pour some more wine into our glasses and ponder Nicoletta's love–hate relationship with Naples. Everyone has a different, passionate view, and I struggle to filter the emotion to get to the essence of an opinion. I stare at Nicoletta and can see the resignation in her face. It's time to divert what is fast becoming a depressing conversation. I compliment Nicoletta on her perfectly plucked eyebrows and tell her all about my hour of indulgence with Filomena at the beauty salon.

'At thirteen, Neapolitan girls are going on forty,' she says with a snort of laughter, then lights one of her Red Merit cigarettes. 'At seventeen their objective is to find themselves a husband, even if he's a lout. They want to be able to say "I'm married", then get pregnant, and have a tranquil life.'

Nicoletta was twenty-nine when she married a writer and intellectual whom she hasn't spoken to now for a decade. She fell in love with his voice, which she heard on a microphone across a crowded room at a Communist Party meeting in the 1970s, and followed till she found its owner.

She giggles as she relays the morning of her wedding, when she woke at 4 am with a panic attack and paced the streets of her hometown in the Avellino district near Naples.

'The entrance of the council building where I was due to get married was ugly, so I went to a florist and asked him to put some flowers there to make it pretty,' she said.

After being married for almost a decade, Nicoletta divorced her husband when she was thirty-eight. She hasn't fallen in love again, and rues the fact that she didn't follow her instinct to separate much earlier.

'Life is fifty per cent chance, fifty per cent destiny,' she sighs. 'If I had known at thirty that I would be here now, without kids…' Her voice trails off with regret.

In an attempt to cheer Nicoletta up, I change the subject and tell her that I'm starting to see Naples as a very feminine city. She smiles and says Naples is like an elegantly wasted *bella signora*.

'There are two types of Neapolitan women,' she says carefully, raising her wine glass to her lips. 'There is the *mamma*: all heart, who screams of tragedy, who would die for her children, who lives for her family, who is very carnal, sentimental and Mediterranean,' she says.

'Then there are those who suck the juice from life. That doesn't mean they're without values or true feelings, but above all they search for pleasure…'

Nicoletta points to Luisa Sanfelice to demonstrate the second category of women. The daughter of a Spanish Bourbon general, Luisa was seventeen when she married her cousin Andrea Sanfelice, a Neapolitan nobleman who bestowed upon her the title of duchess. The pair had a stormy relationship and financial woes.

Following the French invasion and the declaration of the short-lived Republic of Naples in 1799, Luisa attended the many parties thrown to celebrate the new regime, and met a string of men who declared their love for her. Some became her lovers.

Among them was Gherardo Baccher, an army officer and the son of a rich banker, who conspired with his brother to lead the Spanish Bourbons in a military action to overthrow the republic and restore the king to the throne. When she learnt of the conspiracy, Luisa confided in one of her other lovers, who in turn alerted the government and foiled the Baccher brothers' plans.

Hailed by some as 'the saviour of the republic' and 'mother of the nation', Luisa was nonetheless condemned to death the moment Ferdinand I returned to power as sovereign of the Kingdom of Two Sicilies. Many had hoped her youth and beauty would render her a pardon, but the king was furious that the young woman's antics had caused the death of some of his most loyal officers, brutally executed in the final, bloody hours of the republic after their plot to seize power was revealed. At just thirty-six years of age, and a month after giving birth to her third child, Luisa was decapitated in Piazza del Mercato on 11 September 1799.

'She had a difficult life, and to keep afloat she had relationships with rich men who helped her,' says Nicoletta. 'She was severely criticised for this, but she wasn't being a revolutionary just to nab men, she was simply a woman of strong sentiments, who sought pleasure.'

Pulling out some *sanguinosa* – a Neapolitan chocolate pudding that literally means 'bloody' because a dash of pig's blood was traditionally added to the dough – Nicoletta says that Neapolitan women are much more emotionally charged than the average Italian woman.

'Here they search for and manifest sentiments,' she says, tucking into her dessert. 'If a Neapolitan mother loses a child, for example,

her reaction is total desperation, with screaming and drama…
A woman from the North would react much less publicly.'

Nicoletta gets up to clear our plates and I wander onto our *terrazza* to stretch my legs. My phone rings – it's Adriano.

'How are you surviving the *quartieri*?' he asks.

'Great, I'm just settling in,' I say, then admit that I'm still a little hesitant about exploring my new neighbourhood.

'The trick is to make yourself known, because once the locals can place you, they won't cause any trouble…'

Each morning over the next few weeks I buy the newspaper from the *edicola*, or newsstand, beneath my house, engaging in small talk with the newsagent. Around the corner is a flower seller who introduced himself as Antonio and now offers me a smile and a hello when I pass by without buying anything. I stop to pick up some *baba* from a *pasticceria* a few blocks from home, where a gregarious young man, named Nino, updates me on his day and peppers me with questions about Australia, which he dreams of visiting one day.

My neighbourhood project is cut short when I stop in at the bar directly opposite my palazzo to test the waters. At 8 am it is strangely empty, compared to the usual coffee rush hour. Three men stand together at the bar and an elderly lady sits at the cash register. Silence falls before I've even blurted out my order, and I count the seconds it takes for my coffee to arrive so I can gulp it – difficult when the espresso cup is piping hot – and go.

Walking down my street I shake my head in amusement. There was definitely something fishy going on in that bar. But how the hell would a newly arrived Australian, with still no grasp of the local dialect, know what the Camorra smells like?

After work I pop into a hair salon in the *quartieri* and sit down for a trim. As my tattooed, beer-bellied haircutter, Salvatore, sets to work, I hear the roar of a motorbike outside. I turn my head towards the door and smile as I see Nino from the *pasticceria* sitting on a hotted-up bike, a cheeky grin on his face.

'*O Sasà, mi raccomando, trattala bene!*'

Nino shouts out to all and sundry that my hairdresser must 'treat me well'. Now aware of my status as part of the family, Salvatore's brow seems to crease with extra concentration as he resumes styling... and Nino roars off into the 'hood.

'A panza è na pellecchia: chiù ce miette e, chiù se stennecchia

The belly is elastic: the more you put in it, the more it grows

Spring has long sprung when I open the front door of my apartment to find a piping-hot *pastiere* sitting on a tea plate on the terracotta-tiled doorstep. I spy Nicoletta's kitchen door open and I wander across the *terrazza* to see her pulling from her large oven the last of six Neapolitan flans, which are traditionally served at Easter. Moist with ricotta and cereals soaked in orange-blossom water, the *pastiere* is but a currant in the rich fruitcake of Neapolitan *dolci*. Nicoletta says she's cooking up a supply to share with her mother and sisters during the Easter weekend, and then looks at me with a pained expression.

'I can't stop eating,' she says, then recounts what she wolfed down yesterday, twenty-four hours after quitting her two-decade, two-pack-a-day smoking habit: a typical Italian breakfast of biscuits and coffee, a mid-morning pastry, a *panino* at lunch, a packet of chips and a tube of caramels in the afternoon, a bag of *taralli* (savoury, ring-shaped biscuits) upon arriving home, pasta for dinner, and a slab of cake for dessert.

I encourage her to maintain her willpower, but she snorts when I complain that I've put on about half a stone since arriving in Naples.

'*Tu sei molto magra, statti zitta*,' she says, telling me I'm a rake and I should shut up, before disappearing with a *ciao bella* to pack her bags.

I may be slim by local standards, but I've started morning walks to try and regain my pre-Naples physique, kept toned by a more active Roman lifestyle. Arriving in the South in the depths of winter, I was keen to sample the seasonal stodgy dishes: fried *salsiccia* (sausage) with *friarielli* (a green, spinach-like vegetable unique to Naples and typically panfried), plump *polpette* (meatballs) in a thick tomato puree, *pasta alla Genovese* (meat and onion tenderised in litres of oil), and my favourite, *baccalà alla casseruola* (fried cod that miraculously remains crunchy despite drowning in an olive, caper and tomato sauce). Pushing aside the *sfogliatelle* and *baba*, the *caprese* – a dense chocolate cake you can buy as a mini-pudding – is my favourite southern *dolce* to date.

Having left my pushbike in Rome, and not feeling as confident to roam Naples alone after a certain hour, I'm looking less than fly. Yet the moment I step outside my front door, I realise that I have little to worry about. If we are what we eat, Neapolitans are *salsicce*. Flab cascades over the tight belts of men and women wearing low-waisted jeans and many tote their extra load with all the pride of that questionable breed of Australian male who views his beer belly as a national treasure.

Nourishment, explains my friend Manola, is the simplest way for struggling families to show they are wealthy.

'I know poor families who spend all they have on food, to give the impression they don't want for anything,' she said. 'If a child says they have no appetite it's viewed as a bad thing, you know, you have to eat! It's for wellbeing, sure, but it can become a health problem.'

At work one day, I'm not surprised to read a story claiming that only ten per cent of Italians still use the healthy traditional cooking ingredients and methods of the Mediterranean diet, and a survey revealing that people are thinnest in the North and fattest in the South.

Ensconced on the sofa at home after enjoying Nicoletta's *pastiere*, I devour a series of old movies set in Naples and chuckle at their fixation on food, and how it brings not only comfort and solidarity, but is apparently a cure for all ills.

In a classic scene from the 1954 comedy *L'oro di Napoli, The Gold of Naples*, six short films by prolific 'neorealist' Neapolitan director Vittorio de Sica, food is a total preoccupation for Neapolitans.

In *Pizze a Credito*, one of the short films, an impossibly comely Sophia Loren portrays a married woman who runs a primitive, hole in the wall shop that sells fried pizza. When she loses her emerald ring, accidentally leaving it at her lover's house, she tells her husband, Rosario, that it must have slipped into the pizza dough. Having abandoned his dream of opening a pizzeria to buy his wife the precious ring, Rosario drags Sophia around the *quartiere*, chasing customers who had bought pizza that day.

Sophia and Rosario door-knock the Finizio household and find Don Peppino mourning his wife, who has died just hours earlier. When Rosario gently tries to explain to the crying man that they too have suffered a great loss – in one of their fried pizzas – Don Peppino shrieks with grief, realising that he was eating pizza as his wife slipped away.

Later, a group of women haul Don Peppino to a table where a colossal plate of spaghetti is placed in front of him beside a roast chicken and potatoes, a bowl of fruit and bottle of wine, and they order him to eat. It's an attempt to cheer him up, but Don Peppino is last seen with tears streaming down his cheeks, falling face-first into a mountain of pasta.

Another famous scene from Italian cinema, which tells of the poverty in Naples, is in *Miseria e Nobilità*, *Misery and Nobility*, starring the inimitable Neapolitan actor Toto. He plays Felice (which means 'happy'), the patriarch of a starving family that decides to help the son of a poor marquis – who wants to marry the daughter (Sophia Loren) of a rich chef – by posing as his wealthy relatives. When the marquis' servants arrive at Felice's modest home carrying a large buffet, Felice and his malnourished clan cannot contain themselves. As soon as the last servant disappears from sight, they dive upon the food, their bodies becoming as entangled as the spaghetti they grab in handfuls to stuff into their mouths and pockets.

As I watch one classic film after another, I can't help but think that Naples has barely changed. The panorama of the gulf still makes me catch my breath. The same chaos rings out in the street; the poor, yet devout, share their views with the same gesticulations and, resigned to their situation, seem to focus only on survival. The message at the start of *L'oro di Napoli* resonates for me:

> In this film you will see the places and people of Naples. The splendid, humble, sad and joyful aspects of the Neapolitan streets are neverending. We will show you just a little part, but you will find the same traces of that love for life, that patience, and that continuous hope that is the gold of Naples.

Striding home after my morning walk before work, I hear a cheery *buongiorno* behind me. I swing around to see Fernanda, the woman who runs a little fried pizza shop identical to the one Sophia Loren and her grumpy husband run in *L'oro di Napoli*. In Naples, *friggitorie*, or fried food stalls, are everywhere, especially in the *Quartieri Spagnoli*.

Like Loren's pizza seller, Fernanda wears a white apron over her dress, but the similarity stops there. The young, pouting, Marilyn-shaped Loren wears a cotton blouse revealing cleavage that her jealous husband urges her to cover from ogling customers. In her sixties, Fernanda resembles two *nonne* pasted into one with a pair of stocky legs sticking out beneath a housewife smock. Chunky black glasses bridge her nose below her short, thinning hair, tinted blonde and slightly permed. Her grin shows teeth yellowed from the cigarettes she smokes when she's not tending to the fried pizza.

She takes a fist-sized wad of fresh dough, flattens it with her hands before adding ricotta, tomato sauce and bacon; she folds the dough into a little pouch and then tosses it in a huge vat of bubbling oil. The finished product looks a bit like an oversized potato scallop, and like Loren, Fernanda wraps it up in butcher's paper before handing it to the customer.

I met Fernanda when I was doing a story on Neapolitan food for an Australian magazine. Asked to do the run of the mill tourism story at a time when I was starting to feel guilty about my creeping kilos, I pitched a piece on how to get fat in Naples. My idea, an excuse to traipse around the city in search of the best pizzerias, *pasticcerie* and *gelaterie*, was greeted with enthusiasm.

Metres from my front door, I noticed a sign advertising pizza *a volontà* – as much as you like – for two euro *da Fernanda*. Following my nose, I found Fernanda and a group of old hens sitting in plastic chairs out the front of her shop. When I struck up a conversation and I explained my assignment, Fernanda's already puffed-out chest swelled further and she told me that she'd learnt her trade at the age of eight, when she began helping her mother fry pizzas. For almost sixty years she had done little else but toil in her tiny shop.

I asked Fernanda if she lived in the *quartieri* and she pointed to a door directly across the narrow street, little more than a metre away from her shop. She pulled a set of keys out of her apron pocket, grabbed my hand and led me across to her *basso*, unlocked the door and then ordered me to go inside.

Ferdanda's home had one main room, spic'n'span but dark, even though it faced the street. On the left wall stood a glass cabinet crammed with crockery, bottles of alcohol and other random items. To the right was her bed, below a portrait of Jesus hanging on the wall. In one corner of the room a Madonna shrine was illuminated by blue fairy lights. Fernanda then dragged me into the small kitchen area where a tiny table was squashed against a wall, and she opened another door to give me a peek at the pokey bathroom.

Suddenly as lost for words as I was, Fernanda asked if I had a boyfriend, then told me to pop by for lunch one day, no doubt thinking a girl is lost without a man.

I thanked Fernanda for her generosity, but couldn't help thinking my efforts to trim down were being sabotaged at every turn, from Nicoletta's attacks of the munchies and my own bright freelance story ideas, to the dinner invitations of those in my small group of friends.

If there's one thing I miss terribly about Rome it's the culture of eating in restaurants. People do dine out in Naples, but for many it's an unaffordable luxury. Eight out of ten dinner invitations I receive are in someone's home, and pasta is almost always the main meal, particularly if there are many mouths to feed. When Neapolitans do eat out, going to a pizzeria is the logical choice, being the cheapest option, particularly for families.

While foodie opinion is divided on its true origins, pizza's presence in Italy dates back to the Stone Age. After Vesuvius erupted in 79 AD, a flat bread was found in the ashes of Pompeii, alongside other pizza-making implements. When tomatoes made their way from the New World to Europe in the sixteenth century, the Neapolitans pulped them to make a sauce and spread it on pizza made from flour, water, salt, yeast and oil.

It wasn't until 1889, however, that Naples was written into the pages of culinary history as the world pizza capital. On a trip to the city, Umberto I, King of Italy, and Queen Margherita commanded the services of *pizzaiolo* Raffaele Esposito, a pizza maker who concocted three different types for his lieges. One of them, topped with mozzarella, tomatoes and basil – in the colours of the Italian flag – was appreciated so much by Her Royal Highness that it was branded pizza Margherita.

I prefer the thinner-based Roman pizzas to the Neapolitan version – generally flat in the centre and high and crusty on the edge. But I gain a new appreciation for the most staple part of the Neapolitan diet after a chance encounter at the bar I frequent near work. One of the barmen stops me one day to say that his Neapolitan friend Orlando, who lives in Australia, is in town. Within days a meeting is arranged.

Orlando sits on a chair on my terrace and wears a T-shirt with 'Bondi Beach' emblazoned on the front. I soon discover that he's a friend of a friend in Sydney, where he has lived for twelve years. He returns to Naples every two years to see his family, but this time pizza has brought him back.

Orlando is developing a concept for a reality-TV program with three protagonists: pizza; its birthplace, Naples; and a young Australian apprenticed to seven *pizzaiolo* in seven pizzerias in town. When he or she is not slaving before a wood-fired oven, the young chef is toured around town by Pulcinella, Naples' black-masked, hook-nosed mascot.

'People think it's easy to make pizza,' laments Orlando, who has been learning the craft in a bid to make his reality show even more real, and to be the translator between the *pizzaiolo* and the young apprentice should his concept be snapped up by an Australian television station.

'For a start, you can't follow a recipe. You just have to use your hands to feel the dough, watch it in the machine and judge whether it needs water and flour... And if the weather is hot, you can't add too much yeast.'

Orlando insists that Neapolitans make the best pizza in the world. 'Australians are good at swimming and surfing because of the beaches. Well here we eat pizza every day!' he says.

Orlando abandoned Naples for the North when he was twenty-two, fed up with the homophobia and verbal abuse rife in his hometown. In Milan, he fell in love with an Australian man and, in 1991, decided to follow his partner to Sydney.

'In Sydney I found freedom and a quality of life I can't have here, even if I was rich and living in a nice place,' he says.

But Orlando misses the beauty of Naples, from the gulf and all its scents, to the churches, museums and art... not to mention the nutty locals.

'Two days ago I was in Mergellina,' he says, 'and there was an old man on the street who was peeling boiled eggs. I thought he was going to eat them, but he threw them down for a dog walking by. The dog smelt the eggs but then just kept going, and the guy went nuts, screaming all the worst words in dialect... "I saved those eggs for you, but you didn't like them!" It was so funny, so crazy.

'When I'm here I walk everywhere and I never tire of watching these little scenes. You can be on a bus and there will be someone laughing beside you and someone crying behind you. Wherever you go, too, there is a mix of people. You see those who have everything, and those who have nothing…'

But drained after a day walking the streets, watching his back for motorbike *scippo*, Orlando says that Naples is too chaotic for him.

'You have to look right, left, behind…In Sydney you just look ahead,' he says. 'And driving is no pleasure here, you must look everywhere because no one follows the rules.

'In Sydney,' Orlando continues, 'you can go and have a nice breakfast because there are plenty of places to sit down, have a coffee, read the paper, and have time to think and start your day.

'In Naples you have an espresso at home or in a bar where you have to stand up, and you always have a queue behind you, pushing to get coffee too. And the service is always rude.'

'That's not true,' I say, pointing out that at my local bar, despite the chaos, I'm always greeted with a smile and a hello, and invariably get friendly, albeit harried, service. 'In Sydney,' I add, 'I used to go to the same sandwich shop every second day and they always treated me as if I was a new customer, and the only place where I was on name-basis with the staff was a bar run by Italians!'

'Penelope,' says Orlando with a school principal's tone, 'I get that personal service in Sydney too…Foreigners get it anywhere in the world. I advise friends who visit Italy to frequent the same place, because people will get to know you.'

It dawns on me that when people are far from home they often get special service simply because they make more of an effort. I've grown to love making friends with the owners and staff of my local bars in Italy, receiving extra attention because I'm Australian, and Orlando has experienced just the same thing in my country.

While Italian service can be warm and embracing, Orlando's right, it can also be grudging, and sometimes outright rude.

'I'm glad I moved to Australia, because that's where I learned manners…please, thank you, you're welcome,' laughs Orlando. 'In Naples they don't exist. They do NOT exist! Everyday in the street there are so many people pushing you, no one says sorry… In Sydney, even when you go into the supermarket people say hello and goodbye to you.'

I bite my tongue, knowing he's painting a far rosier picture than reality. Like many Neapolitans I have spoken to, he goes on to suggest that I should try and learn a bit of dialect as a way of ingratiating myself with the locals.

'If you can make them laugh they will love it, because they think that if you know their language you must love them – and Neapolitans love to be loved,' he says, then gives me a smile that lights up the terrace.

Orlando invites me to pop into a pizzeria where he'll be working on the weekend, and as he makes to leave I ask him if he can imagine ever returning to Naples for good.

'I had such a hard time when I was young here, but each time I come back I find myself falling in love with the city, I'm finding myself here again,' he says. 'I don't know, but one thing's for sure – I've written my will and I want to be buried in Sydney, where I found my freedom.'

I walk along the Spaccanapoli to Annalisa Durante's local church in the central *quartiere* of Forcella. As I pass a string of restaurants my mouth waters at the smell of freshly baked pizza, and I remember from the diary that it was the slain schoolgirl's favourite meal. In fact, she ate pizza with her family at home hours before she died. Pizza, too, was the final dish a notorious underworld figure enjoyed before he was brazenly gunned down in 2006.

Terrified diners, including children, watched as he slumped face-first into the warm dish.

I enter the church to find Father Merola, who has promised me an interview with Annalisa's father. Apparently, Giovanni Durante can't make it after all but I'm happy to wait my turn to chat to the priest.

I stand outside his office and to kill time I strike up a conversation with one of his police escorts, who starts peppering me with questions about why I'm in Naples. Tiring of having to explaining myself and the tubby man's somewhat cocky attitude, I ask him where his gun is. Standing beneath a Madonna statue he discreetly lifts his polo T-shirt to show off a pistol wedged into the top of his trousers.

I'm saved from having to respond when I hear my name being called, and I'm promptly ushered into a side room furnished with little more than a table, two chairs and a few shelves.

Annalisa's death, Father Merola tells me, generated publicity around the globe not just because she was young, blonde and beautiful.

'It was big news because of how it happened,' he says. 'Salvatore Giuliano knew he was about to get shot at by two *sicari*, and yet he didn't hesitate to walk behind Annalisa and her friends.'

'He knew he was on a hit list, but instead of lying low, he decided to walk around a *quartiere* where the average age is around twenty-five, where people get married at sixteen or seventeen, and every family has around four or five young kids.'

Salvatore Giuliano was condemned to twenty-four years imprisonment in March 2006 for Annalisa's death, but the brutal style of the killing has stuck in the public's memory. His sentence was just one of the many handed down to members of the Giuliano clan.

In *See Naples and Die: The Camorra and Organised Crime,* author Tom Behan writes that 1500 people were murdered in Naples' Campania region between 1977 and 1983 as Rafaelle Cutolo's NCO tried to break the Giuliano clan's strongholds. The power struggle escalated a few days before Christmas in 1980, when NCO members tried to muscle in on the Giuliano clan's contraband cigarette market.

According to Behan, the NCO–Giuliano war was caused by two things: the rapid growth of two distinct Camorra gangs, and the political and financial instability left in the wake of the November 1980 earthquake which killed 2735 people and left 300,000 homeless.

> The war rapidly became a straightforward battle for power, which was fuelled by the billions coming down from Rome for earthquake reconstruction... The highest number of deaths occurred during 1981–1982, when most recon-struction contracts were being awarded. Indeed, during this period some Neapolitans placed illegal and macabre bets, in a system run by the Camorra itself, on whether there would be more gangland murders than days over the coming year.

Father Merola's voice rises with agitation when he says Forcella is famous thanks to the Giuliano family, described by Behan as probably the longest-surviving Camorra clan in Naples. One of ten children, Luigi Giuliano took over the clan founded by his father, Pio Vittorio Giuliano, in the mid-1970s.

Trying to keep track of the Giuliano family tree is difficult. After a reign of more than thirty years, Luigi turned supergrass in 2002, three years before one of his brothers, Nunzio, was assassinated in an ambush. At the height of the Giulianos' power, says Father Merola, the clan was raking in billions of lire each week in illegal soccer betting. And when Argentinian soccer phenomenon Diego Maradona moved to Naples in the early 1980s, the soccer star often socialised with the Giulianos, popping into the Forcella home of Luigi, nicknamed *O' Re*, 'The King'.

In 2003, before Annalisa's death, Father Merola took a stand against the rampant drug trade in the area and fought for funds to have security cameras installed. His first death threat came as he was riding his motorbike home and a scooter rider blocked his path briefly, waved a pistol, and ordered him to 'quit while he knew what was good for him'. Later, he was approached in the sacristy of the church.

'They said, "We live off the drugs – stop or we'll take you out,"' he says matter-of-factly. 'Now, beyond the angel the good Lord provides me, I also have the police escort, whom I also call my angels.'

Soon after he became a priest at the age of twenty-three, Father Merola encountered Forcella's nasty underbelly. In October 2000, he was just hours into his first day at his new church when he was confronted by two men in one of the suburb's narrow, dim streets.

'I was thrown to the ground…I was scared, but friends calmed me and explained that I'd been attacked by the so-called *sentinelli* (who guard the turf for the Camorra), because I was new. They hadn't seen my white collar.'

That day Father Merola understood the destructive abandon of a *quartiere* controlled by the Camorra.

'There and then, with the hands of these two criminals pressing on me, my social work began,' he says. 'I remember thinking, It's not possible to live like this. Something had to be done.'

Judging both Church and State to be ambivalent about the Camorra, Father Merola began writing in vain to the mayor asking for help. But it wasn't until Annalisa was killed that authorities started listening, and since then real progress has been made.

Father Merola tilts his head towards the sunlight that has begun to filter into his small office from a high window to his left. 'We had no street lighting, no school, no post office. It was a desert, but now there are flowers,' he says.

Now Forcella has a school, named in Annalisa's honour, footpaths, better lighting, a post office and even a bus service. Father Merola is toiling to bring about a cultural shift by targetting the young.

'Here in the parish I work only with children, because they are the new generation,' he says. He shifts in his chair and peers through the glass-panel door at the growing queue outside. 'Each day after school we have activities in the church – art, theatre, computer training – to give the children more opportunities than their parents had. We are also able to reach out to the parents, because we have to contact them to involve the kids.'

Often, however, parents are either in jail or have deserted their families, so an aunt or grandmother is the next best thing.

'In the church, children find an extended family,' says the priest, adding that sixty-eight per cent of residents in Forcella have some form of criminal record. 'To eradicate the Camorra, it will take a miracle...Now is the time of sowing seeds, not of reaping. Reaping is for the next generation.'

Father Merola's words begin to wash over me like a sermon, and I wonder how many deaths will occur in the interim, before the next generation grows up.

'Hope is a Christian belief that every now and then gets a bit lost, but as a priest I must try to raise hope in the hearts of people... Hope is not a pacifier, it must be organised. I listen to

God and together with my colleagues I'm organising the hope of this *quartiere*.'

I point out that when horrific incidents occur like Annalisa's death, there tends to be a knee-jerk reaction from authorities and quick fixes without lasting results. But the priest remains upbeat.

'Here we have never let go, we all have dirty hands – I mean, in a work sense,' he says carefully, clasping his hands together and resting them on the desk between us. 'In Naples there's high unemployment, and there is work to be done to raise education levels and help disadvantaged areas like Scampia and Secondigliano to grow. To make them more liveable.'

He admits that even if there was an effective city administration in place, Naples might still be 'Struggle Town'.

'This is a tough city and at times results are not achieved, not because of bad government, but because of Neapolitans who rely on welfare,' he says. 'They are always waiting for help to resolve their problems, but instead every citizen must pitch in.'

Father Merola believes Naples is in a perfect position to exploit two gold mines: tourism and artisanship.

'When the Pope came to visit in 1990 he left saying Naples was the most beautiful city he had been to, because of Vesuvius, the sea, the warmth of the people, and that despite the poverty, the city had a huge heart…'

Father Merola also hopes that efforts will be made to nourish Naples' strong craft tradition, to stop the last generation of artisans dying out. I think of the flourishing handicraft stalls in via San Gregorio Armeno, where Neapolitan craftsmen carve those intricate nativity figurines, or *presepe*, including tiny sheep, goats, baby cribs and Madonnas. When I mention the street to Father Merola, he nods his head and proposes a 'Made in Forcella' brand, and he dismisses my suggestion that shops would struggle to survive with the Camorra in play.

'No, the Camorra is concerned about public tenders and drugs, they don't worry about shops. At the most they just ask for a cut,' he says.

I stand to leave and thank Father Merola for his time; he promises to be in touch with me about meeting Annalisa's father.

Turning at the door, the immensity of Naples' problems beginning to weigh upon me, I ask how he manages to maintain hope when history shows generations of Neapolitans have failed to pull themselves out of the mire.

'The force I have inside comes from the Lord,' he says in a way that sounds almost rehearsed. 'Pope Benedict XVI says that he is a humble servant who works in the vineyard of God. We must all be servants, we must all work in God's vineyard.'

I force a smile and walk out into the afternoon sunshine. I call a friend and entice her to join me in drinking the fruit of God's vineyard.

On a soupy Saturday night just after the mid-August *ferragosto* holiday, when the dirty streets of Naples empty like water gurgling down a drain, I've just confirmed, via a stream of SMS messages, that all of my Neapolitan friends are away. Then Orlando calls and invites me to pop in to a pizzeria where he's working as *pizzaiolo* for the night.

Sluggish from the hot weather but keen to do some exercise, I decide to make the effort. Despite the humidity, I pull on loose jeans so I don't have to carry a bag. I stick my mobile in one pocket and keys in another, along with forty euro, just in case I meet trouble.

The elevator is miraculously working, and as it descends I notice my only piece of jewellery flashing in the mirror. The last time I was home in Australia, Nic, Rob and Erin, the first three friends I made when I moved to Sydney thirteen years ago, gave me a beautiful silver bangle for my birthday. When we realised it didn't fit, I exchanged it for a simple silver ring with thick square sides, which I love more and more as it becomes scratched with wear. When I took off my grandmother's ring months ago in Rome, I couldn't bear the idea of not wearing any keepsakes that reminded me of loved ones. Hardly a delicate piece, I resolve that surely only the most desperate of thieves would covet my birthday gift.

As I walk down my street scooters whir by. On one a man and a woman sandwich their toddler daughter between them. None of them wears helmets. I'm used to seeing children on bikes – tucked in between adults, or standing on the driver's foot platform and hanging onto the steering handles – but I still get a little outraged.

Turning into via Toledo I relax as I see a throng of people, families and kids, walking in the same direction as me. Still early, I take a shortcut through Chiaia's main shopping drag before I reach the gulf. At just after 10 pm the promenade hums with the chitchat of amblers, the banter of African men selling fake bags, and the roar of traffic, from hotted-up scooters to cars pumping techno trash. Gelatos drip and fall from sticky hands, teenagers pash against the sea railing, and heat-induced sleeplessness hangs like a halo over the city.

Within forty-five minutes I reach Al Sarago, one of the many pizzerias in Mergellina, and I spy Orlando the second I walk in. Dressed in white pants and T-shirt, and with a blue apron around his waist that matches the blue bandana he has tied around his head Karate Kid style, to soak up sweat, he stands with his back a metre from a blazing wood-fired oven decorated in pretty blue tiles. His brow furrowed with concentration, he doesn't notice me walk in and start watching as he grabs pockets of pizza dough, smacks them onto his workbench and flattens them with his hands, then strains to read the scribbled orders on a pile stacking up before him.

When I sing out to grab his attention, Orlando plants two sweaty kisses on my cheeks and tells me he's barely qualified to be filling in for the *pizzaiolo,* who has disappeared on holidays, along with most of Naples. He switches into English to moan about the waiters throwing orders before him in three different places and forgetting to keep him supplied with plates.

'Penelope, look at that! You would never see that in Sydney!'

Before me a waiter carries a pizza in one hand and uses the other to chat on his mobile, with customers in full view. I smile at Orlando, taking his point.

He screams to the kitchen for more peas and sausages and other depleted ingredients, and I take a walk around the restaurant looking at the framed photographs. Maradona is the star, posing alongside girls who look like 1980s hair models. Sean Connery and Toto are the only other men I recognise.

I wander back to watch Orlando make a range of pizzas, from the simple Margherita, to fancier numbers involving *friarielli* and *salsiccia.* Gradually he begins to relax and joke and banter with the owner.

I decide to leave just after eleven, knowing I'll be home just before midnight. I tell Orlando that I'm incredibly proud of him, and make a beeline for the promenade, still jammed with rowdy locals. I avoid the shortcut down via Chiaia, which seems to quieten earlier than the other major streets, and walk the full length of the promenade until I reach Piazza Trieste e Trento. A police post is set up alongside an ambulance in the piazza, and as I head along via Toledo the crowd thins to small groups. I stride with purpose, watching the distant glow of the shop sign that marks my street corner.

I'm at the halfway mark when I see a couple about ten metres ahead, standing near the funicular. I watch as a scooter zooms towards us and a hand stretches out and makes a grab for the woman's bag. But she is too quick, or perhaps her attacker too green. As the scooter roars past me I see an acne blemished young boy looking behind him, his expression charged with adrenalin. The whole scene flashes before me as if on fast forward.

Deathly quiet, except for the squeak of my sandshoes, I finally turn into my sloping street. Not far ahead are two young chubby girls wearing tight white shorts and tank tops. I quicken my pace to get closer to them. Their long, meticulously straightened hair reminds me of Annalisa Durante. When she was shot, the people who ran to the scene found her blonde mane glued with blood to the pavement.

I turn the key to my palazzo and look around furtively before ducking through and slamming the wooden door so hard the sound echoes through the courtyard.

Feeling returns to my jelly legs; my chest heaves with relief.

Chi perde ave semp' tuòrto

He who loses is always wrong

News of my first eyewitness *scippo* is met with barely a ripple of interest in the office. True, it's nothing compared to being robbed at gunpoint, and there are hotter things to discuss. The 2006 World Cup is weeks away and debate about the competing teams, which are in furious training for the event, takes precedence.

Three years in Italy has failed to convert me to *calcio*, and as I listen to Marco, Alfonso and Francesco gabble on about Italy's form, I can't even feign interest. Until Benedetta bites. A die-hard Rome fan who worships both the skills and 'athleticism' of the team's ponytailed star striker, Francesco Totti, she seems to know more about the game than the three men combined, and has no fear about putting in her verbal boot to prove a point.

But today I'm more distracted than usual, trying to mentally prepare for an important meeting. After weeks of phone tic-tac with Father Merola, the priest in Forcella, I finally have an appointment with Giovanni Durante, Annalisa's father.

While I'm curious to talk to Durante after reading *The Diary of Annalisa*, I'm not sure how I feel about raising something so personal, and tragic, with a total stranger. When I was working as a journalist for a Sydney tabloid, 'death-knocks' – slang for knocking on the door of someone who has just lost a family member, friend or lover – were just part of my job. It was sometimes hard to justify the intrusion, even though people in mourning often feel the need to talk. There were times when I was welcomed into the homes of people who clearly wanted to share their memories of loved ones.

I cross Piazza del Gesu and head along the ruler-straight Spaccanapoli. Amid the colour and noise I watch as strings of tiny Italian flags are draped across the street. Skirting around stazione Centrale, I head towards the familiar towers. My appointment with Giovanni is at the Centro Direzionale, Naples' central business district. Whether arriving in Naples by plane or exploring the suburbs by car, it's hard to miss this futuristic precinct. Designed by Japanese architect Kenzo Tange, the strange glut of high-rise buildings with mirror-glass windows shoot into the sky like weeds in an unused parking lot.

The main street is a wide paved avenue split in the middle by a series of planter boxes. I pass a few lonely clothes shops and the odd bar before reaching the Chamber of Commerce building, where Durante works putting stamps on books.

A stout man with a boxer's nose holds my stare long enough to show that he's waiting for me. Durante offers me a handshake and a cigarette and we walk over to a planter box nearby. Technically still on the job, he tells me that he must stay within view of his office.

To break the ice, I tell Durante that when I read *The Diary of Annalisa*, I was struck by the close bond he had with his daughter. She wrote about both the affection and frustration she felt towards her mother and sister, Manuela, but more often she wrote how much she adored her *papà*.

'My family was like a team, we were always together and happy, even though we had little money,' Giovanni says. 'Annalisa was the darling of the household because she was always giving cuddles, always joking, and when she saw her friends buy something new, I always did whatever I could to get her the same.'

Annalisa had the same hopes, dreams and materialistic desires as any kid her age, yet she also seemed wise beyond her years. In her diary, Christianity, faith and the drug problem in her neighbourhood are explored with breathtaking sensitivity. When I suggest to Durante that her precocity might have come from living in one of Naples' roughest areas, he shakes his head.

'She was mature from an early age...She never missed school for one day, and she studied,' he says. 'She would tell me so many beautiful things, about nature, the sea, how long flowers took to grow...She loved so many things. The only thing that made her feel sad was that I didn't have a regular job. She'd say, "Papa, if you had a job we could live in another way." But unfortunately I was born into an area...let's call it degraded. But I always did something to support my family. Sold black market cigarettes, cassettes...whatever I could to bring in some crumbs.'

Durante uses that familiar phrase that some Neapolitans bandy about with pride: *l'arte di arrangiarsi*, the art of arranging oneself or doing whatever it takes to survive. I can't help but think with sadness that his employment prospects only took a turn for the better after Annalisa's death, when local authorities gave him work as a sort of compensatory gesture.

Durante pauses to light another cigarette then suddenly apologises, pulling the packet out of his jeans pocket to offer me one again. I thank him but shake my head. To fill the awkward silence, I comment on how vivacious his daughter was, judging by her diary entries. A pained smile flashes across his face.

'At Christmas she said, "Dad, we have to put up street lights and have a party like they do in other zones." And she organised a money collection in the street,' he says, adding that Annalisa also helped him in the toy store he runs with his cousin in Forcella. 'When I went to buy new stock for the shop she would tell me what I should get, and those things tended to sell like hotcakes…'

At home, he recalls, he would often make silly home videos of his daughter singing all of her favourite traditional Neapolitan songs and imitating famous music stars. Among her favourite songs was '*È Bell o' Magnà*', or 'How Beautiful it is to Eat', by local legend Mario Merola.

On the night Annalisa was shot, she ate dinner at home with her parents and aunt and uncle around 10 pm, before leaving to visit some girlfriends. Little more than an hour later, Durante heard gunfire and leapt up to look out the window. He couldn't make out the small figure lying on the street below but the fear of it being Annalisa powered him down his palazzo stairwell to reach the street.

He found his daughter lying still on the pavement. He instinctively put his hand under her head to support it.

'I wanted to help her breathe, but when I moved my hand it was covered in blood and I went into shock,' he says.

Other than the daily visit she makes with her husband to their daughter's grave, Carmela Durante rarely leaves home, even though being there is difficult.

'We don't want to admit what has happened,' he says, absent-mindedly scraping one of his sneakers on the pavement. 'And at home there are so many memories of Annalisa.'

They hope to find a new home in Forcella, but Durante dismisses the idea of leaving the city for good, despite his family's misfortune and the crime that mars the city.

'Why should we leave? I was born here... The bad people should leave, not us,' he says, his voice rising a little.

For all his grief, Durante insists that some good has come from his daughter's death. In Forcella, a school under her name has opened, there is talk of a cinema, and he has proposed a library. But things have only changed twenty per cent, he estimates. When I suggest, as others have to me, that Naples hasn't changed for decades because there hasn't been a clear vision for the city, Durante's voice charges with frustration.

'In Naples, things *must* change, people must push ahead... Institutions must support people, because if they stop, the city stops,' he says. 'The thing needed above all is employment, and harsher laws for the young kids who are committing all these crimes...'

Durante is adamant that this is the only way the Camorra will be beaten.

'It won't be easy, but it can be done. We have to hope and fight,' he says. 'I want people to see the good side of Forcella... Every morning, when I look at a photo of Annalisa, she gives me the energy to cope. Let's hope people can understand how she lived, that there can be a change.'

As Giovanni Durante kisses me on the cheeks and says goodbye, I'm lost for words. I'm incapable of understanding his grief, or the complexities of the depravation in his suburb.

Durante has already started walking back towards his work when I say, not expecting him to hear, that if Naples had more kids like Annalisa then maybe the city's fortunes would turn.

Durante swings around and looks at me with a sad smile. 'No one exists like Annalisa...She was like Maradona.'

A week before the World Cup kicks off, my Rome flatmate Adriano is in town to run a few errands and see his family. Durante's comment has finally sparked my curiosity about soccer: I want to understand why Diego Maradona left such an indelible mark on Naples. I call Adriano, who used to lie on the couch all weekend watching the soccer, and suggest we have lunch.

He arrives on his brother Paolo's battered blue scooter, and we ride to Da Michele. Until now I've been unable to secure a table at Naples' most famous pizzeria. Brandi, in via Chiaia, is the city's oldest pizzeria, but Da Michele – which only serves Margherita and marinara pizzas, with Peroni beer and water – is the locals' favourite, alongside Di Matteo, just off the Spaccanapoli.

Outside the pizzeria, Adriano takes a ticket from a waiter on the doorstep. Despite a small crowd, the turnover is fast. Within ten minutes we are in the door and seated at one of the butcher's paper covered tables and inhaling the baking dough from the wood-fired oven commanded by two rotund men wearing white chef's hats.

Before lunch, I brought myself up to speed on some Maradona facts, figures and key moments, not wanting to embarrass myself in the face of Adriano's encyclopaedic knowledge. In 1984 Maradona signed to play for *Società Sportiva Calcio* (SSC) *Napoli* which, since its foundation in 1926, had only managed to win the *Coppa Italia*, or Italian Cup, only once. With Maradona donning the number 10 guernsey, in the next seven years the squad twice won the *scudetto*, the Italian Football League championships shield, alongside the *Coppa Italia,* the UEFA cup and the *Supercoppa Italia*, or Italian Super Cup. In 1991, Maradona was disqualified for fifteen months when he tested positive to cocaine after a match. He never returned to SSC Napoli, but locals talk about him as if he never left.

In fact, a part of him didn't: in 1993 an Italian court ruled that Maradona had fathered a son by a Neapolitan woman in 1986, but the player refused to undergo DNA tests. It wasn't until 2004, during divorce proceedings with Claudia Villafane, whom he married in 1989, that Maradona admitted siring Diego Junior, who still lives in Naples and has played for a local team. By all reports the young man lacks his father's magic touch.

Adriano and I order and charge our glasses with Peroni.

In 1984, when Adriano was thirteen, word spread like wildfire that SSC Napoli was considering poaching Maradona from Barcelona.

'The news was flatly denied a day or two later, when I was at a street market with my mother, who was buying some pantihose – how many pantihose do women go through!' says Adriano, making me laugh. 'I walked up to a stall of music tapes – CDs hadn't been invented – and I heard a song blaring from a speaker: *Maradona è megl' 'e Pelé*, Neapolitan for "Maradona is better than Pelé".'

For soccer idiots like me, Pelé is the nickname of Edson Arantes do Nascimento, the Brazilian footballer who played from 1957 to 1971. Brazil never lost an international match when Pelé was on the field.

'Obviously,' continues Adriano, 'I bought the cassette, which had a strange compilation of songs, including "Tango of Maradona", which all soccer fans remember.'

Until 1984, Adriano knew nothing about Maradona, only that he was 'the best player in the world', and that, at the age of twenty-three, he was destined to follow in Pelé's footsteps. But as the speculation over Maradona defecting to Naples grew,

Adriano began collecting photos of the player and watching the nightly television news with anticipation.

'Barcelona didn't want to sell him and Naples, it was said, didn't have enough money,' Adriano continues. 'Maradona made it obvious he was keen to play in Naples, but a "no" seemed more probable than a "yes"…and yet the entire city was learning a song about a soccer player who hadn't played for even one minute with the local team. Somehow he'd become the idol, not the soccer player.'

Then came the news everyone had been praying for: Naples had bought Maradona for a reported thirteen billion lire, almost seven million euro. Big money for those days. Italian newspaper *Il Corriere della Sera* said the banknotes had Camorra stamped all over them.

'Everyone was thinking the same thing,' Adriano says as two steaming, wood-fired Margherita pizzas are plonked before us. 'Gianni Agnelli, the patron of Turin's soccer club Juventus, who had until then spent the biggest sums on players, declared: "We're not rich enough to buy Maradona, but we're not so poor that we *have* to buy him."'

If Agnelli, head of car manufacturing giant Fiat in Italy's comparatively rich North, chose a clever way to jeer at Naples, its citizens saw the purchase as a symbol of the South's victory over the North.

'Maradona was "ours" and not "theirs". He was coming to play with an absolutely mediocre squad that had never won anything, in a city considered the poorest in Italy,' says Adriano, lost in the memory, his eyes shining with excitement.

'The city went crazy. Word spread that ten thousand people would be at the airport to see Maradona arrive. There was so much hysteria that he was forced to arrive in Italy secretly and travel to Naples by helicopter.'

Adriano stops to eat his pizza, fast growing cold. I realise mine is, too. Golly, I never thought soccer could be so interesting.

When Maradona arrived at Naples' San Paolo stadium, a crowd of sixty thousand people, who had each paid three thousand lire to be there, went barking mad.

'The grass was the first thing Maradona touched,' says Adriano, who was in the crush. 'I can't swear it's true, but in my memory he bent and kissed the grass...'

No one in Naples, maintains Adriano, declared their team was capable of winning the national *scudetto*, or shield, not just for *scaramanzia*, for luck, because they are superstitious, but because of the club's bleak record. And then the newspapers, mainly foreign, said that if Naples won the shield, the Camorra would have to pay out illegal bets worth up to two hundred billion lire.

'I was going to the stadium and singing all the songs about Maradona, but the word *scudetto* never entered my eardrums and never left my mouth,' says Adriano.

For luck, fans kept mum on the 's' word right up until the night before Naples was to face Milan in the 1986–1987 season final. Riding on his scooter around town, Adriano saw young men climbing every vertical plane to mount blue *Napoli* flags, and teams of people armed with blue paint coating every surface. Apart from the mountains of Maradona song cassettes, fans bought wigs resembling their hero's curly mop and ordered pizza topped with spinach and tomatoes. Shaped in a triangle, the striped green, white and red pizza was a cheesy imitation of the *scudetto*.

'But that word... it was never written anywhere,' says Adriano, who donated all his savings to a money collection for street decorations to support the team.

'Nobody of my generation can forget the earthquake of 23 November 1980, nor what they were doing at that precise moment the windows started shaking and people were running down stairwells. It was a shock, that earthquake, just like the first *scudetto*,' he says.

'Fans could not contain their happiness seeing that phenomenon wearing the number 10 jumper, who crushed every enemy defence. Everyone would arrive at the stadium around two hours before a game to sing songs and jump in the air at precisely the same time.

'It was more entertaining to check the newspapers for the seismometer reading than the match results. I can't remember the term the experts used for it, I just know that eighty thousand people leaping in the air at the same time created a telluric force – an earthquake! Authorities eventually banned jumping at the stadium…As if any rule in Naples would be respected!'

If Maradona wasn't already considered God before the first *scudetto*, he was now more powerful than any pope.

'Everyone knew him. He was dining out in restaurants and hanging with *camorristi*. Intellectuals loved him, they saw the Maradona phenomenon as…' Adriano pauses, suddenly confused. 'Well, who knows, really, everyone saw in him what they wanted. But Maradona himself spoke only of God and his *mamma,* and he got about town with a stream of parasites, like any true king.'

The soccer star flew in his family and friends from Buenos Aires to be by his side. The entourage included a polio-afflicted manager and a gaggle of prostitutes and shady personalities, who easily mixed with the Neapolitan *camorristi*, whose favourite sport was to beat up journalists who were bothering the star.

One of the most telling portraits of the era was a photo of Maradona with Luigi 'Angel Face' Giuliano, then boss of Forcella. The image shows the powerful duo at Giuliano's opulent home, sitting in a black, oyster-shaped pool. At the time, Giuliano was a fugitive.

'But who couldn't love Maradona?' Adriano says with a laugh after seeing my eyebrows lift at the idea of Maradona being on such cosy terms with the Camorra. 'The elites even formed an association of the richest and most influential fans, like entrepreneurs and politicians, and held a competition to capture the "true spirit" of Maradona in poetry. They even built a museum for him.'

The association was called *Te Diegum*, the Neapolitan version of *te Deum,* which is latin for 'to God'. Maradona was received in private by the Pope and other heads of state, including Fidel Castro, with whom he shared an intense hatred for America.

Adriano says that before Naples won its second *scudetto* in April 1990, 'Everyone knew he was throwing sex and drugs parties…that in the morning he couldn't make it to training.

'Later it was revealed that the doctors who were doing his anti-doping tests were being corrupted,' says Adriano, leaning over the table. 'Things got worse. Sometimes he wouldn't even show up for a game. But the strange thing, and unique in the world of soccer champions, was that for all of his power he never became obnoxious. I can honestly say there was no one at the time who ever criticised him. They always defended him. He had a humanity, a…well, who knows.'

A waiter arrives with our bill as Adriano offers his final memory of Maradona: Naples preparing for the 1990 World Cup. The huge event was hosted by Italy and games were played around the nation.

'In Naples, big events are always hugely celebrated, but they are never organised well,' says Adriano. 'And the preparations for the 1990 Cup caused more chaos than the earthquake and the Camorra combined.

'There were construction yards everywhere, dead-end roads, and big developments that promised to change the face of the city. At least that's what the mayor of the time declared, before being jailed for corruption.'

The World Cup began and before too long the event arrived that no one wanted: Argentina versus Italy, on Neapolitan soil.

'Controversy broke out,' remembers Adriano. 'Who to support? A little bit of soberness was called for, but Maradona wasn't sober – two days before the game he invited the Argentinians to his house in ritzy Posillipo for a party. And he extended the invitation to all Neapolitans, saying "Italy remembers you only when it needs you...rebel against anyone who asks you to barrack for Italy – and barrack for ME!"'

Adriano looks at me and laughs.

'I know what you're thinking, he was joking, right? He wasn't. Maradona's appeal to Neapolitans drew a response from the president and every other important figure in Italy at the time. As per usual, Maradona managed to spark sentiment.'

The night before Argentina met Italy at San Paolo stadium, Adriano joined the throng outside Maradona's home to sing Argentinian songs.

'I don't know how to write the words, but I can still sing them,' he says, humming.

The image of my old flatmate passionately singing for Argentina outside Maradona's house is too much. I burst into laughter and Adriano starts humming louder.

The next day he was in the stadium when Maradona, moments before the anthems began, strode across the field.

'He shouldn't have done it, but he was Maradona...He came close to Curve B, where the true Neapolitan fans sit, and he blew a kiss: "Argentina is with you."'

I draw my breath as I imagine the scene. The sporting hero's audacity sends a chill down my spine. Argentina won but Maradona's behaviour contravened the unspoken rules of soccer, and he was vilified in the press. In the next game, indeed the World Cup final, Maradona and his Argentinian team mates faced West Germany. In Rome.

'Argentina was beaten thanks to a wrong penalty. The game was clearly decided by the referees. But everyone knew it would be, even before the game started,' Adriano claims with conviction. 'Maybe Maradona hadn't cottoned on, but he realised as soon as the teams lined up to sing the national anthem. Everyone in the stadium in Rome leapt to their feet and screamed to drown out the Argentinian anthem. But they didn't manage to drown out the famous number 10 who, with giant tears running down his face, declared to the whole of Italy, "*Hijo de puta*" – Son of a bitch – and then spat on the ground. So there he was, the captain of his team, a minuscule dot in the centre of the field, standing with his hand on his heart before a stadium of ninety thousand screaming people.'

In 1992, Adriano says as we stand to leave, Maradona left Naples after a fifteen-month ban for testing positive to cocaine.

'He was forced to flee Naples, like a thief in the night, and as for the rest, I don't know, and I no longer want to know.'

The next day at my computer at work, I reflect on how Maradona began his Italian adventure by kissing Naples' grass, only to leave after spitting on a Roman field. My Neapolitan colleague Francesco, sitting opposite me, is a sports journalist and knows more than a little about Naples' enduring romance with Maradona. Like Adriano, Francesco was in the crowd when Argentina beat Italy in the 1990 World Cup semi-final in Naples.

'During that game, Naples backed Maradona and Argentina,' he confirms, his trademark unlit cigarette hanging from his lips. 'We felt closer to Argentina because Maradona had given us a joy that not even the *Azzurri*, the national Italian squad, could give us. And so the Neapolitan fans enraged all of Italy, and in the final in Rome there was a type of backlash against Naples and Maradona.

'Many Neapolitans said we were wrong to barrack for Argentina, but even today, years later, I have no regrets.'

'Naples,' Francesco says with a blinding smile, 'was so euphoric after its team won the first *scudetto* that some wrote on the wall outside Poggioreale cemetery: "You don't know what you've missed." They wanted their dead grandparents and relatives to join in the party.'

Though Adriano's and Francesco's tales have not made me a soccer convert, they have gone a long way to explaining Naples' obsession with Maradona. He gave Neapolitans a sense of pride and hope. And as for Maradona's elbow rubbing with the Camorra, Francesco is quick to his defence.

'He was no crook or *camorrista*. He was simply the most famous personality in the city. Being a sporting symbol means he was also "manipulable",' Francesco says earnestly. 'His contacts with less-than-clean personalities was hardly scandalous. In the US, most professional basketball, football or baseball players attract shady types like flies, but it doesn't mean that they, too, are crooked. Today, everyone remembers Frank Sinatra for his voice, not his "friends" in Brooklyn.

'For many years, Maradona was under the spotlight in a city that was split in two: the soccer team and Maradona were a spectacle to enjoy after years of sporting defeat, but it also became an occasion for social revenge.' Francesco takes his unlit cigarette between his fingers. 'At the end of the day, every wrong committed by Maradona he actually committed against himself...'

Before I leave work I scan the Naples section of the regional newspaper *Il Mattino*. An article catches my eye.

Under the headline *La morte mi ha sfiorato* – 'Death brushed me' – the *scippo* of a middle-aged local is described in detail.

After dinner with friends in affluent Chiaia, a woman was enjoying a walk along the same sea promenade I pace each morning. As she was walking to her car with friends, a motorbike roared past and made a grab for her bag. But the bag was hooked over the woman's head and she held on. When friends ran to her body, spreadeagled on the tar road, they found her face covered in blood.

With two nose fractures, missing teeth, a fractured left wrist and split lip, the woman made an appeal to Naples' mayor: 'Give me three good reasons why I should stay in this city.' In an open letter to the woman, a Neapolitan doctor who left Naples fifteen years earlier attempts to do the mayor's bidding:

> In the United States I appreciated the effectiveness of a society based on the quantitative measurement of results: I was there two years and it was rich and intense from a work point of view, but in the end I didn't feel a sense of belonging and I returned to Italy.
>
> Throughout my journeys abroad I have not found the same welcoming, the same capacity and rapidity to adapt to change, the same courage and determination that I experience in Naples...
>
> I have decided to face with my family the challenge of Naples and would like to share this experience with all of those Neapolitans of goodwill who, like me, have decided to get involved in the future of this city, my home.

Home. The word resonates as I remember Giovanni Durante saying that he would never leave Naples.

I need to get a sense of bearing. I've been caught up in the gloom, the dark side of the city that fascinates but strangles me. I need to possess the city, adapt to it without fear. It's true that

Naples has a well-deserved reputation, but bad things happen in every city.

I grab my iPod and leave work, hooking my handbag over my head. Listening to music calms me wherever I am, and I've downloaded some new tunes to enjoy. I've swapped the distinctive white headphones with a black pair, so no one knows I'm carrying a valuable toy.

The promenade along the gulf buzzes with activity in the late afternoon. Small stalls do a steady trade selling hot *taralli* biscuits, corn on the cob, freshly made granitas, and raw tripe and fish carved on the spot and drizzled with fresh lemon, alongside bars where the summer masses queue for coffee and gelato.

Families with strollers and couples wander slowly along the concrete walkway, holding up joggers. Young girls wearing stilettos, short-shorts and dangly earrings, and pimply boys with too much hair gel amble along gossiping in dialect I still can't quite grasp.

I pass Castel dell'Ovo and watch late afternoon swimmers jump off the rock wall into the sea. Directly opposite, on a small outcrop of the promenade, families sit on plastic chairs under umbrellas as small dinghies rock in the sheltered bay.

Friends and lovers lie across the large white rocks of the sea wall that stretches from the castle to Mergellina. A group of people play cards at a table they have dragged onto a particularly large rock. I wouldn't be surprised if they camp there overnight. In summer, Neapolitans have a habit of taking the city as if it were their own, as if they were passing time in their own houses. It's a quality I admire. If only they could clean up after themselves.

Towards Piazza della Repubblica, the first of the African street sellers appear, standing guard over row upon row of sunglasses and flashy fake designer handbags. Reaching the piazza I gaze up at the colourful apartment blocks blanketing hilly suburbia, and as I turn back towards the Villa Comunale I notice the fluffy sunset-pink clouds suspended above the park's treetops and wedged beneath blue sky.

On the small beach opposite, people trudge over the black sand on their way home and seagulls squabble over clumps of rubbish. I stop and lean on the grey wall, looking out at the vessels at sea: a few tankers, a hydrofoil ferry returning from one of the islands, and elegant yachts that bob in the pretty port of Mergellina.

Across the gulf, the Sorrento coastline is shrouded by afternoon mist, so too the island of Procida, while the top of Vesuvius wears a cloud cardigan.

I'm mesmerised by the panorama and soothed by the sea, and I remember a conversation I had with Francesco, my old flatmate, weeks after my arrival in the South.

'You will not find the view of the gulf anywhere else. Naples is the most beautiful city in the world…'

Thinking of various places in Australia with rugged, majestic coastlines, I laughed out loud, convinced he was yet another biased local. But as dusk paints the sky and I scan the panorama. I change my mind.

A yearning to feel at peace with the city tugs at me, and as I walk towards home, I start to develop a game plan. I will continue to be cautious, but I have to live a little more. I'll slip on earrings and a nice frock if I feel like it. I'll just stick with the crowds and not take any silly chances.

On my way home, I notice something on the Spaccanapoli that I've heard of but somehow haven't noticed until now.

Mounted on a wall outside Bar Nilo is a shrine which from a distance appears like any of the others that hang from every angle in the historic centre. But up close I see that inside the wooden frame is not the usual serene picture of the Madonna, but a photo of the bushy-eyebrowed Argentinian who gave Neapolitans something to believe in for almost a decade.

'A ciorta è na rota: mentre gira, po s'avota

Fortune is a wheel: while it spins in your favour, all of a sudden it goes the other way

It's barely 9 am but the sun sears my back as I slam the door of my palazzo and hurry to work.

I've just sung out a cheery *ciao* to Antonio, the local florist, when I feel a sharp stab in my foot. Looking down I see blood spurting from my big toe, pricked by a thin piece of wire camouflaged on the bitumen. I rifle through my handbag but can't find the bandaid I know is in there somewhere. So I stick a tissue between my toes to stem the blood, limp home to tend to my wound, then set off for work again.

As I retrace my steps with care, I notice small slivers of wire on the ground every few metres and puzzle over where they have come from. With the same sense of bewilderment, I ponder how each night I hear the rubbish truck stop beneath my apartment to collect the mountains of putrid waste in the bin, but the next morning I find it's still spilling over.

At work, I scan *La Repubblica*. Once again, Naples has made national front-page headlines for all the wrong reasons:

I prigionieri della spazzatura. Napoli assediata dai suoi rifiuti.
Prisoners of rubbish. Naples besieged by its waste.

La Repubblica offers a humiliating glimpse of a problem Neapolitans have wrestled with for more than a decade: a six-kilometre wall of rubbish that ends on the doorstep of Pozzuoli, a suburb that is home to three hundred families. With vehicle access blocked, the community was virtually trapped by refuse and isolated for days until bulldozers finally arrived to push the mountain a few metres away. The residents were freed, but the rubbish remained and was accumulating, growing higher and more stinky by the day at the height of summer, in a zone ironically known as the 'Park of Flowers'.

'This city is a gift from God, one should smell the perfume of the sea. Instead I walk through the streets and it's just unbelievable what I see,' one church leader told the newspaper. 'We must clean Naples on the outside if we want it to be clean on the inside.'

Train carriages of tonne upon tonne of industrial rubbish, much of it from the rich North, arrive in Naples to be dumped or buried illegally in the surrounding countryside. To avoid hefty fees to process waste in accordance with environmental laws, big business is happy to pay Camorra-controlled firms a reduced price to get rid of their dirty linen. The Camorra also uses its might to sabotage council plans to build new dumps, and encourages industrial unrest in the sector.

The battle against rubbish, which oozes from every corner, overflowing from industrial containers and street bins, and lining the street like carpet, dates back to 1994. At the time, space in rubbish dumps and the criminal mismanagement of the disposal of waste had reached crisis point.

Under a 132 billion euro plan announced in 1998, a new system of waste treatment and disposal was scheduled to be in place by 2001. But things didn't go quite according to plan and by 2003 two of the city's rubbish dumps were exhausted, and in 2004 a second emergency rubbish crisis was officially declared.

That was then, and then is still now.

The rubbish problem in Naples is explained in *Napoli Siamo Noi, Naples It's Us*, a rather depressing summary of the city by journalist and historian Giorgio Bocca. Describing the city's waste as a 'gold mine' for the Camorra, Bocca writes that beyond general refuse, the city bleeds with hospital waste, syringes and sullied bandages, all buried to save on the high cost of special disposal. Every so often, the *comune*, or town council, announces that the rubbish emergency has been solved, but then a waste disposal unit goes bust, or a private disposal company doesn't keep to a contract deadline.

I remember my friend Manola talking about the Neapolitan attitude to public cleanliness: 'Watch someone opening a new pack of cigarettes. They'll be standing beside a rubbish bin in the street, rip off the plastic packaging and throw it straight on the ground.'

I realise that I've learnt to turn a blind eye to the putrid piles of household refuse spilling from the waste bin in my street, and the general filth that blankets the city at every turn. But now, indignant about my punctured toe and noticing, once again, the newspaper photos of desperate Neapolitans standing amid mountains of rubbish, I decide to go straight to the source. After weeks of bureaucratic to-ing and fro-ing, I finally secure a meeting with Corrado Catenacci, who was appointed commissioner for the waste emergency in 2004.

I'm told by Catenacci's press office to be *puntualissima* for my 8.30 am appointment, so I leave home a good hour early and dodge dog poo and garbage along via Toledo as I head towards the suspiciously cleaner zone of well-to-do Chiaia.

At Piazza Trieste e Trento the familiar sound of barking greets me as I walk up to Paolo's newsstand. Paolo, possibly the cheeriest man in Naples, pats his mongrel dog and tells the owners of four others to keep their mutts in line as he serves a steady stream of customers.

Where I buy newspapers in Naples has become a bit of a game in recent months. The first thing I see when I walk outside my palazzo is an *edicola,* and at first I bought my papers there as part of my scheme to become known in the neighbourhood. But after a while, I decided that the owner, Stefano, wasn't my type. He was nice enough, but moods are contagious and I sometimes found it hard to shake off his melancholy. My ideal newsagent is someone who, like me, doesn't mind waking up at dawn and might even be chirpy about it, someone who looks on the bright side and reminds me why I want to face a new day, too.

I remained faithful to Stefano until I struck up a conversation with a newsagent in Chiaia on one of my morning walks. Pausing to buy a paper, I asked the young balding vendor if he had any DVDs starring Toto. The classics usually cost anything from ten to twenty-five euro.

'*Aspetta bella,*' he said and disappeared for a few seconds before he came back and beckoned me to follow him into his small cabin. Inside on his workbench were a pile of pirated DVDs starring Toto, Sophia Loren and other well-known Neapolitan actors.

I raised my eyebrows and asked if the DVDs were *buoni,* well-made. He held his hand up to flash his palm in a gesture of scout's honour, and told me that I wouldn't regret my purchase for just three euro. Erring on the side of caution I only bought one, and that night I lay in bed with my computer to watch *Miseria e Nobilità*, *Misery and Nobility*. It's a movie I've seen before, but this one has Italian subtitles so I can decipher the thick Neapolitan dialect.

My relationship with my DVD dealer continues, but the man who won my morning affections was Paolo. Granted, his newsstand has the most enviable position, just metres from glorious monuments like San Carlo Teatro and Palazzo Reale, and within view of the shimmering gulf and Vesuvius. But it's Paolo's sunny disposition and battler values that I appreciate the most. From one day to the next he offers me titbits on his life – failed love affairs and his latest sailing holiday all delivered with dollops of honesty and mischief.

Occasionally, usually on the weekend when I'm not in a rush to get home and shower for work, I stop and have a coffee with him. And when I buy my paper from him on my weekday morning walks, I try and tuck it from view before stepping into my palazzo, and wonder if I'm being silly imagining that Stefano has noticed our relationship is on the rocks. To remove the stain of guilt, I buy a comic book or magazine outside my door once a week.

'*Penelope, fatti una bella giornata!* Penelope, have a beautiful day!' Paolo calls out.

I give him a wink and tuck *Il Mattino* under my arm before heading up via Chiaia towards my 8.30 am appointment with the rubbish commissioner. I stop at a bar for a quick jolt of espresso, pass a string of boutiques and finally enter a glorious palazzo on via Filangieri, where a porter directs me to the first level.

Elena, the head of media relations, greets me with a handshake and a smile that smacks of morning efficiency. A number of

Italian women, including Elena, trace the outline of their lips with a lip pencil, usually deep red in colour, then coat the inside with a lighter coloured gloss. When the gloss fades, the outline stands out even more and reminds me of those mechanical clowns that swallow ping pong balls on sideshow alley. I have no idea if the make-up trend has arrived in Australia, but in Italy it's one of my pet fashion hates, alongside bras with transparent straps, which actually draw attention to the bra, instead of hiding it. I'm sure if I snooped in Elena's underwear drawer I'd find at least one of these crimes against fashion.

Elena ushers me out of the building and into the palazzo directly opposite, where we take an old wooden lift to the fourth floor. We walk into a beautiful foyer with enormous ceilings and antique furniture, then Elena leads me into a chandeliered room with a long oak table, gold velvet-upholstered period chairs and windows facing the quiet street below.

Built like a barrel and wearing a casual navy suit, Corrado Catenacci greets me with a firm handshake and motions for us to join him at one end of the table. I examine his face as pleasantries are exchanged. Probably somewhere in his sixties, the commissioner has a broad face and blunt features.

I draw a breath and get the first thing that's worrying me off my chest. My Italian has deteriorated a little since my arrival in Naples. Due to my work in English and no time to study I can't address him using the formal *lei*, pronounced 'lay'. In Italy, there are two forms of 'you': *tu,* used between family, friends and those on familiar terms; and *lei,* strictly reserved for strangers. I've always had problems with *lei*, which changes the format and endings of the entire vocabulary. I'll start using *lei* with all the best intentions, but within seconds, forgetting my grammar, I'll slip back into *tu.*

Addressing a man of Catenacci's rank as if we are old friends is not only embarrassing, but would be viewed by some as rude. But while I regret my sloppiness, I usually find using *tu* breaks down barriers more easily. In any case, the commissioner tells me he's not fussed, letting me see him as an everyday guy, who perhaps snores at night, spills food on his clothes in restaurants or, like me, commits faux pas like this on a regular basis.

I begin by asking him how he can explain the state of the city's rubbish problem, given it has been attracting global headlines. Even my sister, Lisa, has read about it in a Sydney newspaper.

'Maybe these problems don't exist in Australia, but your country is two million times bigger than our region,' he says, seemingly pleased to have drawn a comparison with my homeland. 'In Italy, we are sixty million on a peninsula, while here in the Campania we have thirteen thousand square kilometres with little space for waste disposal and almost six million inhabitants.'

The conversation winds back more than a decade as we talk about the series of bureaucratic appointments and hiccups in the struggle to confront Naples' ugly side. A local judge has apparently recommended charging twenty-eight bureaucrats, including the Campania region's president, Antonio Bassolini, with a string of fraud-based charges relating to the administration of waste tenders and services.

The commissioner says that notwithstanding public protests, construction of the new Acerra refuse power plant is under way and will be finished in 2007. There are plans for two others and the three plants will burn forty per cent of the region's waste, with the rest deposited in dumps.

According to the commissioner, a big part of the city's rubbish woes remains with the residents who are loath to take personal responsibility for their city.

'When we start digging new dumping areas people protest because they think they're too close to the site...Opposition fades when people realise that millions of euro in schools and roads and the like are part of the development.'

Magistrates and police are attempting to fight the Camorra's stronghold on the illegal dumping of rubbish in Campania, but the man on the street, argues the commissioner, must play a more active role. He's quick to accuse locals of cleaning their own homes to sparkling perfection while brushing aside their duties as citizens to keep the entire city clean. But he maintains that he's seen dirtier cities than Naples, like some suburbs of London and Paris.

As Catenacci pauses to seize a takeaway espresso delivered by one of the soldiers of Naples' caffeine army, I can't resist asking him if he divides his rubbish.

'No, because there are no recycling containers near home,' he admits. 'Here, the culture of separating household rubbish just doesn't exist like it does in the North...'

Tired of hearing the official spiel, I ask the commissioner if he had to think hard about accepting his position, given the long history of the rubbish problem in Naples.

'When I got the telephone call I was given two minutes, maybe three, to decide on whether to take the job,' he said, weariness creeping into his voice. 'Later, I regretted my decision...I've worked for the state for forty-five years, I've been prefect for eighteen years in places like Salerno, Bari, Cagliari. I've worked with governments of the right, centre-right, centre-left and left, but I've never had as many problems as I have now.

'But we are searching to confront them and, if possible, resolve them...We are moving towards a gradual improvement.' Catenacci presses his fingers together then shakes his head in a show of determination. 'Look, in three years, maybe less, the Campania will be one of the most efficient regions in Italy as far as waste disposal…but it will also take a lot of luck.'

Fortune. Luck. Hope. Knowing they are words that Neapolitans throw around lightly in the face of chaos and difficulty, I ask the commissioner if he was born in Naples, and he was.

'Where will this good fortune come from?' I ask mischievously.

'Things often need luck, also in Australia I imagine,' he shoots back with frankness. He looks at me and smiles. 'I haven't had much in my life, I lost two sons, but I'm lucky to have good health – I'm seventy years old.'

The commissioner cuts short our conversation when his telephone rings and I soon find myself being ushered out of the door as he races to his next appointment. In the elevator, I ask Elena with as much tact as I can muster how the commissioner's sons died, my imagination flashing to Naples' seedy side. But I learn that they died shortly after childbirth.

The next day I rise early to meet Elena again. I've accepted a quick tour of the power plant construction site at Acerra.

As we drive out of the centre, Elena pushes the automatic lock on the car doors as windscreen washers and men selling packets of tissues assail us at traffic lights like a swarm of locusts in summer. Hidden behind wraparound, reflective sunglasses, the driver of our hatchback puts his foot flat to reach 150 kilometres per hour. Also with us is Giuseppe Sorace, one of the commissioner's technical henchmen. No one in the car wears a seatbelt, not that anything would save us at this pace.

Pulling up at the Acerra power plant, I see a police car and two officers nearby. It seems a small group of protesters has tried to thwart another day of construction. As Elena trips around in wedge-heeled sandals, I'm glad I chose sneakers as my feet vanish in dust.

In the makeshift site office, the project director explains that work on the plant should be finished by December 2007, already eight months late. Architectural plans are pasted to the walls of every room in the office, giving an air of productivity, yet I wonder if, like so many of the projects mooted to save the city from rot, the plant at Acerra will open at all.

With hardhats on, we follow Sorace around the site, including the football-field sized cement space where the rubbish will be collected, and the makings of a giant industrial oven where the waste will be burnt and transmitted into energy.

'It's a beautiful project – see this hill?' says Elena, pointing at a grassy rise that will be landscaped as part of the project.

I smile enthusiastically.

Back in the car I try to engage in back-seat conversation with Sorace, but he's a man of few words and speaks so softly that I struggle to hear him. I give up and watch a dark black column of smoke rise in the distance as we head back to Naples. I make a nervous joke that the fumes may be coming from one of the frequent street rubbish burn-offs by exasperated Neapolitans. No one laughs. Our driver says in a deadpan voice that it's most likely from the burning of industrial rubber tyres.

I press my back into my seat and wonder if there is a single part of the city from which smoke or waste does not spew.

Work soon turns into a daily grind, with no sign that ANSA*med* will evolve into a more interesting website with photographs. I've presented a report on improving the site to Carlo, but he's a hard man to pin down, flitting between Rome and Naples, where he lives with his family, according to office gossip, in a mansion in swank seaside Posillipo.

But my workmates make it fun; their idiosyncrasies and personalities are endearing. Alfonso's corny gags, along with his complaints about the less rosy side (rubbish, crime, chaos…) of Naples, have us all in stitches; the animated banter between feisty Benedetta and cheery Tania, now chief-of-staff after Mario's retirement; the cheeky pranks of Francesco, ever keen to play basketball around the office; and Marco's infectious energy all contribute to our team at ANSA*med*. We jokingly refer to it as ANSIA*med* – *ansia* being Italian for 'anxiety' – because we're perpetually understaffed and at times more than a little stressed.

It is with Annalisa, however, that I find myself one evening after work, when neither of us can be bothered going home and cooking for one. My outings with colleagues are rare, not because I don't like them, but I still feel a need to protect my privacy and build a social life away from work. When I do go out with workmates I usually find myself with Marco or Annalisa, sometimes both. With a brother who organises dance parties around the city, Marco is a man in the know. One night he dragged Annalisa and me to a 1980s dance party in the seaside industrial zone of Bagnoli.

Annalisa and I leave the office and head to Cantina della Tofa, the restaurant in my suburb where she and Enrico, Marco and Benedetta were confronted by armed robbers. As we walk into the cosy eatery, with rustic orange walls and an 'artistic' clientele, Annalisa says hello to a guy she knows. I glance across at the table. Sitting beside Annalisa's friend is another man, someone I'd call a 'fetch'. With light brown, messy hair, a goatee and a wide smile, he has a sexy air about him.

During dinner, as Annalisa and I get increasingly tipsy and giggle about our disastrous love lives, I steal glances at the man, who seems around my age. When he walks over to chat to some people next to our table, I desperately try and think of a way to introduce myself. Fuelled by white wine, and noticing he's carrying a guitar case on his shoulder, I ask him if he's a musician. Sometimes my originality blinds me.

He kindly humours me. Soon I learn that Francesco Forni is a Neapolitan musician who lives in Rome. Brilliant. Why is it that the guys I find attractive in this city are either taken or in transit?

Trying hard not to slur, a product of fatigue as well as drunkenness, I struggle to keep the conversation flowing. Perhaps for this reason, I find myself telling Francesco that I have a good friend who is a musician in Rome and plays in a band called Cactus; I don't tell him I'm talking about my ex Federico. Before too long we've swapped numbers and as Francesco shuffles out the door I shake my head at my idiocy.

'*Brava!* You got Frankie Bakeries' phone number. *Stupenda!*'

I shriek with laughter at Annalisa's comment, realising the English translation of Francesco's name. Frankie baking-hot Bakeries, indeed.

Half ruing our inability to call it a night, Annalisa and I stumble out of the restaurant and on to Superfly, which has become my favourite bar, for a nightcap. I'm not surprised to bump into Francesco and Carlo, who shower me in kisses.

'How's the house going without my feminine touch?' I tease.

They're quick to point out my miserable attempts to cook them an edible dinner, and the two get back to business, talking strategies for their *Rifondazione Comunista* party, leaving Annalisa and me to slouch on our barstools over vodka tonics served by Antonello, the boyish bar tender who dips into our conversation intermittently.

As I stumble home, too tipsy to be anxious about walking alone, I picture Mr Bakeries' face and hope I'll bump into him again soon.

◄○►

World Cup fever sweeps over Naples and the entire nation, and I let myself get caught up in the action. At work, my colleagues are obsessed with the cup program, and the strengths and weaknesses of the *Azzurri* are dissected and analysed for the best part of the day.

In the streets, Italian flags hang from every angle and at Charlie's Bar, where I stop most mornings on my way to work, a giant television screen is mounted to ensure quality viewing. Naples is arguably even prouder than most Italian cities because the team captain is Fabio Cannavaro, raised in the Neapolitan *quartiere* of Fuorigrotta, and a father of three whose modesty and boy-next-door good looks only add to his popularity.

As Australia notches up its first victory, a wave of patriotism transforms me into Competitive Penny. I'd like to think I'm not a sore loser, but I was always the kid who threw the tennis racket on the court in exasperation and committed the worst fouls on the netball court. At least in water polo my costume-yanking, rib-poking crimes were hidden beneath the water's surface.

In the lead-up to the Croatia versus Australia match, I send my Split-born buddy, Sanja, a few text messages to stir her up. When the green and gold romp home, I send her a message asking if she'll now barrack for Australia against Italy.

'*Mai.* Never,' she responds, and I can imagine her surly face.

Finally the day I've been both praying for and dreading arrives: Australia versus Italy.

Tempted to stay and watch the game at work, I consider the scene should the Socceroos lose.

No, it's best I watch the game on safer ground.

As I hurry across Piazza del Gesu I bump into Francesco, his face flushed from the stifling heat. We stop and buy a few longnecks of Peroni and buzz the palazzo of Manola and Roberto. Thankfully, it's only a small crowd: we four adults and two young boys, Manola's students from her day job with disadvantaged children.

When the two children learn that I'm Australian, they begin teasing me in dialect I can barely understand, then fall silent in awe when I tell them that I can box like a kangaroo. Thankfully, in the pre-match lead-up, the kids get bored and Manola, always churning some delight out of the oven, takes them into the kitchen to bake a cake, shutting the doors behind her.

Wedged on the couch between Francesco and Roberto, I battle the excruciating tension created by a team of Australians whose admirable defence is countered by a failure to attack, and by the repetitive taunts of Manola's charges, let out of the kitchen for the action. In the final moments, I watch with dismay as Francesco Totti nets a penalty goal and races around the field in circles, sucking his thumb in a gesture to his newborn son before his team mates smother him in hugs.

When my protests that my nation was robbed by an unjust, eleventh-hour penalty fall on deaf ears, I do my best to forgive and forget, but opt not to show my face at Charlie's Bar for a few days. When I do find myself back at the bar, I'm forced to swallow a baking serve of humble pie with my *caffè macchiato*.

Four days later, I leave work an hour before Italy is due to face Ukraine in the quarter finals.

I've just bought a bottle of wine to take to Roberto and Manola's when my phone rings. It's Roberto. He and his *dolce metà*, sweet half, have been invited to a dinner at the home of people I don't know. He invites me along but I don't feel like being a ring-in.

Damn. I look at my watch. Less than thirty minutes till kick-off. I scroll the names in my mobile phone…and stop at F.

Frankie Bakeries.

A day earlier I exchanged text messages with Mr Bakeries. So I know he's in town.

Before I have time to lose my nerve, I send an emergency SMS explaining my predicament and ask if it would be okay to join him, if he's watching the action with a bunch of friends.

My heart beats as I stand in a piazza with my bottle of wine, already picturing myself at home on the couch with Nicoletta, who would be good company all the same. I almost leap as my phone beeps, and to my relief it's a fat *sì*, with an address attached. I follow Francesco's directions and find myself standing in front of a pizzeria, staring at a buzzer.

When you're far from home it's easier to take risks and be more courageous, especially to meet people. But right now I'm losing heart. What the hell am I doing? I've had one drunken chat with Francesco and all of a sudden I wonder if he thinks I'm as kooky as I do. I want to watch the game. I want to meet new people. What have I got to lose? I punch the buzzer.

The door clicks open to a flight of stairs and Francesco greets me at a doorway on the first floor. I hide my nerves and give him a cheery kiss on the cheek before he leads me into the dining room. The television is disappointingly small, but the company seems warm. I shake hands with a dark-haired man with blue-rimmed, Bono-like shades, who introduces himself as Pierpaolo. Two girls slightly younger than me sit at the table, along with a man wearing Blundstone boots, which I'm wearing, too. We exchange a knowing look.

As the game begins I charge my glass and glance at the others around me. At half-time I learn that my match companions are in the cast of the Harold Pinter play *The Caretaker*, which director Pierpaolo is pulling together at Teatro Nuovo, a block from my apartment. He is rolling cigarettes and speaking with a sexy, husky voice. I look from Pierpaolo to Francesco and wonder why I have a habit of meeting one man only to then meet his equally appealing buddy.

When Italy romps into the semi-finals, fireworks explode outside and we rush to the tiny balcony. Scooters fly past with two and three people aboard, all waving Italian flags. The street echoes with people singing *bo-bo-bo-bo-bo-bo-bo,* the catchy riff of the White Stripes' song 'Seven Nations Army', which has become the undisputed World Cup anthem of Italy.

Back inside Francesco gives in to his cast mates and pulls out his guitar. As he closes his eyes and sings his heart out in Italian, Spanish and English, I relax completely for the first time all evening. My father plays the guitar and growing up I spent hours singing by his side with my two sisters. Listening to Francesco, I feel very much at home.

We head to Aret' a' Palm, a cute bar beside two palm trees in Piazza Santa Maria la Nova. As I sip my vodka I see a few familiar faces and I chat with my new thespian friends. By 3.30 am tiredness engulfs me and, without a taxi in sight, I hitch a scooter ride with a complete stranger who is a friend of the group.

Rocking up to work on less than four hours sleep, I can barely keep my eyes open. But the adrenalin of meeting interesting new people, and the anticipation of the grand final, keeps me in motion.

A week later I find myself back with Francesco, Pierpaolo and crew at the same apartment, in fact the home of Pierpaolo's ex-girlfriend, who is away on holidays.

When Italy and Germany are nil all at the full-time whistle, the tension is unbearable. Pierpaolo rolls another cigarette and Francesco nervously fiddles with his jeans pocket as the game goes into extra time. I look around the room and every pupil is dilated. No one moves a muscle. No one breathes. When the *Azzurri* boot the ball twice into the goal to win 2–0, we leap to our feet yelling our lungs dry and bouncing off each other's bodies. Italy has made it to the final.

Outside Naples is a screaming carnival of sweat and fireworks. I find myself again at Aret' a' Palm, where Francesco disappears to the bar and I am left chatting to Pierpaolo. At once cuttingly humorous and unnervingly abstract, he's a strange fish, his gaze intense beneath those annoying glasses. Another tortured artist, I guess. When we can't find Francesco in the throng we decide to walk home. Pierpaolo tells me that after splitting from his girlfriend under a year ago he's now okay 'about four days a week'. He appears to think is a remarkable feat, as though his heart literally broke.

'*Dormi da me?*' he asks.

I consider Pierpaolo's invitation to crash at his house. It's three o'clock, there are no taxis in sight and I'm tanked. And I wouldn't mind a bit of TLC, despite the fact that he has more hair on his chest than an orangutan. At least he doesn't wax it like so many Italian Ken dolls. He'll make for a nice cushion.

I wake a few hours later and hear a song I haven't heard for months. As the sad lyrics of Damien Rice's 'The Blower's Daughter' pipe softly out of the stereo I look at the naked body passed out beside me and suddenly hanker for more than drunken rumbles. In the dawn light I spy an ashtray on the floorboards beside the bed and the butt of a filter cigarette, which Pierpaolo doesn't smoke.

I can't sleep so I dress and tiptoe out of the house. Four hours later I'm a robot at my computer, charged by multiple espressos delivered by a young boy from our local bar who doesn't appear to have slept either. Naples, like the rest of the nation, is sleepwalking towards a dream of World Cup victory.

Soccer commentary bounces around the office until it starts to get on my nerves.

'It's just a *game*,' I say wearily. 'Italians over-exaggerate everything in life!'

One glorious second of silence passes before retorts fly at me from all sides. I'm too tired to finish the fight I've started so I turn back to my computer to read an email that's just beeped onto my screen.

Italian theatrics hide great power and determination! With soccer we are very emotional, but against Germany, with seventy thousand people jeering at us, we proved to be strong-willed!

It's from Marco. I smile to myself and look at the clock. Four hours before I can escape home.

Five days later the big game arrives. The World Cup final: Italy versus France.

Frankie Bakeries is in Rome, and while I've been invited to watch the game at my old house with Francesco, Carlo, Roberto and Manola, I decide to accept Pierpaolo's offer to join him and his friend Oreste at a house in the Quartieri Spagnoli. I want to see Pierpaolo, who, swinging from affectionate to elusive remains a source of intrigue.

Apart from the odd scooter roaring towards a television somewhere, Naples is strangely quiet. The air is heavy with great expectation. As I march along via Toledo, scanning the Italian flags hanging from balconies above, I hear a shout.

'*Signora, spostati!*'

Snapping to attention, I see two young boys lighting the wick of a crudely made firework just metres ahead of me. I race around them and hear sparks explode in all directions. The smell of gunpowder lingers as I look back to see the scallywags laughing and running off and people emerging from their apartments to see what all the fuss is about.

I walk up a squalid street, past rows of *bassi* with their doors wide open framing families and friends gathered in front of blaring televisions. I find the palazzo and take the lift to the top floor. Inside the modern, stylish apartment I find Pierpaolo and Oreste with a group of friends, a mix of Italians and French. Dangerous.

Dinner is about to be served. I pile prosciutto and melon on my plate and find a lone chair near the television. Pierpaolo sits to my left on the couch, rolling a cigarette.

The French are feisty until their hero, Zidane, headbutts Italian player Materassi, and they recoil with horror. Pieropaolo, who didn't greet me earlier with customary kisses on the cheeks, is engrossed in the game and barely speaks a word. At half-time he hands me a creamy plate of *pasta alla carbonara* before settling back into tortured silence.

When the final whistle blows, declaring Italy the soccer champions of the world, our hullabaloo is drowned out by the fireworks reverberating through Naples' maze of narrow streets. Far from being a sophisticated pyrotechnics display, it's every person and their cracker to themselves. Standing on the balcony with Oreste, we watch and grin madly at groups of apartment dwellers doing the same in the palazzo barely three metres across from us. Like ants filing out of their earthen nests, young families waving flags descend from their homes and onto the street below. They squash onto scooters in twos, threes and fours and roar off into the madness.

I follow Pierpaolo and Oreste out to the street and over to a huge motorbike. Oreste, who owns the bike, hands me a helmet and orders me to sit behind him, then Pierpaolo squeezes on behind me. I feel safe wedged between two men with the physiques of rugby forwards.

At least, that is, until we reach via Toledo, where a singing, crying, screaming mob in a state of hormonal delirium confronts us. I usually avoid crowds, so I try to keep calm as our motorbike is swallowed by the heaving throng. I see one, then two old cars painted red, green and white that have had their tops sawn off. The cars bounce with young men screaming their lungs out and blowing streamers and horns – a local soccer team.

We finally crawl to a halt in Piazza Trieste e Trento. The fountain has been barricaded with steel since Italy beat Germany and hundreds of fans threw themselves into the water. It's no use. People scale the barricades, throw themselves into the water and emerge with silly grins.

Just as we round the fountain, a teenage boy clad only in underpants and red, green and white facepaint stops in front of our bike, forcing Oreste to jam on the brakes. A war cry sounds from behind and a second boy rushes over and drenches us with a full bucket of water in one, massive dump.

Soggy but cheery, we continue past people carrying mock wooden coffins draped with the French flag, and car loads of families banging cutlery on saucepans. In my entire life I've never witnessed such unbridled chaos; it makes New Year's Eve, the Sydney Olympics or Mardi Gras seem like Rotary Club meetings.

Somehow we make it to Santa Maria la Nova, where we park and make for Aret' a' Palm. Drunk on wine and emotions, I no longer give a hoot about Pierpaolo's mercurial traits. As I straggle out of the bar to hand some drinks to the boys, I spy my workmate Marco across the piazza. His eyes lock mine and his face lights up like a lantern.

'Penny! Viva Italia! Ti voglio bene! Go Italy! I love you!' he squeals.

He practically bodysurfs across the crowd, and when he reaches me he lifts me up in his arms and spins me in circles until my head hurts.

Not as much as it does three hours later when I roll out of bed, have a cold shower and narrowly avoid brushing my teeth with hair gel, before stumbling down my street towards work.

Naples has turned from dirty-grey to black, and I can't help but think of Commissioner Catenacci. A touch of fortune has sullied the city he's battling to clean. I giggle at my semi-delirious wit.

At work, I relive the action with my colleagues and scan the headlines carrying page after page of the *Azzurri* in action photos or huddled in joy. Amid all the good news stories a small column catches my eye. A Camorra member came out of hiding to watch the grand final action at an inner-city bar. Celebrating outside after the game, the *camorrista* dropped his guard and had no time to react when two *sicari* sailed past and riddled his body with bullets.

It's all a matter of *fortuna*.

L'ommo adda essere cumm' 'o presutto: né troppo chiatto, né troppo asciutto, né troppo bello, né troppo brutto

A man should be like prosciutto: not too fat, not too skinny, not too beautiful, not too ugly

Living in Naples is like being bundled into a cantankerous industrial washing machine with a triple spin cycle. It doesn't take long to feel completely wrung out and as stretched as the sheets that drape from every window from *quartiere* to *quartiere*.

Everything seems harder, and the fact that you don't have to look far to find someone worse off than you doesn't bring any comfort. Walking down Naples' streets I've become accustomed to watching my back while dodging rubbish, speeding scooters and human debris, to being bumped and shoved by people who seem to have no concept of the verb 'to speak'. Neapolitans *yell* – across streets, from bar to shop window and into their mobile phones. Sometimes I'm tempted to leave in the earplugs I wear to sleep at night (to block out the bursts of fireworks and the roar of kids doing laps on their motorbikes) until I reach the office. Not that there is any peace there.

If I thought Rome was backward in terms of efficiency, Naples is Neolithic. When I called Telecom to connect the internet at home, it took me three months to schedule an appointment for a technician to come and do the cabling. To get a modem, I had to rush out of work on a day when we were running on a skeleton staff, to wait at home during the one-hour window alotted by Telecom. No one one showed up. I made a second appointment and took a day off work to make sure I couldn't possibly miss the technician. I waited in vain. A third appointment left me at the point of tears. That was four months ago.

On my walks to work, newsagents' posters of the daily headlines ooze with violence, particularly those of *La Cronaca di Napoli,* the newspaper bankrolled by the Camorra. Its front pages splash with the sheet-covered victims of the latest clan killings, and the black and white mug shots of thugs wanted for heinous crimes. I can't deny that the journalist in me sometimes finds the underworld headlines intriguing. But some days they just grate; they're a reminder of the peril that lurks in every corner and at any hour of the day.

Seething at work after another frustrating call to Telecom, my anger turns to dismay as I read an email from my friend Massimo. Last night he went to dinner at a friend's house not far from my first home in Naples, in the historic centre. After midnight, he left to wheel his Vespa outside the palazzo to give his mate Giulio, a local councillor, a ride home. As Massimo started the engine he noticed that a scooter carrying two men, which had passed seconds earlier, had turned around and was heading back towards them.

I knew they wanted us. They ride up beside us and kick the Vespa, making me lose control of it. One of them gets off his scooter and points a gun at my throat. I think he must be out of it and I say, 'It's all okay, stay calm – here, take this', and I give him thirty euro. He looks at me and says, 'You haven't understood a thing!' and grabs my bag and kicks me off my Vespa.

In the meantime, Giulio, who has suffered many robberies and at work has often been threatened by the Camorra, notices the pistol is fake. He looks at the faces of the two hoodlums and realises they have more fear than us. He launches himself on one of the men and shouts, 'Get rid of that gun, bastard, or I'll kill you!'

At this point I think Giulio's gone nuts and I start yelling to try and raise the alarm. Windows open but no one intervenes. It's part of a collusion. Giulio manages to wrestle back my bag as I wrench back the Vespa and finally they take off into the night. We're safe and sound, apart from being bruised and shaken. The Vespa is damaged. But the thing that annoys me most is that we called the police and no one came.

Shaken and upset, I tell my colleagues what's happened and leave the room to make a quick call to Massimo. He tells me not to worry and says he'll call me tonight. Back at my desk I see a new email in my inbox from my colleague Marco.

To speak badly of Naples is too easy, Penny. In all the *Lonely Planet* guides there is nothing but talk of crime, Camorra, rubbish. From Australia's point of view, Naples is a disorganised, chaotic, impossible city. It hurts me that Naples has come to be known by a bunch of clichés!

Wounded by Marco's accusation, I stifle a rush of anger and take a deep breath and remind myself that in spite of his deep love for his hometown, he's usually the first to admit it can drive you to despair.

I read on.

I don't deny that a lot needs to improve, but there is so much: people who work, my parents, friends, so many people who aren't drug pushers; people with cultural interests; people who are courageous, who fight against the Camorra. If it weren't for them, the city would not exist.

A Moroccan used to the poverty in that country sees Naples as mysterious and fascinating, with its underbelly and its narrow, dark streets. Everything is relative. You are not in Sydney, therefore you need to change perspective to see what there is in this city, which is older than all the cities of Australia added up, and more!

The French adore Naples and come from far and wide. I met two French kids who, tired of the ritzy places like Capri and Positano, were charmed by the historic centre of Naples. In Rome and Florence these precincts are full of souvenir shops, in Naples people hang out their sheets – it's a real city! On New Year's Eve I met two other French people who had travelled in Italy's south and were disappointed with Rome because it was like any other European city. But they said Naples was another world.

Marco's words haunt me for the rest of the day. *Damn him.* Fine. Enough of the bad news stories. I'm going to find the joy in this wretched city, which has overcome conquests, earthquakes and doom at every turn. Deja vu? Something tells me I've already made this resolution.

At home that night I flick through some tourist guidebooks and write a list of things to see and do. The next day I make a beeline to the Madre Museum, one of Naples' contemporary art galleries that my pizza-making friend, Orlando, raved to me about before he fled the chaos to return to his adopted Sydney.

As I wind through the historic centre I try to open my heart to the city, returning the smiles of random people and taking in the sights and scents: rubbish, passive cigarette smoke...freshly baked pizza and sweets. Old people sit on chairs outside the shops of their children and stalls open up for business. I arrive at the Madre, tucked away in a side street in a seedy *quartiere* not far from where Annalisa Durante was gunned down. Inside the spartan, white-walled building I buy a ticket and take a lift to see an exhibition by Greek-born artist Jannis Kounellis.

As I step out of the elevator on the third floor I'm confronted by a room full of huge twisted pieces of railway steel lying horizontal and draped in grey prison blankets. It's like a morgue overflowing with bodies. Please, God, not now. Give me joy, give me light.

I push on to the next room where a huge white canvas with an imprint of flowers is framed by twenty-four bird cages holding live budgies. Restrained freedom. I shuffle on to face a black canvas bordered by two metre-long steel slabs. In between them is a series of knives, their handles wrapped in canvas and their cool, clean blades jutting out, ready to wound. I shake my head in disbelief. I came to see art, not what I read in the papers every day. I look to the window and do a double take: the shutter is made of row upon row of hanging knives with wooden handles.

In the next room I breathe a sigh of relief. A serene, bottle-green canvas with bars of musical notes painted in one corner dominates the back wall. Nearby, a man sits on a wooden chair holding a cello between his legs. As I linger he picks up his bow and plays a short piece as if to acknowledge my presence. I spy a fish bowl on a chair nearby and walk over to take a closer look.

Enjoying the soothing melody, my smile disappears when I realise that the two goldfish are not moving. Half-submerged in the water is a thin filleting knife. I'm in an art gallery, I tell myself. I find less confronting pieces by Kounellis in the next room, installations with great chunks of iron, wood, hessian, coal and other raw materials.

On the second floor I'm buoyed by the likes of Yves Klein, Roy Lichtenstein and a few Andy Warhols, including a portrait of Elizabeth Taylor wearing green eye shadow offset by fire-engine red lipstick. I snicker at two photographs taken in 1970 by Italian artist Luigi Ontani. The first picture features a handsome man wearing tanned shoes, grey woollen flares and a striped jumper. The man is lying on his side on a beautiful, floral-upholstered couch, his hair blow-dried to Bee Gees perfection. He's in the identical pose in the second photograph, except for one detail: he's totally naked. I stop to admire his body and wonder what is the acceptable length of time, in artistic terms, to look at a crotch.

Almost two hours later I step out of the Madre with my head spinning from seeing all things new, and I forget to watch my feet. Shit. I do my best to scrape the dog poo off my sneakers. I hurry along through the streets of the Quartieri Spagnoli with a new appreciation for the wire and aluminium sculptures that are peppered around the city. They're pieces of fun, modern art poking out from centuries-old palazzi on many a street corner.

At home, I walk across my terrace and sing out to Nicoletta, who is standing at her kitchen sink washing up. I've missed out on one of the delicious meals I've grown to love sharing with my landlady-cum-confidante-cum-surrogate-mother. I ask her if she knows who makes the sculptures and before too long I have a phone number for local architect Riccardo Dalisi. When I explain Massimo's misfortune, Marco's email and my desire to unearth some of the 'good bits' of Naples, Nicoletta looks at me with amusement, then seriousness when she sees the weariness on my face.

'The Camorra has its tentacles everywhere, but it can't corrupt everything. You have to search hard for the good in Naples,' she says before disappearing to answer her telephone.

I still can't use the internet at home as my battle with Telecom continues, so I pop into the office on a weekend to read about Dalisi. The seventy-five year old Potenza-born designer works with materials like iron, copper and brass, and his sculptures can be found in some of the world's top museums in Paris, the Netherlands, and the US. Joyous, human, hilarious are some of the words used to describe his work. Good, just what the doctor ordered.

Dalisi graduated in Naples in an era of 'organic rationalism' in architecture in 1957, and quickly earned a reputation as a radical in his field. In the seventies he set up the first of a number of 'creative laboratories' in Naples' poorest communities, inviting children to work alongside his students to design everything from furniture to toys. Dalisi won an award in 1981 for his design of a stove-top coffee maker for Alessi, the Italian kitchenware company, and set up a series of workshops in Rua Catalana, an inner-city street, where other artists collaborated to make the coffee makers, and where scores of Dalisi's steel sculptures, inspired by Spanish artist Gaudi, make up the urban landscape.

I call Dalisi and make an appointment to meet him at his studio in Vomero, a *quartiere* rising above the historic centre and reached by funicular. Two days later I catch the railcar from via Toledo up to Vomero, where the chaos in the city centre gives way to relative tranquillity. I follow my nose to the street name scribbled in my notebook. Walking downhill I check the street numbers and pause at a traditional *basso* with its front door wide open. An old biddy hunches in a chair with her television blasting in the background, and the waft of a tomato *sugo* hangs in the air. Pairs of huge underpants and nighties are hanging on a clothes rack at the doorstep. I'm accustomed to scenes of this type in the Quartieri Spagnoli, a bastion of the *basso*, but it's a rare sight in cosmopolitan Vomero.

I find Dalisi's studio and am about to press the buzzer when I hear a noise behind me. I swing around to see an elderly man with a tanned face and white wisps of hair standing on end. Dressed in smart trousers, pin-striped shirt and shiny black shoes splotched with green paint, he stares at me as he licks a chocolate ice-cream. Not impartial to eating chocolate in the morning, I smile as I look at my watch. It's ten-thirty.

'*Salve*. Hello,' Riccardo Dalisi says politely, and leads me up a flight of stairs to his front door. I step into a long corridor cluttered with art crafted from bronze, copper, silver and more. To my left, a row of shelves strain under the weight of coffee makers twisted and shaped into different personalities.

'Here are the bride and groom,' says Dalisi, picking up two machines linking arms, one wearing a top hat, the other painted lipstick. 'And look, these two are making love,' he adds with a cheeky grin, picking up a sculpture of two of the coffee makers melded together.

Dalisi leads me down the corridor, past various doorways leading to more piles of inventive clutter, to the back of the apartment. The large room is filled with sculptures up to two metres high. I run my hands over the smooth surface of the bronze figure of a woman, before gravitating to the balcony and its breathtaking views over the Mediterranean and across to Vesuvius. I'm so often awe-struck by the sheer beauty of the gulf and today is no different.

I follow Dalisi to his office, where mountains of paper scribbled with architectural plans and sketches cover two chairs and a large desk. I sit on top of the paper cushion on one chair and ask Dalisi whether he chose to work with raw materials because of Naples' poverty.

'In a sense, but also because you can work with those materials, if you make a mistake it's nothing. They're also materials closest to man. I've always been attracted to the journey of man, life which pulses...' he says, his voice trailing off. 'When I was young I was very good at mathematics and physics and astronomy, but I gradually descended towards nature and regenerative architecture. I'm a dreamer, but I search to carry my dreams to the land. I live in the clouds, but then when it rains the water meets the land...'

With a voice that barely rises above a whisper, and a sketchy flow of thoughts, I struggle to follow Dalisi, who transmits a delightful air of muddled can-do creativity.

I admit to him that as much as I love the colour and energy of Naples, I'm finding it a tough place to live. I probe Dalisi for his views on the city he chose not to abandon, unlike many of his peers, for the bright lights of the chic North, where the style capital of Milan holds scores of design events.

'I've always felt a connection with this land, my land,' Dalisi says, his eyes boring into mine. 'This is a land of volcanoes, there is a dark side, which becomes beautiful, passion, which becomes love, and then a return to the darkness...But in the end there is always joy. All of the Neapolitan songs, even the most tragic, are full of joy, the mystery of life, and always being on the edge. This is the underbelly of Naples.'

Dalisi begins to hum a Neapolitan tune and I wonder if I've lost him for a minute. Then he continues.

'I was in Milan recently at a book presentation and there was all this talk about how criminals continue to kill each other in Naples. I stood up and said, "But there is so much more, so much energy that could lead to great possibilities. Naples has a

creative force, behind the violence, but it doesn't find a voice…
It turns against itself."'

I ask him what he would do to make Naples a safer, more
livable city.

'I would create loads of small spaces. Like I'm doing at Sanità,
the *quartiere* where my students are working with a group of
children who are making extraordinary things – sculptures,
clothes, small films,' says Dalisi. 'These children are stupendous,
and the idea is to stimulate them, to save them from the Camorra
through creativity. Then their families get involved, their sisters
and mothers come and see the work being done and ask for more
of these spaces… You see, children can save us, if we concentrate
on them. If we work to improve their lives, we can change things.'

As I leave to race to work, I accept Dalisi's invitation to meet
him tomorrow in Sanità, one of the city's poorest neighbourhoods, to see his latest work with kids.

I walk through the city centre and from a bridge take an elevator
down to a rowdy suburb that reminds me of my own
neighbourhood. In front of shops, crates of fruit bake beneath
the afternoon sun, and the footpaths are strewn with litter.

I spy Dalisi on the street corner opposite. He leads me up the
street to a chapel where some of his conspicuous sculptures hang
from wire above the entrance. Inside is a scattering of sculptures
leading to a stage with a red velvet curtain. In a corner, two young
boys rifle through a pile of timber off-cuts looking for bits and
pieces to use in their art projects. One of them eyes me up and
down, picks up a piece of wood and snaps it over his knee in a
show of strength. Show off.

'Riccardo, Riccardo!'

A young boy with glasses and a slight limp bursts into the
chapel and runs towards Dalisi. He opens his hand to show his

mentor a scrap of metal he's been working on, carving a design onto the surface.

'*Bravo,* Mimmo!' says Dalisi, giving the boy a pat on the back before motioning me out of the chapel, past groups of young kids and into *la Chiesa di San Vincenzo*, Saint Vincent's Church. Inside, the cold marble surfaces contrast with Dalisi's modern artworks, which glimmer in the slivers of sunshine that stream in. Before the traditional altar is the artist's own version: a long glass plate held up by two glass angels.

As we walk past a small chapel where a large group of women kneel and chant hymns, I ask Dalisi whether the older churchgoers objected to the space being filled with his outlandish art.

'No…they tell me it's a relief considering all the sombre pieces in here,' he says, dragging me over to a huge papier-mâché figure of an angel, painted yellow and with a red flower attached. The angel is beside a stern bust of San Vincenzo, the church's patron saint. 'He was the only saint who had wings,' says Dalisi before leading me out of the church into a piazza and bidding me farewell.

As I walk away, I can't help but think that it will take more than San Vincenzo's wings, more than an army of angels, to raise this *quartiere* out of its mire.

Turning off via Toledo into my street, I spy one of the many Dalisi sculptures in my neighbourhood, jutting out like a gargoyle from a palazzo stained grey from smog. Having always wondered who was behind the artworks, I feel happy to have tracked down the somewhat dotty but inspiring architect. Riccardo Dalisi may live in his own version of wonderland, but at least he's trying to make a difference.

◄◦►

Rain falls lightly as I step outside my palazzo door, smack two kisses on Massimo's bearded cheeks, then slide on the back of his blue Piaggio scooter, now battered from the late-night mugging.

In recent weeks we've been spending more and more time together, meeting for *aperitivi* and dining out, because both of us live alone and hate cooking. When Massimo comes to my house he knows what to expect: hastily roasted chicken legs and vegetables squashed unceremoniously onto a dinner plate, or an overflowing bowl of over-cooked pasta with an uninspired sauce whose main ingredient is hope. At Massimo's large but cosily furnished inner-city apartment, the home of his late grandparents, we eat *pasta al dente* with slices of fresh *mozzarella di bufala*, cherry tomatoes and basil. Massimo is passionate about music and shares my love of forgettable tunes from the 1980s. He puts vinyl records on the table as dinner mats, and one evening arrives at my place with a few records for the same purpose.

On this drizzly night, Massimo parks outside Superfly; we pull ourselves onto stools, order *negroni* cocktails, and I ask him about the attempted robbery. As the conversation ebbs and flows I take time to study Massimo, his skinny frame accentuated by a loose linen jacket and trousers, his eyes bloodshot and grey hair unruly. A ball of nervous energy at the best of times, he's even more agitated now as he tries to free himself from a complicated, eleven-year relationship. Lately he's been sending me a stream of affectionate text messages and Manola has been teasing me for weeks that he's smitten.

Notwithstanding that I have no desire to catch a man on the rebound, I remain unconvinced about Massimo. I don't have a concrete wish list, but a girl has to have preferences. Not long before meeting the man who would become her husband, my middle sister Sal jotted down eight things she was looking for in a man. Craig qualified for six, and now they are a family of five.

Massimo is a generous, intelligent, loving soul who, at the age of thirty-eight, openly admits to wanting to start a family. But when we're together, either because he's so tense about his current relationship conundrums, or I'm too busy being annoyed that I can't fall for him, I struggle to totally relax. Sure, we share a few laughs, but not the belly-aching kind. And now, more than ever, I want to laugh in the face of my struggle with Naples.

Before long we're back on the scooter throttling towards Massimo's parents' place for dinner, an event I've been assured will be totally casual. Perhaps. To be safe I traded my favoured street-urchin look for one of casual elegance, slipping off my sneakers for a pair of heeled, suede shoes to go with jeans and a smart jacket. My dress sense in Naples has been a revolving wardrobe. When I arrived, common sense told me to dress down. At first I resented it, having learnt to be more stylish in Rome, but before long I embraced my old, casual dress sense. After spending time with foxy Neapolitan girlfriends like twins Anna and Claudia, whom I met at Superfly and who live in my street, I again changed tack and now try to make an effort without being too flashy. Deep down, though, I know I relish the opportunity Naples gives me to embrace my grunge sensibilities – which means that tonight I feel overdressed in heels.

As we wind our way uphill I look out over the city luminous beneath a lowering sky. We swing into a driveway and Massimo turns a key to activate an electric sliding gate. It's the most exclusive entrance I've encountered in Naples.

We park, unhook our helmets and catch a private elevator up to the apartment. A door swings open and Massimo's parents, Giovannella and Federico, greet me with huge smiles and kisses, as if I'm a long lost member of the family.

'We've heard a lot about you,' says Giovannella, Novella for short, before ushering us inside and taking my coat.

I stand and admire my surrounds. Two enormous living spaces are decorated with antique cabinets and tables busy with porcelain knick-knacks. There is a 1970s blue velvet lounge suite, chandeliers hang from high ceilings and intricately patterned wallpaper adorns every surface. It's kitsch-cool to the absolute extreme.

Tall and slim with a swimmer's broad shoulders, Novella orders us to sit down at the dinner table and serves *tortellini in brodo* before she swipes my plate to serve a second bowl brimming with a spiral pasta and pumpkin and herb sauce. Soon the *secondi* plates – cuts of roast lamb, meatballs, sausage and *friarielli* – are doing the rounds. Novella urges her son to eat but I notice that like Massimo she eats like a bird, pushing food around her plate as she smokes wafer-thin cigarettes.

The conversation turns to Massimo's sister, who is currently working for a non-government agency in Africa. Novella is happy that her daughter is enjoying her work, but admits that she'd love her to come home, meet a nice boy and settle down in a house nearby. In a flash I see myself living with Massimo and having a ready-made babysitter for our bambini. Every Sunday, like ninety-five per cent of Italians, we would bundle up our offspring and travel the short distance to Federico and Novella's house to enjoy a long family lunch.

Sitting beside me, Federico, who has just retired as chief editor at a local television station, talks about refurbishing his boat to take out on the harbour this summer. Novella drags out photos of the boat, and I admire images of a tanned, shirtless Massimo a decade earlier, before his jet-black hair turned grey.

The evening passes in a pleasurable blur, Massimo's parents making me laugh with anecdotes of life and family. At 2 am it's still raining lightly as we stand at the front door putting on our coats. Fussing that I'll get wet, Novella gives me a raincoat while Federico, remembering a comment I made about my love for actor Gregory Peck, gives me a pat on the back and tilts his head towards Massimo.

'He's no Gregory Peck, but he's got the scooter,' he jokes, in reference to the Vespa that Peck rode with Audrey Hepburn in the classic *Roman Holiday*.

As I lean into Massimo's bony frame on the way home, I stare at his red Converse sneakers with approval. Perhaps because many Neapolitan men are vertically challenged, a great number of them wear a style of unsightly canvas sports shoes with fat white soles. Massimo is a step ahead of the rest.

Tipsy and happy from an evening in the bosom of a family, I kiss Massimo's cheeks and pretend not to see his lingering gaze before I disappear into my building. As the elevator rises I realise my folly. I adore Massimo's parents as much as the man himself. I'm in love with the idea of having a decent, honest man with a fabulous family: I want a better reason than work to stay in a city that fascinates and scares me.

But I'm not smitten.

Missing old girlfriends to gossip with, and low on mobile phone credit, I send a mayday SMS to my mate Viviana in Rome, who has met Massimo.

He's sweet, sincere, tender and I know he genuinely cares for me, but my heart doesn't skip when I see him, but then the perfect man doesn't exist, but I don't want to settle for second best, but am I too picky? Oh, Christ, will you marry me?

'*Sìììììììì!*' she replies, making me laugh, adding:

I am also pretty demanding. The perfect man doesn't exist, but if your heart doesn't skip then there's no point. Massimo is sweet, but he's too messed up right now. Anyway, you're so young, you have so much time!

Eight years my senior, Viviana probably feels more pressed for time, but at thirty-two I feel like I need to at least work out what country I want to live in. Australia or Italy?

Dinner at Massimo's parents' brought comfort, reminding me of what is missing in my life. I want to feel settled. I want to have more than twelve boxes to my name. I want to live in a house full of my own furniture. I want to create a home with someone I love. I want to wake up and roll over to snuggle up to my partner. I want to overcook pasta for two.

I crawl into bed and create my first Ideal Male wish list.

- Funny (thus sexy)
- Affectionate and communicative
- Informed and curious
- Loves music
- Ideally a chef, or good cook, or a sailor to feed my love for the sea
- No ex-girlfriend issues dating back two decades
- Healthy relationship with his mother
- Wears decent shoes

If, like my sister, I must relinquish two points, the chef-sailor can go (we can always eat out, or hire a boat), ditto the decent shoes (as Nicoletta often tells me, small fashion oversights can be addressed later). I do a quick cross-check. Massimo currently ranks five, arguably five and a half if I allow half a point for his father's boat.

I reflect on my evening with fondness for Massimo, but also with an overwhelming sense of emptiness. Finally resigned, if

not a little embarrassed, about having reached such a pathetic
point in my desire for affection, I switch on my iPod and fill my
eardrums with 'Fill You in', one of my favourite songs by Josh Pyke.

Now there's a hole in the ground where I used to lay down
and I can't fill it in.
And there's a colouring pad in the back of my head and I
want to fill you in.
And I was nothing more than an impression of myself and
I want to fill you in.
Yeah you could lay your body in the hollow where I used
to be and you could fill me in.

I bid goodnight to Josh and for once forget to stick in my ear
plugs. The rain has kept the rowdy street urchins indoors.

In a state of nervous excitement, I eat breakfast standing at my
kitchen window and stare out at the dark mass of Vesuvius. At
its base, lights from houses and cars in villages flicker on and
off in the dark until the sun pokes over its peak and rays of light
shoot across the sea horizon.

I down an espresso in two gulps and dress with purpose: T-
shirt, loose jeans with big pockets for my wallet and mobile
phone, and sneakers. I tuck my camera into a small bag and
hook it carefully over my neck. Just before 9 am I leave home
to meet Gianni Maddaloni, a fifty-one year old Neapolitan who
runs a judo school on the fringes of Scampia and Secondigliano,
suburbs notorious for street crime and the scene of the brutal
Camorra *faida* in 2004 and 2005.

The son of a professional boxer, Maddaloni also dabbled in
the ring before he gained his black belt in judo and began teaching
martial arts. When his children, Pino and Laura, came along,

Maddaloni often took the toddlers with him as he worked at different gyms. A few years later he realised he had a problem when Pino started winning judo championship after championship and he couldn't afford private gyms to help his son make it all the way to the Olympics. He sold his car and pooled his finances, and in 1993 Maddaloni opened his first gym and judo training school. In 1998, he began offering disadvantaged kids training for free. Two years later, Pino won judo gold at the Sydney Olympics. But a greater victory was to come.

Addressing a local sports event in December 2005, only months after the *faida* bloodshed, Pino was unaware that in the audience were the heads of five powerful companies from the rich Veneto region in the North, including Gilberto Benetton, patriarch of the famous Italian clothing brand. Moved by Pino's words, the five executives donated ten thousand euro each to his father, allowing him to build a better, bigger gymnasium not far from the old site in Miano, near Scampia.

On my way to the train station, I bump into my workmate Tania, who knows about my appointment.

'I thought you weren't going to take a bag?' she says with a worried look on her face.

'I've only got it for my camera, in case I want to take photographs,' I explain, and tell her I'll see her at midday, when I start work.

'I know you know how to look after yourself, but be careful,' she says in her motherly fashion before scurrying off.

I'm a little bit early for my 10 am appointment, so I let three trains pass before I board for Secondigliano, the last and thirteenth stop on the line. I read a newspaper until the train stops abruptly, then jump off trailing a posse of teenage boys all wearing jeans that threaten to fall off their hips.

At the metro gate I see a tall, solid man with cropped hair. We shake hands and Gianni Maddaloni leads me to a small green hatchback; I hop in the front and say hello to a young boy in the back, one of the judo students. I've been well-warned never to visit this area on my own, so I take the opportunity and ask Giovanni whether he has time to give me a mini-tour. He nods and starts the engine.

We wind past shops that sprout randomly from the rubbish-strewn pavement until we reach a long street that slices between dirty apartment blocks rising from overgrown paddocks.

'In this area, there are around ninety thousand people in a space that should house five thousand,' Maddaloni says. He points to some older-style apartments called the *vele*, or boat sails, for their pyramid shapes. I've read countless newspaper references to the ugly housing blocks, so I know we've reached the suburb of Scampia. 'Every palazzo has up to fifty families of seven or eight people, every *vela* has over three hundred families. It's unbelievable.'

I don't know what I expected, but as I stare out the window I feel a sadness growing. The thing that shocks me the most is the absence of life. There are no shops, no people in sight. It's like a real-life science fiction movie where the entire population has been exterminated by an invisible force. I've seen poverty-ridden suburbs in my own country, and have backpacked in third world countries, but I've never seen such desolation, such a miserable consortium of concrete and grime.

Maddaloni tells me we're driving along viale della Resistenza, or 'boulevard of resistance', a wide, dead-straight road flanked by a strip of dirt and grass that slopes down into a small ravine.

'See that,' he says, nodding at a lone tree in the centre of the ravine where a few people gather. 'That's the tree of death. The druggies meet there to shoot up.'

Maddaloni takes his eyes off the road and looks at me for a moment; it's almost like he's gauging my level of interest. He turns his head again and I notice the muscles twitch in his neck. He wears a T-shirt, despite the cold weather, which exposes his strong arms, and he speaks with the composure and authority of a school principal.

'Here, children don't go out – their parents don't want them to be in the middle of things. But when they reach eight or nine, they have to let them go, and the kids see...too much. Their conditioning is total.'

At the end of the road, he pulls up to an iron security gate. To the left of the gym, says Maddaloni, is a workshop of carpenters where his students can learn a trade, to the right a group of Jesuits where some kids attend bible studies. A young boy opens the gates and we park in front of a large sign beside the entrance of the gym:

Codici Comportamentali del Clain dei Maddaloni
Comportment rules of the Maddaloni Clan
Faith
Courage
Humility
Altruism
Temperament
Respect for others
Do not steal
Respect the gym
Help the weak
Only then can you be a part of the clan

'You see, "clan" can be a good word, not necessarily linked to the Camorra,' Maddaloni says.

As we step from the car, he explains that of his three hundred judo students, almost ninety per cent cannot afford to pay for their training. But thanks to the fifty thousand euro grant, he can give them free uniforms, training kits and lessons, with most kids attending morning and night, up to six hours a day.

We walk into the large gym and over half the floor space is covered in green matting for judo sparring. Weight machines fill the rest of the space. We sit on a push-up bench below a banner that reads, 'Impossible Is Nothing'.

'To open a gym like this is a huge thing, and to let people come for free...it's beyond the Neapolitan mindset,' he says proudly, watching his charges warm up. 'Everyone told me I was crazy, but we did it. How? It was something I felt inside, something I had to do. Sport is the right of every child. Here we aim to teach the children fundamental principles, like order, obedience, humility. And judo is all about respect – respect for the adversary.'

Maddaloni says that he teaches with gentleness rather than severity. 'In this way you can have a dialogue with the kids,' he explains. 'If a child respects you, you get even better results. You need to lead by example. If the trainer has principles then a sensible child will pick up on this.'

According to Maddaloni, the children who train with him change dramatically after attending judo school and establishing friendships with the other kids.

'At the start you see children who are violent, who strike out, but when they start to develop skills, they mature...One of these aggressive kids now gives presents to his mum on Mother's Day! This is a huge result.'

Maddaloni admits that he's had countless offers to work in other cities, but he refuses to leave the *quartiere*. He grew up in an apartment in one of the *vele*, and his mother still lives in the area.

'I'm not a practising Christian, but I'm Christian. I think this gives me the force to continue,' he says simply. 'If I hadn't chosen sport, I could have been a Camorra boss like so many others here...But I was lucky, I had good parents – and work. I believe in two things, sport and work. If we give these to the people only good things will flow from it.'

When I ask Maddaloni what will become of his students, whether his work will ultimately make a difference, he's more circumspect.

'You've seen this area – there's no commercial centre, no shopping centres. If this changes then there will be opportunities for work. This is what's wrong here – there's nothing to do. The kids are forced to move to other cities.'

Maddaloni stands up to join his class, leaving me to chat to three of his pupils, Guida, Rusciano and Diguida.

Straddled on a work bench, practically sitting on top of one another, the three boys are endearingly candid about what they get from training with Maddaloni.

'Other than learning from the master,' says Guida, a skinny lad with neat black hair combed flat, 'we've all become friends. We're a family, we help each other.'

The boys agree that living in the area is tough. All of them have suffered bullying and episodes of violence.

'But this sport teaches you self control,' points out Rusciano, a thick-set youth with an earring and gold chain around his neck. 'And we've all learnt not to respond to provocation.

'When I was younger my parents were super protective, I had no contact with anyone. This place is no place to grow up, there's too much delinquency, ignorance that causes robberies, violence, drug pushing...But coming here gave me the connections I needed. I'm more sure of myself now, I don't feel like a target.'

Guida says he wants to be a photographer, Rusciano a policeman, and Diguida, an overweight kid who seems the shyest of the three, wants to pursue something in the ambit of sport. And all of them are sure they want to stay put.

'I don't know if I'll stay in Scampia, but in Naples for sure,' says Guida. 'I can't abandon my hometown. I want to try and make this city better.'

The boys get up to start training and I go over to Maddaloni to say goodbye. He gives me two T-shirts with the inscription of the gym on the back.

'I'll wear them on my morning walks,' I tell him.

We shake hands and I make for the parking lot to meet a young man who has agreed to give me a lift back to the station. Outside I spy Pino Maddaloni, judo Olympic gold medal winner and hero, alongside his dad, to the young kids who stream into the gym every day. I tell him that I think his father is an inspiration.

'Dad insists kids need a meeting place,' says Pino, crossing his arms against his broad chest. 'This sport doesn't make you rich, but you learn values, and I think this can change your life. All of Dad's students manage to get work, go to university...Dad believes in them, in this gym, and I'm behind him one hundred per cent.'

Like his dad, Pino believes sport is crucial for a child's physical and personal growth.

'You're Australian, you have a culture of sport. But in Naples you can pay up to four hundred euro a month to play soccer. It's a crime!'

Looking at me curiously, as if suddenly wondering why an Australian has bothered to come to Naples, let alone the wild north of Scampia, Pino asks me where I live. When I mention the Quartieri Spagnoli, he gives me a smile of approval.

'Life in Naples is hard, and in the *quartieri* life is arguably harder on some,' he says. 'But living there you'll see the real Naples, people who live in *bassi,* who stretch their arms and can touch the window of their next-door neighbour...this is Naples.'

When I raise his Olympic victory, Pino is quick to place it in a broader context.

'I live with these kids, I know everything about them. Dad and I go and pick them up most mornings, we train and we compete as one,' he says, his eyes starting to glisten. 'If I cried on that podium in Sydney, it was because when I saw the Italian flag I saw all of their faces, all of the sacrifices we've made together. Without them, I'm nothing. I helped them understand that even if you are born in the *vele* you can reach the top.'

I look at Pino's face, full of simple determination, and I smile. I feel privileged to have spent some time with a family so loyal to their hometown, and so determined to make it better. I bid him farewell and my young driver drops me at the station and kindly waits until I'm through the gate before he leaves.

On the train I look at the people around me and wonder how many of them live in the *vele*, how many remain in a suburb that seems to have died decades ago, but still manages to spawn poverty, drug abuse and violence.

Emerging from the metro, I pause in Piazza Dante and let the noise, the grime, the suffocating chaos of Naples assault my senses.

For the first time it brings relief, not tension.

At home I find my first bill in Naples. Telecom has charged me 240 euro in connection fees for a service I still haven't received. *Grrr.*

Avutato 'o vicariello, mine è vermicielle

As soon as the funeral has finished in the street, throw on the pasta

When you're a foreigner in a new city, it helps to have a few creature comforts to keep you sane. My two weapons against the daily onslaught of the unfamiliar are music and the sea. I bought my iPod before I left Rome and loaded it up with all my favourite songs. My Naples-born flatmate Massi said that he would never carry his iPod around in the wild South, but I feel safe enough with my black headphones as a disguise.

Each morning before work I put my iPod on shuffle, stick it in my tracksuit pocket, and pace along the gulf for around an hour, dodging scooters whose riders mount the wide, pedestrian promenade to avoid the traffic. In Naples, I've never seen such unabashed road disobedience, and I doubt it occurs in any other Italian city. Approaching Castel dell'Ovo, I tilt my head to the left, breathing in the sea, watching the moored boats bob in the marina, and doing my best to ignore the bumper-to-bumper cars on my right.

I've become accustomed to seeing the regulars: in the warmer months, a man with a small stall sells lemon-flavoured iced drinks, and an elderly woman who wears a strange engine-driver hat, takes off her long denim dress and strappy silver sandals to sunbake topless on the same smooth flat rock every day. Most mornings I pass the same clusters of runners, a few solitary fishermen, and my imagination runs wild speculating on what the lone scuba diver near Castel dell'Ovo is searching for in the early hours of the morning. That's the thing about Naples: its reputation makes you think the worst. I ask a local fisherman one day about the scuba diver and blush when I hear the answer. He's only checking clay pots.

I stop at Piazza della Repubblica, just short of Mergellina port, and take in the outlines of the island of Procida and the great Vesuvius, before heading towards home via Villa Comunale, whose pretty gardens are peppered with sculptures and palm trees. I window-shop along ritzy via Chiaia before stopping in Piazza Trieste e Trento to buy the morning news from Paolo, who gives me a free paper, a kiss on the cheek and a cheery *buona giornata*.

The promenade takes me past some of the city's most prestigious hotels, including the Excelsior, famous for its roof-top restaurant, La Terrazza. Since it opened in 1908, the Hotel Excelsior has attracted eminent guests, from royalty, including Italy's King Vittorio Emanuele II, to movie stars like Charlie Chaplin, Humphrey Bogart and Tony Curtis. On the recommendation of Carlo, my boss, I call the hotel to make an appointment to speak to the director, Vincent Pagano.

Sporting a smart, tailored suit (I want to at least try to fit in), I arrive at Hotel Excelsior at 9 am sharp and pause at the entrance while a rake in tuxedo tails opens the brass and glass doors. I walk to the marble reception desk and a few minutes later a bespectacled man in a starched white shirt and grey suit approaches and offers me a solid handshake. Vincenzo Pagano leads me to the elegant breakfast room where tourists help themselves to the sumptuous buffet. He asks one of the male staff, who wears a white jacket with tails, black pants and cummerbund, to send a light breakfast to the rooftop, then guides me to a lift with polished brass fittings and timber panels.

On the terracotta-tiled terrazza, surrounded by white wicker chairs and glass-topped tables, I take in the view and marvel again at Naples' beauty.

We sit down at a table and I ask Pagano if he was born in Naples. With a proud *sì*, Pagano says he started his career at Hotel Vesuvius, a few steps along the water from the Excelsior, when he was seventeen.

'My father was a businessman and my mother a housewife with a small shop, but I realised I'd never have much opportunity to go far, so I chose hotels,' he says. 'Pretty soon, though, I realised my options in Naples were limited, so I took a job in Hamburg, where I knew some people.'

In the years that followed, Pagano worked in the UK, France and Switzerland, learning every aspect of his trade, moving from bellboy to front office manager and mastering new languages. By the age of twenty-nine he was director of a hotel in England, but was drawn back to Italy to work in hotels on Ischia and Capri and others in the Campania region, before returning to the Hotel Vesuvius in Naples.

Two people he'd worked with thirteen years earlier were still at the hotel: a bellboy who had been promoted to head doorman, and the manager who had told him that he'd never amount to anything. Pagano had to hide a smirk. He had returned to his hometown to take up the hotel's directorship.

Another member of the hotel's penguin squad arrives with a small silver-service trolley. The waiter places toast and pastries before us and I resist the *frolla* for approximately half a nano-second before loading it onto my plate. From this waterside bunker of luxury in a city battling poverty at every turn, I sink my teeth into my ricotta-filled pastry and ask Pagano how he views the city.

'Naples makes news, but in reality what happens here happens everywhere,' he says. 'It's true that Naples is disadvantaged compared to Rome, Florence and Venice, but that's partly an historical fact. It has a different culture – it's Mediterranean. It has suffered over decades, been invaded, survived.'

When I suggest that Naples offers a wild beauty unrivalled by other Italian cities but remains on the 'tourist outer', Pagano interjects.

'Naples is the most evocative tourist city in Italy, with history, monuments, churches, art and museums, the sea, Vesuvius, and the incredible beauty of nearby Capri, Ischia, Procida, Sorrento … But while attracting artists from Goethe to Picasso and being recognised as a city of the Grand Tour, it's now seen as a gateway to other locations.'

A custom in the sixteenth century, the Grand Tour was embraced in the eighteenth century by English aristocrats expected to travel through Europe to study its classical past. Rome and Naples were obvious highlights of the trip. In the 1950s, when Naples' airport and transport system were still primitive, the rich arrived in their limousines, en route to Sorrento and the islands, but they always returned to Naples before heading off to other tourist spots like Florence and Rome.

'After the 1950s,' continues Pagano, 'Naples was badly run and it changed from a tourist city to a transit city. And until 1994 crime ruled the streets, but when the G7 was held, the city was transformed. It was like Switzerland or Australia – the most beautiful and cleanest city in the nation. And then the rot set in.

'The city is governed by people who only want to profit, they don't work for the people. Their idea is not of civil service, but the *poltrona* – a safe armchair in a safe job,' he says, then asks me not to repeat his last comment. I convince him that I've heard worse. 'Let's just say that the government has interests,' he says.

'But surely if Naples could clean up its act for the G7 it can do it again?' I ask.

'Look, people do respond. During the G7 everyone was good, clean, honest... the city was a salon. When we *want* to, we know how to behave... But when we see bad government, we wallow.'

I flush self-consciously. I know I've been doing just that lately, but as each day passes I'm realising how much I'm growing to love the city, its disarray, its clash of cultures and social classes, its generous and mind-bogglingly optimistic people. I miss Rome for my friends, but right now I have no desire to live there again. The Eternal City seems sterile compared to the abrasive reality of Naples. It makes me curse in frustration at times, but challenges me to use all my energy to stay afloat.

I tell Pagano that, although the violence irks me, Naples has won me over.

'It's a city you either love or hate, and I can see from your expression that it's a city you like, which means you have found positives,' he says.

He apologises for taking another *cornetto*, then cites his wish list to revitalise the city: change sentencing laws so *camorristi* serve full jail terms, promote Naples more directly as a tourist destination, and encourage a more collective culture, instead of everyone fighting for themselves.

'Then,' he says, wiping icing sugar from his mouth, 'I'd give industry a chance to expand. If you go to the home of a successful businessman here, you may enter a poor *quartiere*, a decrepit palazzo, but you walk into a house fit for God. In Milan, you enter a beautiful palazzo with a porter and a shiny elevator, but find a very modest home...Do you understand the mentality?'

'That people hide their wealth?'

'Yes! I would encourage industry to invest, to be showy – to give people pride.'

I tell Pagano that I love how Neapolitans possess their land, put beach chairs on the sea wall, and how Naples is a mixing pot, with the rich living alongside the poor in every *quartiere*. But part of the problem, I suggest, seems to be that the rich are reluctant to understand the plight of the poor, the cycle of poverty.

'Yes, it's true. But again that relates to history...In times of severe hardship, if you managed to get a *cornetto* you'd hide it and take it home to your children. This attitude of hiding assets has lingered. It's a type of paranoia, a fear of envy, it's superstition,' he says.

'I'll give you an example. If I was asked to be director-general of all the hotels in Italy, and not just this one, I wouldn't want anyone to know. It would bring bad luck.' Pagano dips his hand into his trouser pocket and pulls out a key ring with five plastic tokens attached. 'This may surprise you,' he says, lowering his voice, 'but I carry this to chase away bad spirits...I never go anywhere without it.'

I smile at this quirk. Pagano tells me he has travelled to Australia three times and loved Perth so much that he dreams of returning there to build a villa.

Lately I've been trying not to think of Australia. I have a strong feeling that if work gets better (and I meet a fabulous local), I could easily stay in Naples for good.

—◦—

I'm slowly making new friends, like twins Anna and Claudia, who drag me out for a tipple every so often, never earlier than 11 pm. The twins, who are around my age and both recently graduated as architects, are far from identical and have very different personalities. Anna, with jet black hair in an elfin cut, is outspoken and the life of any party, while wavy haired Claudia is a brunette, and far more reserved. But I love them both for their frankness, generosity and engaging company.

On a brisk autumn night I wait for them beneath my flat; they have invited me to the thirtieth birthday bash of their architect friend Chiara. I watch them walk the short distance downhill from their house. With her short locks slicked into a chic style and a slash of red lipstick on her pretty face, Anna is hot to trot in a vintage black dress, a string of pearls looped around her neck, and a red handbag to match her red heels. Her wavy brown hair cascading down her shoulders, Claudia, too, looks foxy in a black dress she has paired with white shoes. I'm a little dowdier in jeans, but with a slinky top, French shawl and my black, suede, steel-studded Marc Jacob heels on, I'm feeling pretty fly myself.

We walk down to the corner and meet Matteo and Emma, friends of the twins, and head to Piazza del Gesu, where street urchins smoke cigarettes and loiter in groups. I follow Anna into a crumbling palazzo on the corner of the piazza and we're greeted by a bouncer checking off a guest list. With standing room for two people only in the lift, Anna and I whistle up the stairs to the top floor of the palazzo and walk into the party.

Pagano's description of decrepit buildings hiding luxury homes comes to mind. Modern minimalist, with three huge terraces showing off views to every angle of the city, it's the sort of house I dream about owning.

Anna and I charge our glasses and find Claudia and another girlfriend, Orfina, also an architect.

'Girls, there's plenty of talent here tonight,' I say, having noticed a few appealing types.

'Don't forget to play your foreigner card,' says Orfina with a wink. 'Naples is so provincial, all you have to do is say you're Australian and you'll be adored.'

I laugh along with the girls but secretly bristle. While it's true that being Australian, my 'curiosity' status, makes flirting easier, I maintain that Italian men mostly view foreign women as brief romp material.

I turn to see my old flatmate Francesco standing with Roberto and Manola. I push through the crowd and greet them all before we catch up on a few weeks of news. Manola and Roberto have just arrived from dinner with both sets of their parents. Manola's last boyfriend never met her parents and she never thought it was important, but Roberto's elderly father insisted on the occasion. In poor health, it seems he wanted to meet his potential daughter-in-law before it was too late. The dinner went well, judging by the beaming faces of the two lovers.

As we chat I scan the young and trendy around me and wonder where these people hide during the day. I feel like running around giving them my business cards.

I move to the wine table and strike up a conversation with a man who offers to pour me a glass of red from the bottle he's just opened. He introduces himself as Enrico and saves me from my ever deteriorating Italian: he lived in London for three years and is happy to speak English.

I discover that Enrico, upon returning to his hometown four years ago at the age of twenty-six, decided to open a youth hostel.

'When I came back from London I took a job looking at tourism data and I noticed a gap in hotel accommodation,' he explains. 'So I talked to my best friend, who is smart and also happens to be very rich!'

Enrico's laugh is infectious and I tell him that I'm nonetheless impressed with his business venture at such a young age and in a city crippled by unemployment.

But his face hardens a little as he recounts his four-year battle to get council approval to open the hostel. If he'd known how much red tape he'd have had to face, he says that he wouldn't have bothered.

'The hostel's great, but if I could, I'd go back to England. Not because of things like corruption, or even the Camorra, but because of the bureaucratic culture here,' he says.

Like Pagano, Enrico believes Naples is impossibly beautiful. 'The historic centre hasn't been destroyed like it has in other cities. The streets are 2500 years old and the Quartieri Spagnoli has architecture that most of Europe has lost...You find something similar in Barcelona's gothic quarter, but it's so touristy there,' he says.

I tell Enrico that it took some time before I could walk through my neighbourhood without feeling on edge, and how I see tourists every day standing on via Toledo, gazing up alleyways into the *quartieri*, too scared to enter.

'Naples,' he says, turning to look at the DJ, 'needs a little bit of fantasy to change. Have you heard of *neomelodica* music?'

I nod, recalling the pop trend I've seen on local television stations, a bizarre style of professional karaoke where singers perform for hysterical crowds.

'It's shit music but it's hugely popular. Why don't we start a massive publicity campaign with the divas of the *neomelodica* to sing about how cool it is to wear a helmet, to clean the streets, to be a good citizen? It would work because Neapolitans are conformist! If it was trendy to respect the law, they would!'

I laugh out loud, imagining heavily made up, belly-flashing Neapolitan *neomelodic* singers standing at traffic lights and public parks, calling on their fellow citizens to be good.

'I'm serious,' says Enrico. 'What do we need? We need a Councillor for Creativity, that's what. It's marketing jargon, but we need focus groups, quality research…'

But if Naples gets organised, becomes a tourist destination, I argue, then all the charm will be lost.

'Maybe…' he admits. 'But there has to be a halfway street.'

We exchange numbers (I figure Enrico's hostel might be worth checking out for visiting friends with tight budgets), and I join Francesco nearby. He's talking to a tall portly man with a white shirt and deep tan who caught my eye at the start of the party. Watching him earlier, embracing friends and entertaining the small group gathered around him, I had hoped for an excuse to meet him. Francesco introduces us before disappearing into the terrace throng.

I learn that Valerio works for the city council and is the right-hand man of Naples' city manager. I struggle with my Italian as the music blares and start to feel nervous because I can't understand everything Valerio is saying. And being a bit tipsy doesn't help. Embarrassed, I find myself making excuses to find a friend and disappear into the crowd, but not before exchanging numbers and noting his trendy black sports shoes.

I spy Anna and Claudia nearby and we opt to leave the party. Our heels click on the cobblestones on our way home, and I feel happy for having met some interesting new people, Valerio in particular.

A week passes before I receive the text message I've been hoping for. On Sunday morning, an invitation arrives from Valerio to catch up for a coffee after lunch; he's a few blocks from my house enjoying the meal in the bosom of his family home.

At one o'clock I eat a hastily cobbled together salad, alone on my terrace, imagining Valerio with envy, surrounded by his family and feasting on course after course of Neapolitan delicacies. As I dress, pre-date nerves take over and I wonder what I'm letting myself in for. It'll probably be a half-hour meeting, if that.

I arrive outside the local bookshop where we've agreed to rendezvous. He's dressed in a beige cord jacket and jeans, and I remember why I was attracted to him. I like men with a bit of bulk: all the better for hugging. He looks up and I notice he seems a little nervous, too. It's gently disarming. We kiss each other on the cheek and he suggests a ride on his motorbike.

We weave in and out of traffic on his sporty Yamaha and park near Castel dell'Ovo. The conversation flows easily as we walk to a little bar at the nearby marina.

Over a couple of coffees, we chat about our jobs, and Valerio says how much he loves to return to Naples at the weekend after a week on the road for work.

'To me this city is like a kaleidoscope,' he says simply. 'I miss the colour and the light, and the scents, especially of the sea…'

I look at Valerio as he talks, his voice soft and sweet in contrast to his manly frame. He lights another cigarette and tells me about a nightclub he runs with three of his friends in the historic centre.

'We got sick of what was on offer,' he says, and I try to chase away an image of him surrounded by a bevy of female admirers. 'We only open it when we want. Next Saturday is my birthday and I'm having my party there – you have to come!'

I smile and accept the invitation before the conversation takes an unexpected turn.

'I don't know if I told you at the party last week, but I've just accepted a job as manager of a small province in Tuscany,' he says. 'It's going to be a big challenge, but I need a new focus, and they've offered me a good package, too.'

My heart heaves, even though I know I'm being ridiculous given I barely know the man sitting beside me.

'So it's true what they tell me – all the good Neapolitan men leave town for better opportunities?' I joke.

'Ah, but a part of my contract is that I can leave work at five every Friday, so I can be home in Naples by nine.'

He suggests a ride along the coast and I have to stop myself from hugging him with excitement. My Vespa rides are few and far between in Naples and, even though I've been in Italy for years, I still get a thrill from being on the back of a motorbike, even better one driven by a swarthy local.

Valerio snakes along the waterfront and my heart soars at the sight of the ink-blue swell and the idea of an afternoon in new company.

As we wind through Posillipo, we take a detour past Villa Rosebery, its landscaped gardens peeping above a wall. Valerio tells me that it's the residence of the Italian president, Giorgio Napolitano. I already know this snippet of information but I don't let on, so he feels like an excellent guide.

We pass the beachside village of Bagnoli, where I've only been at night and I tell Valerio that I'd love to live around here. But when we get to seaside Pozzuoli, full of cute cafes and a community buzz, I change my mind.

'You want to live anywhere new!' Valerio laughs.

'Ah, but there is a common theme,' I retort, waving my hand towards the sea.

We sail along the coast, past Baia and Bacoli, before arriving at Miseno as dusk falls. Valerio leads me up to the cliff edge, and we stand at the lookout to watch the lighthouse. It feels like Naples is a million miles away.

When my teeth start to chatter from the chilly breeze, we walk to a cosy bar on the beach and order a beer. Just as they arrive, Valerio is distracted by a phone call. He chats briefly and then hangs up. It was a friend who has just separated from his wife less than a month after their marriage.

'I have to meet him in about an hour…It could be a long night,' he says.

Not wanting to pry, I ask him what he thought went wrong after such a short marriage.

'I think my friend never really wanted to get married, maybe he was convinced by other people…'

We agree that the older you get the bigger the risk of settling for something that is good, but not perfect, for fear of being left on the shelf. I tell him of the wish list my sister Sally made before she got married, and the one I've just formulated.

'Okay, so what's on it?' Valerio asks.

Feeling a little silly, but determined to be my daggy self, I give him a quick run-down, adding that trendy shoes and cooking skills are negotiable.

'Well, I don't know what you think of my shoes, but I can tell you that I only know how to cook a few dishes, like any bachelor, and I have cans of tuna and beans stockpiled in my kitchen.'

I reassure him that his shoes have definitely passed the test.

'So, what's on your wish list?' I tease.

'Obviously intelligence, a strong sense of independence… ummm…practicality, because I'm hopeless in that respect.'

I've definitely failed on the last front.

'What else? I like a woman who doesn't wear make-up. I think those who do are trying to hide something.'

I'm only wearing a touch of mascara.

'And then, I love affectionate women…although my last few girlfriends were a little cold. I don't know why…'

Beats me, I think silently, resisting the urge to psychoanalyse the man.

Valerio kicks his engine into gear and we head back to Naples, this time taking the highway. I wonder if I've made as good an impression on Valerio as he has on me. When he shudders from the icy wind, which his body is shielding me from, and without thinking, I take my hands off the handles behind me and wrap my arms around him.

'Well, you did say you like affectionate women,' I shout over the buzz of the motor.

Ouside my palazzo I kiss Valerio on both cheeks, secretly wishing he had no plans so we could go to dinner, or maybe see a film. Anything to spend some more time together.

'*Ci sentiamo presto*,' he says, reassuring me that we'll talk soon.

At home I have a hot shower to defrost and rake over Valerio's words. I wasn't left with an overwhelming impression that he was interested. Annoyed that I'm even bothering to dwell on the indecipherable, I hop into bed to watch *Tootsie*, a movie I haven't seen for years. Dustin Hoffman's cross-dressing antics make me giggle out loud and before long the events of the afternoon have drifted out to sea.

As the barometer drops, a harbinger of winter, I take a week off to spend time with my sister Lisa and her husband, David, who are visiting Naples for a week.

After hugs and kisses at the airport, we jump in a taxi back to my neighbourhood, where I've organised accommodation in a bed and breakfast in my street. They're slightly jetlagged but excited to see my new home, so we meet up with my workmate Marco, and head down towards the marina to lunch at the legendary restaurant La Bersagliera, which specialises in seafood.

We sit in the warm autumn sunlight and enjoy antipasti dishes of fresh seafood, sautéed clams and fried anchovies, before a delicious serving of *schiaffone* pasta with a sauce of *fantasia del mare,* or fantasy of the sea, swimming with octopus and fish.

After lunch, Lisa, David and I stroll along the water to Mergellina and then wind back towards home, passing apartment buildings on Chiaia's *riviera.* David, an architect, waxes lyrical about the fading splendour of the facades. Through their eyes, I'm seeing Naples anew, and I'm reminded of just how beautiful it is. I realise that I've been taking my surrounds for granted, just as I did in Sydney, and Rome.

The next morning we walk down to Beverello port and jump on a ferry to Capri, where I've booked two nights accommodation. I'm excited because I've never been to the famous island, known as a playground for the super rich.

We dump our bags at the reception of our modest hotel and set off for a walk to Villa Jovus, built by the emperor Tiberius, before settling down under a grapevine-laden pergola at a nearby restaurant for a long lunch. We feast on fried zucchini flowers, rabbit stewed in a tomato and onion sauce, and a locally produced red wine. After lunch we head to a rocky beach for a lightning dip and later find enough tummy room for a slice of homemade lemon cake at a lone cafe.

That night, David is suffering from a jetlag-induced cold, so he stays in while Lisa and I wrap up and walk to Capri's famous piazza. Along the way we pass Pucci, Moschino, Prada and Dolce e Gabbana, and other Italian design stores.

'I've never seen so many of these brands in one place – not even in Rome or Milan,' says my sister, whom I consider to be a style guru. 'I think I'm going to have to buy a jacket.'

I roll my eyes but she protests that she really does need to shop because she has packed too lightly.

At Bar Piccolo we order two glasses of champagne at forty Australian dollars a round and settle back to watch the action. At the port earlier in the day, we were swamped by tour groups of day-tripping Japanese and Russians, but tonight the piazza isn't overcrowded. Still, it's not hard to imagine how it heats up in summer, with scores of wealthy Italians passing lazy weekends in designer resort wear. Capri has priced regular tourists out of the market; we're staying at the only budget hotel in town. But there is nothing to stop me making a day trip whenever I need some peace. Capri is like a church compared to the rowdy *quartieri*.

'You know, Pen, I can see how Naples is a tough city, but I reckon you've picked the right area to live in, and the trick is to escape for trips like this, to get out of the chaos…' says Lisa, as if reading my mind.

We order another round, this time of Pinot Grigio, and I tell Lisa how much I've grown to love Naples, but feel that I need a better reason to stay in Italy. While I'm grateful to be employed, my job is hardly creatively satisfying, and my single status seems unlikely to change.

'I met a cute guy at a party last week, but I have a feeling he's seeing someone else,' I say, inviting some sibling 'free advice'.

'Don't be too quick to judge, Penny, but don't waste too much time figuring him out – act fast, while you're still *bella*,' she says with a wink.

'Easier said than done…' I moan, and we pull ourselves off our chairs and wander back to the hotel.

On our second and final day on Capri, we walk almost three hours from one side of the island to the other, following a rugged coastal track. With a wild, mountainous beauty, Capri is like a huge park, landscaped in part with pretty white houses and iridescent pink bougainvillea, and ruggedly uncontained in others, with inaccessible cliffs and bays.

'Look, here's the flower of love,' says Lisa, noting the botanical description on a plaque nearby.

I grab it from her outstretched hand, thinking she's giving it to me as a corny good-luck token.

'Actually, I wanted to give it to my husband,' she says in a soppy way, taking the piss out of herself.

I laugh and watch her give the flower to David, who plays along, solemnly tucking it behind one ear.

I think of my conversation with Valerio about settling for less in love for fear of being alone. No relationship is perfect, but spending time with Lisa and David I'm reminded of what is worth waiting for.

Back in Naples, I play tour guide for them, and when Saturday rolls around I get a text message from Valerio, telling me that his party starts at 11 pm at his bar. I'm ecstatic.

I don't want to go alone so I call Anna and Claudia, but neither of them can make it. Earlier in the day I bumped into Francesco, who told me that Roberto's father had passed away, weeks after fulfilling his wish of meeting Manola. The funeral is tomorrow, so it's certainly not the time to ask some of my friends if they want to go out.

Lisa kindly offers to come out with me when she sees my crestfallen face, but she's pooped after a day of sightseeing and backs out quickly when Marco sends me a text saying he's up for a night out.

Rain is pouring as I walk to Piazza del Gesù to meet Marco at a bar for a quick beer before the party.

'So glad you could come,' I say, kissing Marco hello. 'But Valerio can't think you're my squeeze. We somehow have to make it clear that you have a girlfriend in Paris.'

'Don't worry, we'll work something out,' he says seriously, then mocks me with a toothy smile.

My phone beeps. It's Valerio asking where I am.

'A good sign!' Marco says with excitement, pulling me to my feet.

The nightclub is at the end of a dark, narrow street that leads to Roberto and Manola's house. One night on my way to their place I swallowed fear when some young hoods in a car passed by and yelled at me. With Marco by my side I feel protected.

We step inside a small, dimly lit bar where a few people sit on divans. I see Valerio at the DJ mixing board and when he looks up he hands over mixing duties to a man standing beside him and walks over to give me a hug and kisses on the cheek.

'So you were getting worried about no one showing up, so you sent a stream of messages to fill the place,' I tease, before introducing him to Marco.

'No, I sent a message to you,' he says rather seriously, locking eyes with mine.

He leads us to the bar and returns to DJ duties, leaving Marco and I to jostle for standing room among the disco crowd, with their too-tight jeans and lycra tops – an obvious fashion hit with both sexes. I sneak glances at Valerio as he mixes music and floats to the bar to chat with friends.

Suddenly the song 'Billie Jean' blasts on and Marco and I spring onto the dance floor. Marco grabs the hat off a man who has just walked into the bar and sticks one hand over his crotch and makes exaggerated pelvic thrusts. Doubled over in laughter, I apologise to the man, who humours Marco for about thirty seconds, before reclaiming his hat.

Valerio makes his way through the crowd and we dance in three until we get thirsty and head to the bar. We find the barman pouring rum from a bottle down the throat of a woman leaning backwards over the bar. The music pumps, the crowd heaves, and the light bulbs hanging above the bar swing wildly. Good god, I think, in a moment of semi-clarity. Someone could lose an eye.

'What would you like to drink?' says Valerio, who at 3 am appears as happily loaded as Marco and I are.

'Rum!' says Marco with a devil's grin.

Before I know it, arms come from nowhere to pin my back to the bar. I follow orders to open my mouth, and I feel a rush of warm liquid at the back of my throat, which I down with as much poise as I can muster in the circumstances, before stumbling away from the bar. Apparently having suffered the same fate beside me, Valerio holds his eyes, stinging from a splash of the alcohol, before wiping some of the sticky liquid off my cheeks. How romantic.

At 3.30 am the shout goes out that the bar has closed and Marco and I sidle outside. Valerio's friend Federico drops Marco and me home, but not before we stop at a tiny cafe for a slice of piping hot Margherita pizza, an insurance policy against a hangover.

A few hours later I'm at the funeral of Roberto's father. The church is packed with friends and family of the respected magistrate, and I watch Roberto standing at the front of the church, his bandy legs supporting his slim frame. I breathe deeply.

I've attended Catholic masses a few times in my life, and often, in recent years, for funerals. From the moment I enter a church of any denomination, I fill with a mix of envy – for those who have faith – and a fear of mortality. Both feelings often bring me close to tears. Today, running on next to no sleep, the sensation is worse than usual. I watch the priest bless the coffin.

I think of my own father, who has just celebrated his sixtieth birthday, and try to imagine his arms wrapped around me. Fixing my eyes on the ornate ceiling of the church, I try to hold back welling tears. When the service ends I join friends and family to embrace Roberto, and outside, more hugs and kisses are exchanged and I leave feeling strangely uplifted.

I walk through the maze of tiny streets in a daze, and meet up with my visitors for our last long lunch together.

I've organised an *aperitivo* with Valerio and Nicoletta, who wants to talk to my brother-in-law about architecture.

I meet Valerio on the street and take him upstairs. As we walk across the terrace he looks at the lights of Naples flickering around us.

'*Mamma mia, che bella vista,*' he says.

I introduce him to Lisa and David, who are already enjoying the view, and he follows me into the kitchen to open some wine.

'You can't use a Pink Floyd album as a placemat!' he says in horror. I giggle and insist it was already scratched.

'This is one of my favourites. It's blasphemy! I'll bring you a different one you can use as a mat.'

Outside Valerio and I act as translators for David and Nicoletta and we talk architecture until the wine is finished. Lisa and David head back to their apartment, having agreed to meet me in the morning, and I warm to Valerio's suggestion to have a glass of wine at a bar nearby. I ignore my exhaustion when I remember that the following day he leaves Naples for the working week.

We hop on his bike and head to Chiaia, stopping for a slice of pizza before propping ourselves up on stools at a *vineria* in the chic *quartiere*. The conversation turns to Nicoletta, whom I describe as my mother, friend and confidante.

'I personally couldn't live with someone like that, she has a very strong personality,' says Valerio, adding that she dominated the conversation the moment we sat down.

'She just wanted to talk to David about architecture,' I say, feeling the need to defend the woman who has been so kind to me. 'She can be difficult, but we have a good relationship, an honest friendship…If she's in a bad mood I steer clear of her and vice versa, and we catch up for a meal about once a week… I like her company.'

The conversation bubbles away and we find ourselves talking about our favourite films.

After citing *The Godfather* among others, Valerio smiles. 'It's a bit daggy, but when I'm down I always watch *Tootsie*.'

Working hard not smile too widely – because shared movie tastes are certainly not among the founding pillars of successful relationships – I tell Valerio that I have it at home and often watch it for the same reason.

At just past midnight we pull to a halt at the entrance of my palazzo.

Too tired to be nervous about what may or may not happen next, I walk towards him and give him a huge hug, happy that my family, both Australian and Italian, have met someone I'm fast developing a crush on. Pulling out of the hug, we kiss French instead of Italian-style. Valerio smiles and then waits for me to find the keys to my palazzo door. I push it open and give a silly wave before stepping inside. When the door slams behind me I walk two steps and do a little jig to the elevator.

The next morning at work my phone beeps. It's Valerio. He wants to know if I have time for a coffee before he gets the train.

I never leave work; there's never time. *Until now.*

I bark an update at Tania on what news is ready to send, promise I won't be long, and jump in the elevator to meet Valerio below my office.

As we walk to a bar nearby, I confess I'm feeling sad about Lisa and David leaving, and I'm afraid I'll have a *piantella,* 'a little weep'.

'There's no such word, Penny, but be careful, because in Neapolitan *chiantella* means "a fling",' he says with a chuckle.

We down a coffee and he walks me back to my office where I give him two quick, soft pecks on the lips.

As the elevator rises to my office, I think that surely it's a good sign that he has been in touch so soon. Christ. The worst thing about dating is not wanting to appear super-keen when in reality you're leaping out of your skin to get to know someone new. Then why do I have a hunch that Valerio may not be single? Am I just being defensive?

I dash home at five to meet Lisa and David, who have one hour to kill before their flight leaves. With a grin I can't seem to wipe from my face, I bring them up to speed on the night's events.

'Pen, he probably saw your copy of *Tootsie* on your shelf,' says David, rolling his eyes with mock exaggeration.

'Oh David, how? She has so many!' says Lisa, giving me a look of support.

Thankfully my fear of getting teary is short-circuited when the taxi arrives early and there is no time for a lingering goodbye. I hug my sister hard, kiss David on the cheek, and watch them disappear from sight.

À vita storta te porta à morte

A dishonest life leads you to death

Naples has wormed its way under my skin, as my Italian friends predicted it would. The city's glaring contrasts are a source of constant wonder: the rich and the poor living on top of each other, from flashy suburbs like Chiaia and Vomero, to shadowy Forcella and the Quartieri Spagnoli. The layers of cultural and natural beauty, alongside the poverty-stricken suburbs on the periphery, like Scampia and Secondigliano. The chaos, the confusion, the nosy, noisy, but ever sunny locals, the disrespect for time and the law and the ever-present threat of crime is frustrating, often frightening and all-consuming. Charles Darwin could have elaborated on his theories with a brief spell in Naples, where only the fittest seem to survive.

Which all helps to explain why I'm not too fazed – at least not yet – by the fact that my job is not turning out as I expected. Within months of arriving in Naples, I enthusiastically handed a report to my boss, Carlo, full of ideas for building a bigger, better website, which I had been promised was in the pipeline. I've come to realise that 'bureaucracy' is holding the project up, and it will probably take months to bear fruit.

I'm disappointed but remain grateful not only to have a contract for twelve months but also to have found good work in Naples, something that never fails to raise eyebrows when I strike up conversations with new acquaintances.

And, despite the fact that I'm far from being a roving reporter, instead glued to my chair to edit stories filed by correspondents, thawed relations with my workmates now make the daily grind enjoyable, and often side-splittingly fun. We're united in trying to make the best of the situation, and jokes fly around the office from morning to night as we take the micky out of Naples, its inhabitants, each other and the inconsistent quality of the stories that flow in from around the Mediterraean.

Every day I make an effort to skim *Il Mattino,* the local broadsheet, to follow the ongoing debate on Naples' rejuvenation. Page after page is filled with the opinions and ideas of Antonio Bassolino, president of Campania, Rosa Russo Iervolino, mayor of Naples, Cardinal Crescenzio Sepe, archbishop of Naples, and a cast of other politicians and personalities. Day after day I read of plans to revitalise the *Mezzogiorno*, or Southern Italy, and Naples with infrastructure, new urban zones, innovation, greater police numbers...When I read aloud that the Italian prime minister, Romano Prodi, thinks Naples will only be saved by something 'shocking', jokes ricochet around the office as freely as the rain of bullets fired by the Camorra in the almost-daily clan killings.

'More than anything I'd say Naples needs electric shock therapy,' says bureau boss Enrico with his clumsy guffaw.

The joke reminds me of a scene the previous day. Frustrated by indolent correspondents and bickering colleagues, Enrico beat his fist against a glass panel near my desk. I was showered in glass from the partly shattered window, but my shock almost gave way to a strange form of admiration: I'd never witnessed such a lively outburst in a work place.

As I pause to read *Il Mattino* one morning, in between translating a story from Italian to English and calling our local bar to order a round of three different types of espresso, I glance at a story with an interview with local councillor for development and culture, Nicola Oddati. Noting that Bassolino and Iervolino are both in their second and final terms, Oddati calls on them to reflect seriously upon criticism of their leadership, and give the city *una scossa*, a shake, before they leave office.

Still awaiting a reply from the minders of both the mayor and the regional president about my interview requests, I leave a message at Oddati's office to see if I can pin him down in the interim. He calls back immediately and suggests we meet at his office at the PAN Museum of Contemporary Art that afternoon. Either Oddati is incredibly generous with his time, has nothing better to do (like a good chunk of the portly population), or is keen for more media attention.

After work I walk through elegant Chiaia to reach the PAN, housed in a distinctive, dust pink building. A security guard ushers me through a white-walled gallery and into a lift that whisks me to a spartan office with a reception desk.

A door opens and I recognise Oddati's funny moustache and neatly cubed goatee from the newspapers. We shake hands and I give him a discreet once over as he turns to walk to his desk. Dressed in jeans, a sports jacket and those terrible thick-soled canvas shoes, he's the embodiment of smart-casual.

As we sit down I mention a comment Oddati made in *Il Mattino* which I found disturbing: children born during the term of the current government are more likely to become drug dealers and *camorristi*.

'What would you do if you had your way?' I ask Oddati, who toys with a packet of Tuscan cigars on his desk.

'The problem is there has always been, and perhaps there will always be, two cities, which in some way manage to feed each other. On the one hand there are the idlers, extremely generous but hardened, and on the other, the noble class, educated but with a social egoism which leads to neglect of others.'

Lighting a cigar after asking my permission, Oddati says that the Camorra offers kids the chance to earn big money and enjoy the sort of lifestyle that regular salaries have no hope of supporting.

'The middle and "elite" classes have taken a leap,' he says, standing to open the French doors behind him, with a view over one of Chiaia's flashest shopping streets. 'But we haven't been able to reach the heart of the working class, both in the peripheries and the historic centre. Here you find the baby gangs, young criminals who were born in the term of our government.

'Something has changed. In kids today there's a mix of arrogance and apathy about life. It's something politicians have failed to address. We've failed to reach the underbelly of the city,' he says, and offers to light a cigarette I've pulled from my bag. 'How can we instil the idea that it's more important to have consideration for others than to become rich?'

I'm not surprised to hear that Oddati, like Riccardo Dalisi and Giovanni Maddaloni, believes the only way to make a difference is through educating the young. He throws around ideas like keeping schools open every day for sport and cultural activities, but when he talks of rejuvenating the historic centre by knocking down historic palazzos to make way for parks, shops and restaurants, my hackles are raised.

'Yes, but that will ruin Naples' uniqueness,' I protest.

'Sure, there will be some who will criticise us for wanting to "empty" the historic centre, and using our power to squeeze out the underclass, but actually it's worth the risk,' Oddati says evenly. 'Otherwise the historic centre will always be in the hands of the Camorra. It's a jungle – even the police won't go near it, they'll get beaten up.'

I ask how he hopes to educate a populace that doesn't know how to use a public rubbish bin. I suggest that if the papers are any indication, there is a lot of talk and little change.

He laughs and takes a long puff of his cigar, considering my charge. 'No, Penelope, things change. We have to be optimistic. The worst thing in this city is the attitude of "you can't do that". We have to take radical decisions, and we have to have courage.'

That night I lie in bed reading the latest issue of the national *L'Espresso* magazine, with a cover story called 'Lost Naples'. As I study the picture on the front I suddenly feel queasy. At first glance I didn't bat an eyelid at the victim of a Camorra ambush lying beneath a sheet, one arm poking out on the grotty street. Pictures like this are a dime a dozen in the dailies.

Upon closer inspection, I notice the crowd pressed against railings behind the body. There are primary-school children, their arms folded against their chests casually, as if the gruesome image before them is as normal as eating a *cornetto* for breakfast each morning.

The *L'Espresso* article is written by young local Roberto Saviano, whose first book, *Gomorra*, a gritty, Tarantino-esque account of the author's experiences growing up in Camorra territory mixed with meticulous research into the incomprehensible scope of the underworld economy, has scooped literary awards and provoked furious debate in literary and political circles.

Saviano is a friend of my workmate Benedetta and she has given me his phone number. I'm keen to trace him, but within a week of the *L'Espresso* article coming out, the story breaks that he's under police escort after being threatened by the Camorra. Benedetta tells me Saviano has gone to ground outside the city.

As I swing the office door open, I hear raised voices from the corridor. Having listened to the radio on my morning walk, I have a hunch what the hullabaloo is about. In the past six days as many people have died in Camorra ambushes. I listen to the tense conversation about the latest shooting, a man gunned down at Porta San Gennaro, metres from the homes of my colleagues Tania and Khalid.

Playing the devil's advocate, I try and suggest to Tania that nothing has really changed. Every day the papers are saturated with news of the fresh blood spilt by *sicari* on motorbikes.

'Pen, maybe, but not like this, not in the centre of the city,' she says, handing me a story from the ANSA news wire, which describes how a mother found herself caught with her two children in the crowded city street when the murder happened. As bullets whizzed past their ears the woman told her children not to worry, that it was only fireworks.

Later, Tania emails me to explain her shock.

At first it seemed impossible, so close to home. But then, when I saw the body under a sheet, I realised, maybe for the first time, just how dangerous this city is. Before, shootings always happened in suburbs like Scampia or Secondigliano. The fact that the Camorra doesn't stop at anything, not even in front of mothers and children that pass by Porta San Gennaro, it makes you reflect...

The thing that comforts me is that I know I won't stay in Naples forever. It's a beautiful city and it gives so much. But let's stop saying 'bad things happen everywhere'. Here it has taken control. Let's admit it and let's try to do something about it. It's useless to bury your head in the sand. I try to be optimistic, but when things like this happen, it's so hard...

Reading Tania's moving email, I feel guilty about my reaction, but when I read that the forty-nine murders in the first ten months of 2006 are actually fewer than the same period in 2005, my scepticism flares again.

When the Naples-born Italian president, Giorgio Napolitano, describes his anguish at the spate of killings *nella mia Napoli*, in 'my' Naples, Prime Minister Romano Prodi announces a visit, and Mayor Rosa Russo Iervolino attacks the media's 'dirty campaign' to depict Naples as the Far West.

With the debate raging around me, on the news service, the television nearby, and heated conversations between my colleagues, I struggle to concentrate on the job at hand. I jump when my phone rings.

It's Valerio.

I blush and step out of the office onto the balcony. Hooting car horns and noisy Neapolitans make it hard for me to hear, but I gather he has bought two tickets to a music concert that night.

'Sorry, to see what?' I say, eyeing a housewife on the balcony opposite lighting a cigarette.

'Gianmaria Testa...I think you'll like him.'

Before I leave work I google Testa. Who said you can't prepare for a date? I soon learn that the singer–songwriter is touring to promote his latest 'concept' album, entitled *Da questa Parte del*

Mare, From this Part of the Sea, exploring immigration. I'm up to speed on his politics by the time I meet Valerio outside my house at nine.

At the theatre three blocks away, the stalls are filling fast, so we go to the second floor where only a few couples sit. As the concert begins, I lean forward in my seat in the dark and listen to Testa's deft guitar playing and the soft, simple lyrics, which weave intricate tales of the hardships faced by those fleeing their homelands.

My mind wanders to my time spent in Rome in the Questura visa office, where I witnessed first-hand the struggle faced by so many people from so many countries to stay in Italy. Closing my eyes for a moment to avoid the glare of the stage lights, I let Testa's words and beautiful melodies transport me back in time. I can almost smell the nervous sweat, feel the collective desperation, see the stress-lined faces of the people I rubbed shoulders with for hours on end.

Suddenly I feel Valerio's arms wrap around me. I turn to see his face light up when he hears the first notes of a more upbeat tune, obviously one of his favourites. The warmth of his spontaneous bear hug reaches my heart. I kiss him on the cheek.

When the concert ends we hop on his bike and head to Chiaia, whose nightclubs are too try-hard cool, too ritzy, for my liking, but where one of Valerio's exes of years ago is having a thirtieth birthday drink.

Near the outdoor bar I see a small group of girls, who, almost without exception, are dressed in the regulation tight jeans or denim mini skirt, toothpick heels, chunky belt, cleavage-revealing top, dangly earrings and long, hairdresser-straightened hair. I'm proudly sporting my Aussie-made Blundstone boots, casual jeans, a jacket that hardly meets the local standards, and my scraggly long hair pulled back in a piggy tail. I can't help but smile at the contrast.

Having offered my best wishes to the birthday girl, I turn to chat to some people I met at Valerio's party. An hour later, and as annoyed as I am by the stream of scooters and cars moving within millimetres of the bar crowd, Valerio suggests we head to his nightclub for the next drink.

As we drive along the bay, he suddenly swings his bike over to the side of the road.

'Let's have a chat for a second,' he says with a strange tone in his voice.

Eeny, meeny, miny moe, catch another commitment freak by the toe…I brace for the worst.

Valerio clears his throat and begins to tell me that a few months ago he split up with his girlfriend of three years. The relationship was stormy and he feels the need to be independent. To my annoyance, tears sting in my eyes, but I manage to remain composed and respond without being too revealing, or asking too much. Valerio seems to be issuing me a warning that he is, for now, damaged goods.

Thrown, I tell him that I'm grateful for his honesty, but suggest that we just wait and see what happens. Oh Christ. Who knows? I don't even know where I want to call home.

'Come on, let's go. Enough serious talk!' I roll my eyes jokingly.

We drink and dance for a few hours then head to Valerio's house in Vomero, the *quartiere* on the hill above the city, which seems so quiet compared to my neck of the woods.

I admire the small but cosy living room of his cute 1960s one-bedroom apartment before catching sight of the small bedroom alcove. Mounted above the bed is an enlarged photo of Valerio wearing black sunglasses, a big blue sky framing the shot.

I accidentally laugh out loud, but Valerio doesn't seem to take offence.

'Everyone does it,' he insists. The photo was taken shortly after he moved into the flat, turning it from a dump into a bachelor pad. Putting up the photo was an act of 'self-affirmation', he says. Maybe, I think silently. This man has baggage to burn.

Waking early the next day, I wait for Valerio to stir before we jump on his bike and join two of his friends. We weave out of the city, along highways romantically littered with mounds of rubbish, and on to the beach.

The day passes breezily and before long we're back in Naples and walking into a restaurant just after midnight to dine amid a raucous crowd of night owls. It's almost 2 am by the time Valerio drops me home.

Under my doona I feel the crack between my two single beds, and remember Valerio lamenting that he'd found himself sinking in the middle in his efforts to stay close to me.

Damaged or not, the man's affection is growing on me.

I stand at the large Feltrinelli bookshop at Piazza Martiri and read the paper. I'm killing time before I meet Giovanni Corona, the public prosecutor who was on the tail of the Camorra at the time of the bloody clan *faida* of 2004–2005, when fifty-seven people were killed in little over six months.

An ANSA colleague who works on the floor below our office has recommended I talk to Corona, who seems to have a reputation as a big-noter, but is an impeccable source.

I look up to see a man with large biceps and sandy, styled hair halt his silver scooter alongside me. Corona hops off his bike and opens the back container. I drop my gaze. Those bad shoes sure do get around town.

Corona hands me a helmet and restarts his bike engine. '*Sali!*' he says, ordering me to hop on the seat behind him.

Smiling despite myself at the casual note of my first formal meeting with a public prosecutor in Italy, I slip on the helmet and feel grateful that I'm wearing jeans.

As Corona weaves his bike in and out of the late afternoon traffic, I shout into his ear, telling him about my background as a journalist and my curiosity about what makes Naples tick.

'Well, the first thing I would say is that you must write a feature on me, which you can simply call "Him",' says Corona.

I can't help but laugh; Corona is undeniably corny but he has his delivery down pat.

He pulls up at a bar opposite Castel dell'Ovo and over a round of Campari soda, fills me in on the various criminal court cases he has worked on. In 1999, at the age of thirty-four, he was seconded to the *Direzione Distrettuale Anti-Mafia*, or anti-Mafia prosecution squad. There, he delved into the drug-fuelled economies of Naples' north, including an investigation into Paolo di Lauro, the notorious head of the clan operating in Secondigliano and Scampia, the ugly backdrop of the *faida*.

'Around this time,' Corona says in a high-pitched voice, 'I thought the Camorra was a bit like the Mafia, with a boss who gave orders to foot soldiers, an organisation that had rules and an unwritten code. It controlled territory thanks to good relations with the police and the powers that be. In that sense there was a mutual respect: an understanding that the Camorra wouldn't push the boundaries.'

Delving into di Lauro's turf, however, Corona soon changed his mind.

'I realised that there was no boss, but zones were controlled by six or seven small groups that were siding with each other or fighting,' he says, nibbling the peanuts before us. 'There were no rules, simply vendettas between groups and affiliated people, those who had gained power because they were crueller and more blood-thirsty than others in getting a slice of the drugs market. And above all there was the *sistema...*'

I remember author Roberto Saviano's observation that the word Camorra is used only by cops and journos these days and has been superseded by the *sistema*, 'the system'. I read in Saviano's article that clan members proudly describe themselves as belonging to the *sistema* of various family controlled zones. The *sistema* was created by Paolo di Lauro in the early 1980s, says Corona, and had escaped the attention of law authorities, largely because he operated in a sprawling zone in Naples' north, removed from political interests.

But when Corona and his cronies began obtaining arrest warrants and nabbing the small fry of di Lauro's clan, cracks began to appear in the empire. And when di Lauro went into hiding, the final blow was dealt by his son Cosimo.

When Paolo di Lauro was in charge, he was taking a neat, if not large, chunk of drug profits, estimated at around 500,000 euro per day, from the twenty piazzas he controlled in the northern suburbs. But when Cosimo took the reins, he decided to give his operators a fixed wage, stripping them of the relative autonomy they had enjoyed. Before long, the older members of di Lauro's clan began to resent their new boss, enough to form the breakaway group called the *scissionisti*, the secessionists, also known as the *Spagnoli*, the Spaniards, because many fled to Spain to save their hides.

In September 2004, recalls Corona with what seems like a photographic memory, the first *faida* blood was spilt, with authorities thrown into a state of panic by the sudden warfare between di Lauro's clan and the *scissionisti*.

'No one could understand anything, because when someone was killed, it was often so brutal it took time to decipher who it was, let alone why,' he says.

One such case was a man who was suspected of giving information to the authorities that led to the eventual arrest of Cosimo. His body was found in a sack; he had been tortured beyond recognition, his wounds included gouged eyes and a cross slashed into his flesh.

'By now,' says Corona, 'everything I ever thought of the Camorra flew out the window. If I'd ever thought that *camorristi* had principles, that they didn't harm women or children...During the *faida* some young kids shot dead a woman in front of her children. The alliances of old times, based on honour and friendship, no longer existed. Debts were paid directly in blood, there was no form of control.'

Paolo and Cosimo di Lauro are still locked up, but Corona is ambivalent when I ask if he feels like he made a difference in the fight against the *sistema*.

'No,' he says matter-of-factly. 'I guess you could say that we showed that if there is a commitment, something can hold. If there's an effort by the state to stop the feuding, there will always be arrests, because in the end you can always catch people.

'But you can't think that you can resolve the problems of Scampia, Secondigliano and the whole question of Naples with force only. You have to think of prevention, how to stop the crimes happening in the first place.'

Corona eyes my empty glass. 'I'm hungry, let's go and eat,' he says, disappearing to pay the bill before I have time to argue.

I had no intention of declining; Corona is too interesting.

Over dinner at a friend's restaurant on the gulf, Corona laughs as he remembers a magistrate colleague's theory on how to rid Naples of crime.

'He claimed the only way to get the city back on its feet was to go to the worst zones, take all the newborns and deport them to Australia,' he says, smirking at the memory. 'In Australia these kids would live on new soil, breathe fresh air. They wouldn't be influenced by the culture of bullying and injustice, of making money on the street, this culture of laziness that grows until you no longer want to be a better person.

'My colleague was suggesting this to some *camorristi,* who didn't really get what he was saying…They just thought he wanted to steal their kids!'

Over slices of plain salted pizza, fried fish as appetisers and *secondi* of swordfish, calamari and prawns, Corona lists his ideas to reform the city. Not surprisingly he talks of greater investment in poor areas and more focus on education – but not just for children.

'It's the Neapolitan attitude, even that of the rich, to avoid paying taxes, to cheat the person next to you, while the economy is based on kickbacks,' he says with a shake of his head. 'But if there was a campaign to change the culture, to denounce it, maybe things would change.'

Corona has been under police escort since 1998, when they uncovered plans by the Camorra to kill him, and he started getting death threats: cards in the mail, bullets in packages.

'I've never thought that an escort could save me – if they want to get me, they can,' he says without flinching. 'I'm not afraid, but obviously I worry about my family.'

Corona tells me he's separated from his wife, who has custody of their two young children, but he sees them every day.

A bottle of *Rucolina*, a type of bitter digestive made from rocket, is placed on our table as Corona and I talk about women in the Camorra. He claims they're more brutal than their male counterparts and agrees when I suggest he means women like Pupetta Maresca, a legendary female clan leader of the 1950s.

'Strangely enough, I know her nephew,' he says, signalling for the bill. 'He runs a nightclub nearby – let's go.'

I make an effort to appear nonchalant, but adrenalin pumps through my veins at the thought of meeting Maresca. She entered Naples' criminal history in April 1955 when she married up-and-coming Camorra boss Pasquale Simonetti. Barely half a year would pass before Simonetti was killed by a hitman hired by his former business partner. Six months pregnant, Maresca took the law into her own hands. Arming herself with a pistol, she entered a bar near Naples' central train station and fired a volley of bullets into the former business associate. Maresca was sentenced to eighteen years jail for murder, but was paroled in 1965.

I'm curious to know what Maresca, who must now be in her sixties, thinks of the renewed bloodshed in Naples, where she apparently still lives. Perhaps tonight I can plant the seed.

I leap behind Corona on his bike and we wait for his friend Enrico, the owner of the pizzeria, to start his own scooter.

As we head along the gulf, Corona and Enrico drive side by side and chat, something I see the locals do often in 'small-town' Naples, but never saw in Rome. I suddenly feel very Neapolitan. All I'm missing are the high heels, serious tan, exposed cleavage and a little more belly.

Arriving at the nightclub in Fuorigrotta, we park our bikes and walk into a room packed with people aged from their late teens to early forties. On a dance floor couples tango before an admiring audience.

'As you can see,' says Corona, eyeing the crowd, 'the demographic is lower to middle class, more or less honest citizens.'

I follow Corona's lead to the bar, where he introduces me to Massimo, a bald, smiley man with a rich tan, which he displays to effect with a carefully unbuttoned blue cotton shirt. Corona explains my interest in speaking to Pupetta Maresca.

Massimo looks at me curiously before telling me his famous aunt is currently writing her memoirs and can't talk to anyone. Arguing that I would be happy just to talk to Pupetta and not interview her as a journalist, he agrees to chat to his family and see what he can arrange.

I take a vodka tonic Massimo shoves in my hand and move with Corona and Enrico to a free space in the throng.

'You realise that I've placed myself in the lion's mouth,' says Corona with a wink. He then tells me that during clan warfare two years ago one of Massimo's relatives was shot dead outside the nightclub we're standing in.

I thank Corona sincerely, playing to his routine, and size him up as we stand sipping our drinks amid the smoke and colour. At forty-two he's nothing short of fascinating, but my instinct bristles at his showmanship. His generosity is offset by something slippery, but he could prove a good contact.

Minutes after walking in my front door an hour later, I hear the beep of an SMS message on my phone. *I like you a lot, Penny. I hope to see you again, as soon as possible. A nice kiss.*

Giggling out loud at Corona's attempt at English, which doesn't quite hit the mark, I realise how much fun I've had tonight, but know I'm going to have to play this new acquaintance – a mature *provolone* – with extreme care.

Nun credere o' santo sì nun he' visto 'o miraculo

Don't believe in the saint if you haven't seen the miracle

Blood may be thicker than water, but in Naples it takes on whole new properties and proportions. *Sangue* spills every day in clan warfare, but it can also 'come back from the dead'. Well, that's if I'm prepared to put my faith, shaky at the best of times, in the true believers.

As autumn arrives I count down the days to 19 September, a red-letter date on Naples' calendar, when everyone takes a holiday to celebrate the city's patron saint, San Gennaro.

In the chronicles of Neapolitan history, San Gennaro was a bishop in Benevento, south of Naples, who died a martyr in 305 AD when he was beheaded during Roman emperor Diocletian's Christian persecutions. According to legend, San Gennaro's body and head were saved by an old man and taken to a safe place, where a local woman filled two phials with his blood. Somewhere between forty to a hundred years later, depending on which version of history you believe, during an operation to move San

Gennaro's relics to Naples' catacombs, the saint's blood, which over time had solidified in the phial, began to bubble. Since that day, San Gennaro's blood has miraculously liquefied three times a year: on the first Saturday in May, on his feast day in September, and on 16 December, marking the 1631 eruption of Vesuvius, believed to have been halted by the saint's intervention.

To the faithful, San Gennaro has saved Naples from wars, epidemics and natural disasters, all of which I find incredible, if not laughable. But my scepticism is shot down by history: the various misfortunes that have struck the city when San Gennaro's blood failed to liquefy include a plague that killed tens of thousands of Neapolitans in 1527, and the 1980 earthquake, which claimed almost than three thousand lives.

In 1991, three Italian scientists examined the wacky phenomenon in a paper entitled 'Working Bloody Miracles', published in science magazine *Nature*. The trio thought the blood's transformation could be attributed to thixotropy, whereby certain substances liquefy if agitated – a little bit like tomato sauce.

I decide there is only one way to discover the truth.

I rise early on 19 September and down an espresso and some breakfast before heading to the city's famed *duomo*, where San Gennaro's blood is stored, arriving at 7.30 am sharp. As I wait for the ceremony to begin, I examine the crowd: groups of old women clutch rosary beads, and young kids hold cards printed with the images of saints and the Madonna, rather than basket-ball stars.

I strike up a conversation with a middle-aged couple beside me. Aniello and Alessandra, both artists, tell me they have attended the ceremony for the past three years. I can't help being a smarty-pants and wonder out loud how San Gennaro's blood can, on the same day, both liquefy in the *duomo* and ooze from the stone in the nearby town of Pozzuoli, where he met his death.

Aniello raises his eyebrows. 'Haven't you seen a miracle before?'

As we wait for the church to open, the couple explain what I'm about to see. To get things rolling, a group of *parenti*, or 'relatives', of San Gennaro gather inside the church in the adjoining *Cappella del Tesoro*, Chapel of Treasure. The *parenti* watch one of the phials (God knows where the other one is) mounted on a gold-gilded altar, and wail and sing, urging the saint to perform his miracle. Regardless of where the blood actually liquefies – be it in the chapel, or after it has been carried to the front of the church before the congregation – when the 'miracle' occurs, an official waves a white handkerchief, prompting those watching to do the same.

The church doors suddenly swing open and the crowd surges forward in a sprint to bag a front pew. I wedge myself next to Alessandra and Aniello, keen to hear their commentary during the service.

Rolling rosary beads in her hands, Alessandra tells me that San Gennaro has become a big part of their lives.

'A strange thing happened…There were signs, which I can't elaborate on, but together we became devoted to San Gennaro. We decided that, of all the saints, he was ours,' she says, holding up a pendant of the saint attached to a chain around her neck.

The voice of the bishop rings out.

'From this point you can ask something of San Gennaro, like a new house or job,' she whispers into my ear.

'What about love?' I say.

'Well, that could be more difficult. But you can try.' Alessandra giggles and motions for me to follow her.

We walk to the back of the church and into the chapel. The strange incantations of the *parenti* fill the small space, a cross between a Gregorian chant and a muffled conversation. Alessandra walks to the altar and drops to her knees to pray. In front of her, beneath ornate chandeliers illuminating the red carpet and shiny wooden pews, is a bronze bust of San Gennaro cloaked in a red and gold embroidered cloth. Among the *parenti* I recongise one of the elderly women who was in the queue outside the church. She rubs rosary beads and murmurs words I can't decipher. The funereal atmosphere is tinged with a nervous anticipation.

Alessandra's eyes glisten with tears as she leads me back to our seat. With the clock creeping to 8 am, I stare at the huge organ across from us and scan the gold and marble furnishings and sombre frescoes.

At the front of the church to the right is a small platform for the media. With my press card in my pocket, I decide to join the throng to get a better look at the action. I step onto the stage and jostle with TV cameramen to position myself at the front of the scrum.

The assembled crowd hushes as a flock of bishops in white cloaks and red sashes walk single file to the front of the church. The crowd parts like the Red Sea for Moses to allow Cardinal Crescenzio Sepe, whom I recognise from the papers, to float down the aisle and join other clergymen near the altar. A rotund man with raccoon eyes, Cardinal Sepe is conducting his first San Gennaro ceremony before a three-thousand-strong crowd.

At 8.55 am church bells peal and the organ cranks into action, blaring from a speaker above. From the back of the church, two men wearing red and black robes solemnly carry an ornate mini palanquin, almost a metre high, to the front of the church. Straining my eyes, I can see they carry a small phial of blood encased in a small wooden box.

The crowd bursts into sudden applause when Cardinal Sepe declares that the blood appears to have half liquefied.

'*San Genná…fai presto, fai presto!*' From somewhere in the crowd, the desperate voice of a woman urges San Gennaro to 'do it quickly'.

I look down at the crowd and see mobile phones raised high in the air: Italians love recording every moment with their *telefonini*.

Twenty minutes later the crowd cheers again as Cardinal Sepe, his face beaded with sweat, announces that the blood has almost liquefied. As far as I can see, nothing much has changed in the phial.

Hand fans flutter and all eyes remain glued to the blood.

A whoop rings out as a grey-haired man in a black suit finally waves a white handkerchief and Cardinal Sepe grabs for his own, wiping away tears of emotion. It's official: San Gennaro has worked another wonder.

Below me I watch an American TV journalist ask an old woman in the crowd why she is crying.

'*È un miracolo, miracolo*,' gasps the woman, on the verge of passing out.

Cardinal Sepe takes the phial and holds it up to the crowd. He turns it to demonstrate that the blood is as fluid as the tears streaming down faces in the crowd.

'Our patron saint, Gennaro, with his blood, has handed back Christian hope to our dear, tormented city,' says Cardinal Sepe, visibly moved, his eyes roving. 'It's no chance that today the word of God, which rewakes our conscience, wants to remind us that we are the salt of the earth and the light of the world…We have to believe, we have to hope that our diocese, our region, can rise again.

'God teaches us that to change the world, all we need is a pinch of salt. The Lord doesn't ask us to be heroes, rather just a small grain of salt capable of giving flavour to an entire dish, capable of preserving food. Naples has a real need for this, of women and men of good will…'

Hope, blood, food, crime. All that's missing is Diego Maradona.

I watch as dignitaries, including Campania President Antonio Bassolino and Mayor Rosa Russo Iervolino, kneel before Cardinal Sepe and then rise to kiss the phial before being swallowed by the crowd elbowing to exit the church.

Stepping into the morning light, I pull an apple out of my bag and take a huge bite. After close to two hours the sugar levels in my own blood are low. Small stalls are doing a roaring trade selling *torroni*, or 'big towers', the long blocks of fudge-like chocolate traditionally sold in Naples at Christmas, but also on other special occasions like today.

I stop to buy one and strike up a conversation with a family waiting beside me. I smile as I hear the father is named Gennaro, which is also the name of a Neapolitan friend of mine.

'The fact the blood liquefied quickly is a good omen for the rest of the year,' says Gennaro's wife, Graziella, who sticks some *torroni* in her handbag to take to lunch with the couple's extended family. 'And it's true, according to my grandparents.'

Graziella takes me by the arm and practically frog-marches me into a nearby bar, where Gennaro insists on buying me a coffee. The couple's son, Giuseppe, stands munching on a *frolla,* one of Naples' famous *sfogliatelle* pastries, as Graziella makes the most of our acquaintance. Am I married? How old am I? Have I got a boyfriend? At first Neapolitans' nosiness annoyed me, but now I like that I have an excuse to be inquisitive without apparently offending anyone.

When I shake my head in response to the question about my *ragazza* status, Graziella shrugs her shoulders and smiles. '*Beh*, you are so young…Don't worry, you'll find someone good!'

Graziella's pronunciation of *buono*, or good, makes me giggle out loud because in Naples, 'u' is more marked than in Rome, almost as if it comes straight from the heart – a bit like the locals themselves.

I bid Graziella and family goodbye after she insists I scribble down her home number 'in case I ever need anything', and head home along via San Biagio dei Librai. It's one of my favourite streets in the old town, intersected by via San Gregorio Armeno, the famous strip where all the *presepe* figurines are sold. Christmas is nearing and business is picking up as locals, and not just tourists interested in a souvenir, flock to buy the tiny nativity figurines.

I stroll past pizza stands, shops selling *limoncello*, antiques, books, and the Maradona shrine beside Bar Nilo. A stroll through the heart of Naples always turns up something new, and reminds me of the old Italian films I love so much.

As rain starts to fall I wonder whether locals are blaming San Gennaro for the inconvenience. In spite of the pomp and ceremony, or perhaps because of it, I can't help but think his 'miracle' was somehow rigged. Maybe they just stick the phial under a flame or rub it in their hands to turn the congealed blood to liquid. However they do it, at a time when Naples is reeling from fresh clan killings, there is no way Cardinal Sepe would not have made the red stuff run in his first attempt.

Italian Prime Minister Romano Prodi is in Naples to help thrash out a new anti-crime plan in a period which Italian President Giorgio Napolitano describes as one of the bleakest in the city's history.

'Naples cannot die – we need concrete commitments,' Prodi said on the eve of his visit.

In a public opinion poll in *Il Mattino*, there is overwhelming favour for the army to be called in for extra security and to help put a stop to escalating violence. In the same newspaper I look at the latest sheet-covered body of a Camorra widow, whose two 'boss' sons had already been gunned down by rival clans, and see a comment by famous Neapolitan musician Mario Merola.

'*Me fa male 'o core*,' moans Merola in Neapolitan dialect: the city's recent crime wave is hurting his heart.

The next morning I read the update on Prodi's visit. Ruling out the need for the army, the national government has signed a security pact with local authorities and released a raft of new measures: at least one hundred new police officers to boost the thirteen thousand-strong force, more police patrols in danger zones, new officers to investigate clan finances, millions of euro towards public lighting and surveillance…

'The Camorra had better understand its reign is coming to an end,' warns Giuliano Amato, Italy's minister of the interior. 'There will be no more crime sanctuaries, and those who refuse to comply will pay.'

My phone rings – it's Valerio.

'*Ciao, Penny, che fai?* Hi, Penny, what are you up to?'

It's a chilly Saturday and rain pours heavily. I don't feel like moving so I suggest Valerio comes around for lunch and then maybe we can go and see a film.

When I hang up, reality hits home. *Che idiota!* I can barely cook to save my life, let alone kindle a relationship.

I sprint across the terrace to find Nicoletta standing in her kitchen, dicing cherry tomatoes as a delicious savoury scent wafts from her oven. Seeing a table set in beautiful linen in her dining room behind her, I figure she's expecting visitors for lunch.

She smirks when I tell her the bind I'm in. '*Che cosa hai nel tuo frigo?*' she says, casually enquiring about the contents of my refrigerator.

Within minutes we're standing in my kitchen. I watch as she takes a long eggplant, quarters it and cuts out the core before dicing it and placing it on a plate. *'Sale!'* Nicoletta barks, asking me for salt, which she sprinkles over the eggplant, explaining that it will draw out the bitterness.

She opens a big can of tomatoes, cuts off their ends and cores them, telling me she has removed the too-chewy bit, before putting them into a frying pan she has coated with olive oil. Having discovered (with a grimace) that my garlic is mouldy with age, she grabs a clove from her kitchen and returns to place it in the pan with a fresh basil leaf. Then she orders me to buy some fresh *mozzarella di bufala* from Anna, the *signora* who keeps her corner store open until lunchtime on Saturdays, and disappears.

I yell out to her when I get back ten minutes later; she reappears within seconds, grabs the eggplant and squeezes it over the sink, forcing black juice to gush out. She then tips the eggplant into another pan, fries it until it's golden, then adds the tomato sauce. I follow orders and cook some *rigatone* pasta Nicoletta has spied on my shelf, while she returns to her kitchen to finish her own lunch. I sing out when the pasta is *pronta*.

I watch as she deftly drains the pasta, tips in the tomato and eggplant sauce, mixes it gently, and then pours it into a baking tray lined with oven paper. Finally, she drops cubes of the mozzarella into the dish.

'Okay, done. Five minutes before Valerio comes just put this in the oven and the cheese will melt... Then take it out, leave it to sit for five minutes to absorb the sauce a little more, then sprinkle some basil on top... and *voila*, you have *pasta al forno Siciliana.*'

'Sei da sposare! You're marriage material!' I say, before giving her a huge hug.

Nicoletta stares at me and shakes her head. *'Sei una causa persa!* You're a lost cause!'

'*Sì. Sì, è vero, ma della verità… Ti sei divertita!* Yes. Yes it's true, but say you didn't have fun!'

She rolls her eyes and mutters '*in bocca al lupo*', 'in the mouth of the wolf', an Italian euphemism for 'good luck', before disappearing across the terrace.

I change quickly and stand in front of the bathroom mirror, remembering Valerio's comment that he doesn't like make-up. While I never doll myself up that much anyway, I stifle a strange desire to paint myself like Paul Stanley of Kiss fame, complete with black star over one eye. Why am I thinking so much about what he likes? I curse out loud at the agitated woman in the mirror.

Valerio rings to say he's outside my palazzo and I buzz him in. I open my door to find him in a dripping raincoat, a tray of sweets from the *pasticceria* in his hands. When he attempts to take his goodies to the kitchen I order him out, saying that a surprise awaits him.

We snack on a plate of *prosciutto crudo* and *provola*, smoked mozzarella, as we wait for the pasta to bake. I take it out and let it cool before serving two hearty portions into deep bowls. As I place a plate before him, Valerio raises one eyebrow.

'Okay, okay, Nicoletta gave me some tips,' I admit, when he tastes the dish and showers me with compliments.

He's right. The pasta is delicious. Good. Now I have at least one new dish to add to my skinny repertoire.

Pouring some *aglianico* wine into our glasses, I ask Valerio what he thinks about the newspaper poll showing public support to use the army to help deal with the current crisis.

A shake of his hand tells me he's not in favour. 'In the short term, there needs to be an investment in reorganising the police force to combat criminal activities,' he says in between mouthfuls. 'There is a major police station minutes from your house, but do you see any patrols? If I were in charge I'd have these officers in action, on the beat.'

'But is this current spate of murders an exception or just media hype or,' as my magistrate friend Giovanni Corona speculated, 'simply a ploy to distract attention from the Prodi government's struggle with the budget?' I ask.

'Who have you been hanging out with? Spare me the political fantasy! Let's not joke about it, there have been 114 deaths since the start of the year. I don't know if it's a Camorra war, but it's certainly a grave thing to underestimate. The Camorra's moments of silence are normally linked to a convergence of clan interests: influence, the markets, are equally distributed and affairs run smoothly. So recent events are signs of an agitation, or change.'

As I tuck into my last mouthful, I wonder why the hell I'm grilling Valerio about Camorra politics on a romantic date, but he continues, seemingly lost in his thoughts.

'Naples will move ahead, regardless. It's a city that can absorb and metabolise anything. The capacity of Neapolitans to *arrangersi*, to "get by", is equalled only by their ability to compromise.'

'I wonder if Naples will ever love itself enough to change for good,' I say, standing to clear our plates and grab a bottle of grappa from the kitchen.

'Naples loves itself, the locals have a visceral connection to the city,' Valerio says. 'In the 1990s, Mayor Antonio Bassolino created a sense of community that had extraordinary results. But sometimes Neapolitans love their city so much they pretend nothing is happening…You know, "focusing on Naples is convenient for the national government". Bullshit. The situation is serious. To *really* love Naples means to not hide it, and to change it.'

Valerio opens the tray of sweets, beautifully packaged in glistening gold paper and ribbon, and explains the three different types of *torroni* he has bought: coffee, white chocolate and hazelnut, and rich chocolate. Beside them are a few mini *baba* and *sfogliatelle* for good measure. The phone rings and Nicoletta, lunching with a friend across the terrace, cheekily asks me if I have any sweets. I load some on a plate and deliver them with pleasure.

The rain has stopped so Valerio and I head outdoors for a long walk before the film and the conversation suddenly takes a turn I wasn't expecting. In few but precise words, Valerio tells me that if his ex made it known that she wanted them to get back together, he would most likely agree.

My belly, round with pasta and sweets, does a sickening flip. Thankfully, I don't have time to respond because we spy Valerio's friends Federico and Illaria standing outside the cinema. We file inside to watch the thriller *La Sconosciuta*, *The Unknown Woman*, a film about a Hungarian woman with a dark past who migrates to Italy. My concentration falters as I occasionally glance at Valerio in the dark.

Later I kiss Federico, Illaria and Valerio goodbye before starting the short walk home up the hill. Within seconds I feel warm tears flowing down my cheeks, brought on by the sad film and Valerio's earlier comment.

At home, I sit down and write Valerio a letter. Trying to sound strong and indifferent, I tell him that while I didn't have any expectations of what could be, I had at least hoped he could enter a possible relationship with an open mind.

'I'm sick of being the nice, fun girl, the go-between girl, the girl who mends hearts,' I say simply. 'And for now, I can't be a friend when I feel affection for you.'

Spying Nicoletta's light on, I walk across the terrace and knock on the glass kitchen door. She lets me in and I sit on the couch to vent my frustration, sniffling all over again.

'Treasure, it's nothing you have done, sometimes timing is just wrong,' she says, trying to comfort me.

'But, Nicoletta, he was rich!' I say, attempting a joke. She had warned me not to date starving artists but men with sizeable bank accounts.

'*Madonna mia*,' she says, slapping her forehead in mock horror. 'If you had told me that I would have taught you how to cook a second course!'

Nicoletta gives me a long hug before I drag my feet across the terrace, tuck myself under my doona and tune out with my iPod. I think of the wish I made as I sat among the faithful to watch the miracle of San Gennaro. Alessandra, the woman sitting next to me during the service, was right.

I wished for something too complicated, a miracle in its own right.

Days after my experience in the *duomo*, my Neapolitan workmate Francesco tells me that a re-release of the 1966 film *Operazione San Gennaro* is being screened tomorrow at Teatro Bellini.

Directed by Dino Risi, revered as one of the masters, if not the father, of Italian comedies, the film was one of the last starring comic genius Toto, who died in 1967. The plot, says Francesco, revolves around three American thieves who attempt to steal the treasure in the same *duomo* where San Gennaro's blood is stored, while the city is distracted by the annual Festival of Naples, a singing competition which began in 1952, ran for twenty years, then started again in 1998.

Francesco uses his contacts to secure me a ticket to the screening, which will be introduced by Risi himself.

After work the next day I hurry up via Toledo, past Piazza Dante and take a right to arrive at the theatre just before 9 pm. Gathered outside is a well-dressed crowd, men with cravats and bejewelled women in furs clutching designer handbags. Dressed in my usual street-urchin style, I feel decidedly underdressed.

I elbow my way to the front desk and discover that I actually have two tickets waiting for me. With the movie starting within half an hour, I scan my list of friends and send a message to my workmate Marco, who lives close by. He replies immediately and I'm relieved when he shows up fifteen minutes later. Marco is not the most punctual of my friends.

Inside the theatre foyer a flash of cameras greets us, with local media eager to snap Risi, a small man with a shock of white hair and black spectacles, and other dignitaries whose importance is lost on me. Marco and I walk up a flight of stairs and enter the theatre, an expanse of blood-red velvet seats and curtains, with seven levels of viewing booths to the left and right. Beautiful cupids, nude except for strategically placed foliage, are painted on the cavernous ceiling.

Francesco has outdone himself. We have prime seats only a few rows behind the VIPs. Marco and I stop chattering when a microphone bursts into action and Risi stands up, aided by a friend. The audience hushes as Risi clears his throat.

'There are many anecdotes tied to the making of this film, but what I remember above all is Toto, who was extremely ill and almost blind,' says Risi, far from sprightly himself but with a voice that fills the theatre. 'And yet, when I asked him if he was able to go on, he replied: "My work is generating laughter, and even if I'm feeling bad I'll never show it."'

The audience erupts into cheers before he takes a serious note.

'I don't have any types of devotion, but I have a great sympathy for saints like Gennaro,' he says, still relying on his friend's arm to keep him steady. 'I was born in Milan but I wish I was Neapolitan. I have always been in love with Naples. I know this city will pass this ugly moment. Looking into the past one realises that there have been worse times. The city has many saints who protect it. Things will get better.'

The crowd claps their approval, with some people standing to pay tribute to the diminutive Risi, before the lights dim. As the film starts, offering glorious panoramas and street shots of Naples, Marco squeezes my arm in the dark, full of joy and passion for his hometown.

With a heavy use of dialect, I miss at least a third of the jokes, but I laugh all the same at Nino Manfredi's and Senta Berger's exaggerated acting, and the bad Italian accent of Harry Guardino, in the role of one of the American thieves. I wonder if my accent is as grating.

In a small scene showing the miracle of San Gennaro, women crush up against the front of the church, crying and wailing. I can't remember seeing such mass hysteria when I watched the ceremony last week.

By eleven the show is over and Marco walks me halfway home to Piazza Dante, raving all the way about the classic film he hadn't seen until tonight. I assure him that I'll be fine to make it home alone and promise to watch the movie on DVD, so I can appreciate more of the scenes.

'Let me know when you do – I'll explain the jokes you still can't get, idiot,' he says playfully before hugging me and turning on his heel.

A bowl of piping hot lentil and broccoli soup is plonked unceremoniously before me as I grab my wine glass and chin-chin with Anna, Claudia and Orfina.

We are dining at Il Buon Gustaio, a one-room trattoria near the daily market at Monte Santo, not far from my home. Being fairly regular clientele the larrikin staff know most of us by name. I pause to watch the main waiter, Salvatore, lean over a table to run through the never-changing specials. I've seen him do the same thing scores of times, but I still marvel at how much enthusiasm he puts into his spiel.

Orfina regales us with the story of her last date – in fact only an SMS rally that lasted three minutes before the man in question pulled out. I join in the ensuing conversation (about the weaker sex) with almost too much glee. Thank God I have some strong women, Nicoletta included, to turn to in Naples.

Salvatore arrives with my favourite dish. Try as I might, I can't go past the cod, or *bacala*, fried and drizzled in a tomato sauce with capers and olives. The fact that the batter coating the fish is still crisp under the heavy sauce is one thing, the rich, salty flavour another. I think of the man gunned down as he dined at a pizzeria. If I had a choice of my last meal in Naples I'd eat *bacala;* I chase away an image of my face planted in my cod, blood mixing with the sauce.

After a round of grappa and *limoncello,* we head out onto the streets for *La Notte Bianca*, The White Night, a national street festival that runs all night on a Saturday. It's the second time it has been held, after the inaugural event was written off as a disaster when thousands of Neapolitans were trapped underground in the metro while trying to get to the city centre. Perhaps for this reason, this year the city has been divided into various entertainment hubs for the different events to take place.

I see in the program that there will be a silent protest in memory of victims of the Camorra, with mute spectators painting their faces white. I want to go, but it's a matter of being able to get there through the crowd. We meet up with another group of friends, including Roberto and Manola, and head to see satirical writer and journalist Stefano Benni, whose books have been translated into twenty languages.

Benni is illuminated on a stage at a beautiful historic palazzo near Piazza del Gesu, and his voice reaches out in the dark as he reads '*Le Piccole Cose*', 'The Small Things', a poem that details the depressing course of a relationship from romantic beginnings to domestic drudgery. I laugh out loud, and when he belts out a tribute to actor Toto, he has the audience screaming for more.

Moving on, we pass one of my local haunts, Aret' a' Palm, where a man in a tent reads tarot cards and some African jazz is in full swing on a stage nearby. Three people in black suits and rubbery Toto masks pass by. White sheets hang from buildings and wrap around the palm trees in the street. We stop for a beer before heading to Piazza Matteoitti, where the fascist-era post office building stands. Before too long saxophonist Enzo Avitabile has the crowd bouncing. Touted as the only white man to have flanked James Brown on the stage in a series of European concerts, the Neapolitan musician, yells Manola to me above the crowd, works pushing hospital gurneys to make a buck.

Some of our group heads off to a concert too far away for my energy levels. I walk with Anna, Claudia and Orfina to Piazza del Plebiscito, crammed with spectators watching one of the biggest concerts of the night, including a performance by Pino Daniele. My friends have all raved about him, but they soon jeer; his performance is apparently a fizzer. When he finally cranks out a romantic melody from the 1980s, my friends burst into song. I watch as Anna's eyes glisten with tears and wonder what buried moment she's recalling. All of a sudden I wish that I could sing along, too.

Tired of queuing at a bar to use the bathroom, I send a goodnight SMS to my friends and weave home through the thick crowd shuffling along via Toledo. At home, I switch on the television and and find that bizarre *neomelodica* music, a type of karaoke with a huge local following. The festival tonight has been a good introduction to the Neapolitan music scene, but I'm keen to know more about the traditional *canzone Napoletana* as well as *neomelodica*.

My phone beeps with a message from my old flatmates in Rome, Massi and Adriano, who are at Aret' a' Palm.

My boots are already off and my body is no longer made for walking.

Almost three months have passed since I first contacted Telecom to get internet connected at home.

When Nando, our IT guy, sees my look of desperation during my umpteenth phone call to Telecom, he takes matters into his own hands. Through a contact, he succeeds in getting the cable, which was installed in my home months ago, finally activated. And the next day he walks me home and hooks up the modem he has kindly donated to the cause, thus saving another endless delay from Telecom, who were insisting they had to install it.

Within minutes of arriving home I finally have internet, albeit not a fast connection, but in one of the city's oldest *quartieri*, I'm just thankful to be connected. I plant two kisses on Nando's cheeks, thrust a tube of *baci* chocolates I bought earlier into his hands, and bounce around my small living room, much to my friend's amusement.

I spend the night surfing the web and sending emails, resisting the urge to make contact with Valerio, whom I've happily let fall off my radar.

I hear Nicoletta chatting on the phone and think of one of her favourite sayings: 'Men are like phone boxes – the ones that aren't occupied don't work.'

Men and San Gennaro, who needs them?

And if there is a God, his name is Nando.

È malu tiempo a mare e 'o cefalu va caro

The sea is at storm and the fish is expensive

As I thrust some coins into the open palm of Paolo, my *giornalaio*, he hands me my newspapers and breaks into tune, drawing smiles from the other early morning risers who stop by his outdoor newsstand. Rocco, the fur-balled dog with cascading flab and walrus-like front teeth, whom Paolo lovingly refers to as his *fidanzata*, or girlfriend, spreads out languorously in a wind-protected possie.

'Do you know that song?' he asks. 'It's called "Penelope e Ulisse". It's all about Penelope weaving her shroud, waiting for Ulysses to return.' He scribbles down the name of Renato Carosone, the man behind the song.

At home I hit the web to read that Carosone, born in Naples in 1920, was considered one of the major protagonists of what is known as *canzone Napoletana,* or Neapolitan song, a style of music strictly performed in the local dialect (to which I'm unfortunately still deaf).

The musical genre officially burst onto the stage on 7 September 1837, during a songwriting competition at the inaugural Festival of Piedigrotta. The event was dedicated to the Madonna of Piedigrotta, a famous church in Naples' well-to-do suburb of Mergellina, where I first got off the train from Rome with my flatmate Adriano, to enjoy a cappuccino and *sfogliatella* in the sunshine.

One of the most famous hits of the *canzone Napoletana* is 'Funiculi Funicula', which claimed the top prize at the Piedigrotta festival in 1880, lauding the newly opened, and now defunct, funicular on Vesuvius. The festival died out in the 1950s, but not before decades of emigrants from Naples and Italy's south had exported the music to the far reaches of the globe.

Neapolitan poet, playwright and songwriter Salvatore di Giacomo is also often credited for inventing the genre in the late nineteenth century, mixing classical arias and chamber music with the traditional *taranta* – a bongo-driven rhythm from Italy's south accompanied by whirling couples who, according to folklore, dance frenetically to cure themselves after being bitten by the allegedly deadly tarantula spider.

The *canzone Napoletana* was carried on after World War II by performers like the Pucci tie-wearing Carosone, whose song '*Torero*', or 'Bullfighter', written specifically for a Spanish tour, hogged number one on the American hit parade for more than three months, and was translated into twelve languages.

Carosone toured the world, playing at New York's prestigious Carnegie Hall, and his songs featured in films starring Sophia Loren, who crooned '*Tu Vuò Fà l'Americano*', 'You Want to Be an American', in *It Started in Naples*, also starring Clark Gable. In 1960, as crowds of screaming girls created Beatle-mania, the then forty-year-old Carosone unplugged his microphone, saying he'd rather finish on the crest of the wave than be washed away by what he dismissed as the 'new armies in blue jeans'.

As I pour my first espresso of the day, I scan *La Repubblica.* Naples has hit the front pages again, but this time with the headline 'Farewell Merola, king of the *sceneggiata*'. Mario Merola, a Neapolitan singer and actor famous for reviving the traditional Neapolitan musical soap opera, known as the *sceneggiata,* has died. The seventy-two year old's funeral is scheduled for tomorrow.

Coming to the fore just after World War I, the *sceneggiata* is a type of staged musical that explores the domestic woes, betrayals and loves of ordinary people, all sung or spoken in Neapolitan dialect. Music hall performances, which supposedly drew audiences away from 'legitimate' theatre, attracted a hefty tax. So the *sceneggiata* evolved from the music hall to avoid the tax.

Most popular in the 1920s, the musical soap opera resurfaced in the 1960s. Merola, who hailed from a poor family, worked as a longshoreman at Naples' port before one of his songs, '*Malu Filgliu*', 'Bad Son', propelled him to fame. His popularity soared during the 1970s and 1980s, and he recorded around forty albums and acted in a string of Italian movies.

La Repubblica describes Merola's death like the collapse of a monument 'that represented the good and the bad of a vast part of Naples…' I remember how Giovanni Durante, the father of Camorra shooting victim Annalisa, described his daughter's love for music, in particular the songs of Merola. He sure must have been a power to influence today's teens, almost two decades after his career high.

Intrigued, I swap my morning shift the next day for a midday start and head to *la Chiesa Santa Maria del Carmine* for Merola's funeral.

When I arrive, the piazza crowd is so thick I have no hope of getting close to the church. I wedge myself between a police truck and a stationary Vespa whose young, male owner kneels on the seat to get a better look, his eyes hidden beneath enormous, fake, designer sunglasses. The church's intricate campanile, Naples' tallest, towers above the crowd.

An hour before the 11 am ceremony is scheduled to begin, the crowd surges and I turn my head to see the human tide has almost completely jammed the street. As I swing back around I do a double take. About two metres away is the down-and-out chap that I often see on via Toledo trying to sell balloons. Today, balloon man is empty-handed, his face deflated.

I look up to the banners hanging from balconies filled with beige dots for faces. *Senza di te finisce Napoli* – 'Without you, Naples is finished' – reads one, in reference to a song that contemporary Neapolitan crooner Gigi d'Alessio is supposed to have dedicated to Merola. *Oggi si e' spento il sole a Napoli* – 'Today the sun was extinguished in Naples' – laments another. A loud-speaker mounted on top of the church hisses into action, and an elderly male voice reminds us that we're in the house of God, of the Madonna, and that if a corridor of space leading into the church is not cleared, the funeral service and sacred mass cannot proceed. Mario Merola's fame is literally blocking the arrival of his coffin.

At midday the funeral is still not under way. Disappointed, I elbow my way out of the mob and rush to work. Two hours later an email arrives in my inbox from my friend Enzo, a local singer whom I'd arranged to meet but couldn't find in the throng.

I stayed right until the end. I wish you could have, too, because many things I hoped you could witness indeed happened in the end. When the body was carried out you could feel the emotion. In front of me was a group that began to flap white handkerchiefs in perfect synchrony. It was a salute, and it made me think of the ovations for bullfighters, like I once saw in Barcelona: the same gesture for moments of pain and joy. We in the Mediterranean have exaggerated gestures! After a little while an old woman in front of me fainted. Then came the fireworks.

Neapolitan religious fervour is rich. It's a little bit like Arabs at the Mecca. Certain things, however, I can't understand: Merola's son gesticulating madly like an actor more conscious of the public than his father nearby; and Merola's wife wailing, 'Come to me in my dreams.' Why say it out loud? I don't know what the anthropological explanation is for this type of expression of pain. Maybe they fear their emotion is not real, or maybe it's to exorcise it. Anyway, it made me think: Will Naples be the last Italian bastion against Western civilisation, against the cult of law and order, 'money is time', of balance, of good manners?

On Merola's coffin there was a scarf of the Palermo soccer team. And there was a gadget you use in a casino to play chemin de fer – Merola had a weakness for gambling. We Neapolitans seem like pagans, polytheists. And the funeral was a bit like that. Merola himself once said, 'I believe in God and Padre Pio', one of the most famous saints in Italy. But maybe he didn't realise that this made him a bit of a heretic. Have you ever noticed all the shrines throughout Naples dedicated to the Madonna, the saints, and all the souls in purgatory?

Naples is a city of kings; we're accustomed to personality cults. We had a king for centuries, a separate sovereign, and then the reign of Italy. It's not by chance that Mussolini had many followers in Naples... Berlusconi also wins a stack of votes here, but on a personal level, not for his party. There is a tendency here to sanctify people.

They say that Merola was a king. For me he was an artist. Maybe you didn't like him, maybe you didn't agree with his world, but you couldn't deny he was a grand interpreter. Many snob him without trying to understand the popular culture he represented: his simple logic, his world of good and bad, his sense of honour, of justice.

They say that a part of Naples has gone, and when I arrived this morning I understood what they meant. I felt a loss of a part of Naples that maybe I didn't belong to, but it was part of my upbringing. I don't know if someone from Vomero, from Chiaia, or other affluent zones, can understand.

I think about Enzo's comment on Naples' historic class divide as I read coverage of the funeral the next day, with photos of the estimated crowd of twenty thousand, including Italians from every region, and foreigners from as far away as Australia. On top of the crowd, Merola's wooden coffin floats like ship wreck on a high swell.

Amid the fanfare, with tributes streaming in from the Italian president and politicians of every colour, Naples' mayor, Rosa Russo Iervolino, has caused an uproar by citing a recent book that describes Merola as being a kind of *guappo buono.*

In Naples in the mid-1600s, well before the Camorra became the economic power it is today, a *guappo* was a community leader, a type of social policeman. He would threaten violence to resolve problems, like disputes between families, or to pressure men to marry their pregnant lovers. *Guapperia,* the 'way' of the *guappo,* was built around a code of honour that disappeared as the criminal element of the Camorra evolved. 'We must revive the *guapperia,* its pride and generosity,' the mayor declared. But her critics claim there was never a positive side of *guapperia*, rather, like the Camorra, it was always about the abuse of power.

At least Cardinal Sepe, who also attended the funeral, fails to ruffle feathers: 'Merola was like the ambassador of this city, reflecting the good and the bad, the shadow and light.' According to *La Repubblica,* Merola represented 'forty per cent of Naples, the indigestible plebs who embody a little of everything: gratuitous violence and absolute generosity, obstinacy and tolerance, tears of desperation and the belly laugh, destitution and wealth.'

Bemused by the cultural cringe, I picture the crowd I was part of for an hour yesterday and accept the most simple analysis that Merola's funeral was all show and all heart, for better or worse.

Just like Naples.

During a walk through the historic centre I spy my friend Mario Spada, a photographer who gets about town on a gorgeous, fire-engine red Vespa with his mongrel terrier, Wallaby.

A mad rugby fan, Spada, whose name in English means 'sword', is a self-taught snapper whose unforgiving photos of Naples' dark side – of young kids selling drugs and lurking in the city's darkest *quartiere* – has earnt him a string of accolades.

He's surprised by my interest in the local music scene, and we talk bands, including 99 Posse and Almamagretta, whose hip-hop, reggae-driven sounds inspired a huge national following which peaked in the 1990s. Reggae has never been my preferred groove, but Almamagretta wins points for the fact that British band Massive Attack asked them to help remix some of their biggest hits. Massive Attack's connection to Naples is through the band's Bristol-born frontman Robert '3D' Del Naja, who has Neapolitan relatives and shows his love for Naples' soccer team in album dedications.

With a wagging tail, Wallaby hops onto his master's Vespa. Pulling on a helmet to scoot to a job, Mario recommends I contact 'A67, a band that plays a hip-hop, rock and jazz fusion and hails from Scampia, the area of the Camorra *faida* in 2004 and 2005. Later in the day, Mario sends me an SMS with a telephone number for 'A67's singer, Daniele. I ring him and we arrange to meet at the group's studio on Naples' periphery.

Doing some speed reading beforehand, I learn that 'A67 takes its name from *Legge* 167 of 1962, the parliamentary bill that allowed for the creation of the horrible concrete jungle of Scampia, without shops or community services, and which so depressed me when I visited Gianni Maddaloni's judo gym.

'A67's 2005 debut album, *A Camorra Song'io, I am the Camorra*, won acclaim in Italian musical circles and overseas for both its sound and political message. Most recently, the band won the 2006 'Voices for Liberty – A song for Amnesty International', and has collaborated with the organisation on community youth initiatives.

On a freezing December night I board a train after work and am met at the station by Luciano, the band's drummer, and his girlfriend, Paola, who drive me back to the small studio, painted in bright reggae colours. Soon the group is assembled around me: singer Daniele, a short, feisty twenty-eight year old studies philosophy; Luciano, thirty-one, runs a music school next door; lanky saxophonist Andrea, thirty-four, works market stalls in Rome; electric guitarist Enzo, thirty-one, works for cleaning company; and bassist Alfonso, thirty-one, is a computer programmer.

Daniele says the group evolved naturally, as a response to what he describes as their 'difficult social circumstances'. 'We simply wanted to bring to light the problems of our *quartiere,* which are only acknowledged during episodes of high crime, or election campaigns,' he says.

When I tell the group of how my visit to Scampia affected me, they seem surprised I made the effort, such is its reputation.

'The landscape doesn't allow socialisation,' says Alfonso, rolling a cigarette. With his jet black hair tied in a small pigtail that accentuates his boyish good looks, I've been sneaking glances at Alfonso since he entered the studio. Until now, Daniele has been doing the talking, but I'm keen to hear more from 'A67's bassist.

'There are no piazzas or meeting places,' he continues, 'there are just buildings, and each is an island, closed to the others.'

Admitting that I can't understand the Neapolitan dialect Daniele sings, I ask him to explain the meanings behind some of the group's songs, which I have listened to at home.

'Our songs are about our history and the Camorra, about love, politics, dreams realised and broken, and about hope,' he says. 'Our first album confronts the mentality of the Camorra. We believe that before being a criminal empire, the Camorra is above all a mode of presenting oneself, an attitude. In Naples, a simple glance can cause a fight or even death. Often you hear "What are you looking at?" and this hostility comes from honest people because they've grown up with it. That's what's behind the album title, *I am the Camorra*.'

'Are you talking about Naples or Scampia?' I ask.

'It's a problem in Naples and in the South generally,' says Daniele, before asking me if I know the phrase *cavallo di ritorno*. I nod.

Loosely translated as 'horse that comes back', it refers to an illegal practice widespread in the Campania region, and linked to the Camorra, whereby a robbery victim strikes a payment deal with the thief to get the stolen goods back – without bothering to go to the police. Historically, the term refers to the horse that was lent to help a person return home after striking the deal.

'If you get robbed in Naples,' says Daniele, 'the first thing you do is *not* go to the police. The point is, it's not drug sellers and *camorristi* who practise the *cavallo di ritorno*, but honest citizens who wake up each morning and go to work. For reasons beyond their control, honest people, not just in Scampia but in all of Naples, must compromise their values –'

'Compromise also mean bribes,' Alfonso interjects, leaning forward on his chair. I'm glad to have an excuse to study his face. His skin is as pale as his eyes are dark, and in a soft, slightly raspy voice he articulates his opinions carefully, as if sensitive to the fact that Italian is not my first language.

'The moment you open any store in Scampia and many parts of Naples, you know that apart from the usual taxes, you will have to pay a tax to the Camorra. Or perhaps you will be forced to buy stock for your store from particular suppliers connected with the Camorra.'

'What's it like to grow up in Scampia?' I ask, sensing the group is keen to wind up our chat and start their jam session.

'Penelope, it's very boring,' jokes Daniele, before his face hardens a little. 'It's complex, because kids here live within a code, and they're shielded from other realities…It's hard to explain, but I was fortunate to go to university because my father did everything he could to send me. But at the same time I grew up in Scampia, my best friends are from Scampia…I know two realities.'

Luciano, sitting silently with his drumsticks in hand, pipes up when I ask what has changed since the group began singing.

'When we were making our first disc the *faida* broke out. There was pandemonium, people were dying every day, but amid all this I believe people were thinking hard about what was happening…'

According to Daniele, Naples is like Gomorrah, the biblical city that, alongside Sodom, was destroyed by God for its sins. *Gomorra* is also the title of Roberto Saviano's book on the Camorra.

'We don't lambaste the state, even though it has managed things poorly,' he says. 'We're simply tired of this general attitude of rationalising everything as a "means to survive".'

The boys nod in unison when Daniele says the Camorra can be defeated, notwithstanding the blurred line between the legal and illegal economies.

'On a cultural level it'll take generations to change... But the State must also do its duty, create new jobs, offer a real alternative to those who live on the margins. Above all, though, it must break the chains that bind the illegal market to the legal one. But this means the state must battle right until the bitter end against the Camorra, even destroy a part of the national economy, and of course, some industrial sectors will go into crisis.'

The band considers itself among the group of young Neapolitans, including author Saviano and film director Paolo Sorrentino, who are creating art with a social commitment.

I jokingly ask them what they like most about the city, explaining that I've grown to love it.

'Why?' asks Alfonso, turning the question back on me.

I blush, not sure if I can explain. It's a question I've been asking myself a lot lately, without coming up with neat answers.

'Maybe it's because of my own nature... Neapolitans are both welcoming and sticky beaks, and I like that. And I like the human contact...' I begin before Alfonso saves me.

'In Naples the word meaning "effort" or "difficulty" also means "work",' he says with a laugh, as if summing up the Neapolitan work ethic. 'As a way of greeting, the first thing you say is, "What are you doing, where are you going?" so there is already a desire to enter your personal sphere. It's like an open house, in the sense that the line between public and private is very narrow.'

Daniele clears his throat, signalling to the others to gear up. From beneath his jumper hood, he looks me directly in the eye.

'You know the Neapolitans, you know how beautiful they are. You know that most of them are good honest people and that unlike what you read in the papers, you don't get off the train and immediately get robbed or shot like in a Wild West film,' he says.

'There is a sense of life, how you *live* life. The philosophy here is so different from other Italian cities. It means to live every minute of the day, without thinking of the past nor of the future, to live in the present moment. It's perhaps closest to South American cultures…a mode of facing life, the world, others… It's not by chance that we're so welcoming.'

'And then,' says Andrea, fingering his saxophone and flashing a mischievous grin, 'there is exceptional weather! There are millions of things to see, from Pompeii to Roman villas, and the food –'

'See Naples and die of overconsumption!' Alfonso cuts in, standing to walk to the small studio stage. 'We have pizza, *spaghetti alle vongole*, the best coffee in Italy…!'

Daniele pats his beer belly with mock affection, as if pregnant. 'And to eat together in Naples is a way of staying together. The sense of family here is very strong, especially during the holidays, like Christmas…What are you doing for Christmas?'

'Probably spend it with my old flatmate Francesco, like last year, with his family,' I say.

Satisfied that I won't be an orphan for Christmas, Daniele nods at Luciano, who taps three times and 'A67 cranks into rhythm. Looking the part of an America rap star, all gesticulation and attitude, Daniele growls out the lyrics of 'Don Raffae', a catchy interpretation of a hit by the late, much-loved, Italian singer–songwriter Fabrizio De Andre, all about *Nuova Camorra* clan boss Raffaele Cutolo.

The wads of cotton tissue I've stuck in my ears (following Alfonso's lead) protect my hearing but still allow me to appreciate the polished tunes of the group. They play a fun version of rap and hip-hop with moments that remind me of British ska group Madness.

Two hours later we sit in a circle to eat takeaway pizza, and it's past eleven when we rug up and walk outside to face the bitter chill.

'I'll give you a lift,' Alfonso says, refusing to drop me at the metro station nearby.

I hop in his car with a smile. Initially shy, Alfonso's comments during the evening seemed ingenuous, with a healthy dose of self-deprecating humour. I'm glad to be his private audience.

As we wind back through dark, unfamiliar streets towards the city we talk about life and travel. I tease Alfonso that he is a *mammone*, still living at home appreciating all the services of his *mamma*. He is quick to point out that he has lived in Sweden, Belgium and London. And his working parents, he argues, are hardly home, so he has all the space he needs. For now it also makes financial sense.

'I turned down a job with tenure and a good salary because I wanted to dedicate myself to music,' he says. 'I've just started a three-month contract to teach computer skills.'

I confess to Alfonso that I struggle with dialect and there were times during the group's rehearsal that I couldn't understand a word.

'We weren't talking dialect, we were talking *parlesia*,' he says with a laugh. 'It has been around in Naples for about a century, used mostly by the *posteggiatori*, the musicians who walk into restaurants and play instruments for coin donations,' he says, making me think of the old violinist who always shows his face at Il Buon Gustaio, my local trattoria.

'It's similar to the blues or jive talk of the Harlem ghetto, so it's tied to illegal immigration and designed so others can't understand it,' he says, adding that it's a mix of Neapolitan and Rom dialect, among other influences. 'In Naples, when you learn a musical instrument you learn the *parlesia* together with the major scale. My first music lesson was conducted entirely in *parlesia*. Sometimes I accidentally slip words into everyday conversation, and no one can understand! To use *parlesia* also affirms that you're a musician.'

'How cool,' I say, envying the secret jargon and vowing, once again, to get my head around Neapolitan.

As Alfonso pulls up to my palazzo I'm suddenly tempted to suggest a drink, but instinct tells me to wait. Instead I say how keen I am to learn more about the *neomelodici*. He can help: prominent local *neomelodica* personality Sergio Donati is the brother-in-law of 'A67's guitarist, Enzo.

'I'll call Enzo tomorrow and arrange an interview for you,' he says, as conscious as I am of the silence in the car now that it's stationary. I wonder if he, too, wants to suggest a nightcap but lacks the nerve.

I give him a hurried kiss on the cheeks and jump out of the car. He waits while I put the key in the entrance of my palazzo and heave open the dwarf-sized door and disappear.

Alfonso. Alfie. The Fonz. Call him what you will, but tell me he's only attached to his bass guitar.

At home I slip 'A67's first album into my iBook and I realise that the sound is almost shot, my computer so old and badly maintained that dust must have practically destroyed the speakers.

As I listen to the group sing their social cause, I notice that Nicoletta's bedroom light is still on and smile at my landlady's insistence that I seek a partner with a fat wallet rather than an artistic sensibility.

All fine in theory.

As Alfonso weaves his small car in and out of traffic, he gives me some background on Sergio Donati, who lives in Scampia, not far from Giugliano where he lives.

Accustomed to dodging Vespas as I walk through the Quarteri Spagnoli, hearing noises at every turn, the quietness of the late evening here in the outer suburbs kind of irks me. Apart from the odd roadside stall selling fruit, the isolation brings a sinister air.

'Sergio produces *neomelodica* albums, so he's not in the limelight, but ten years ago he was a star, and even today when he walks down the street people stop him all the time,' Alfonso says.

We pull up in a small deserted parking area off a highway and wait a few minutes before Enzo arrives. He leads us through some steel gates to a bleak concrete apartment building, where we take the lift to the fourth floor and knock on a door.

Sergio Donati's wife, Anna, Enzo's sister, greets us at the door and fusses over us, ignoring our attempts to decline food and placing a plate of cheese, salami and pickled vegetables on the table with two bottles of rose wine. We sink into a puffy, L-shaped, red leather sofa and I glance to my left, to the open-plan kitchen, and to my right, to the lounge room dominated by an enormous television screen mounted on the far wall. I feel like I've been teleported to an AVJennings display home on the Gold Coast. It's showcase spic'n'span.

Sergio Donati appears from a room dressed in a synthetic white tracksuit. He looks like a boxer, his blunt facial features rendered more menacing by a three-day growth. The only thing that gives gentleness to his face are his small, deep-set eyes, which flicker like sapphires in the light.

Penelope Green

We're introduced and he lights a cigarette and launches into a history of how *neomelodica* music was born. In his view, the first to experiment was Neapolitan singer–actor Nino D'Angelo, who worked alongside Mario Merola performing theatre *sceneggiate*. D'Angelo's 1982 album, *Un Jeans e una Maglietta, A Pair of Jeans and a T-shirt*, was made into a film which in Italy beat the box office takings of the huge international hit *Flashdance*. Around the same time, Donati, then not even in his teens, began experimenting with music and video, eventually producing low-budget programs for local television stations.

'Leaving behind the influence of D'Angelo, which was a mix of Neapolitan and Italian music, new pieces emerged…strange melodies, like a light classical tune mixed with a modern dance beat,' he says.

Notwithstanding a passion for music and a drive to produce new sounds, it was television that provided the crucial leg-up for the new musical sensation. In the mid-1990s, Donati and three friends created VideoTeamItalia, a television channel devoted to *musica neomelodica*, turning the trend into a cult phenomenon. During transmissions, home viewers were encouraged to telephone the station and request and dedicate songs, making it more interactive. Donati had a hunch he and his mates were on a winner, and in its first year, VideoTeamItalia had a peak following of two million viewers.

When I ask Donati if he thinks the genre took off because people dreamt of becoming household names like Nino D'Angelo and, more recently, Gigi D'Alessio, he shakes his head.

'Its success lies also in the fact that it was music of the *quartiere*, of the family, in dialect,' he explains. 'To the people, it became almost like a relative, a partner, a friend, do you get it? A familiar, homemade music.'

Neomelodica singers now outnumber their audience, jokes Donati, who has cut about six of his own albums, but now produces for other musicians and plans to ride the trend until his CDs wind up in the bargain bin.

When I broach the death of Mario Merola, Donati says that Merola's music brought goose bumps to the skin because the singer never lost his grand passion for music, or for Naples.

'In music, Naples is perhaps the city most difficult to conquer in Italy,' he says. 'To have a dance hit in other places you throw four little words together with two chords and hey, presto. But in Naples you can't do this. Contrary to appearances, the market is more demanding. Not all artists here win fame.'

Alfonso and I drive towards my place an hour or so later, I ask him what he thinks of comments from Italy's minister of the interior, Giuliano Amato, that the *neomelodici* glorify the Camorra.

Among the stars who defend their artistic freedom or claim their music has nothing to do with the underworld is Tommy Riccio, who enjoyed a hit with '*Nu Latitante*', 'The Fugitive'. The song's on-the-run protagonist pines for his family, perhaps like the modern-day *camorristi* of the *scissionisti* who fled to Spain as the *faida* between clans in Naples' north broke out.

'Amato is right, it's worrying that small kids listen to this popular music and they become fascinated,' says Alfonso, who parks and slips the Depeche Mode CD we've been listening to into a case and hides it under a seat. 'In "*Nu Latitante*", Tommy Riccio sings about the sentimental side of the fugitive, so he legitimises the Camorra. This is dangerous because we're talking about kids so young they still don't know bad from good, and in Naples the line between the two is so fine anyway...'

'How? Give me an example,' I prod as we walk up the street to my house.

'Okay, you spoke to Annalisa Durante's father, no? When he was interviewed on television once, he was asked what work he did. He replied that he sold pirated CDs. Then he was asked who gave him the merchandise he sold, and he answered the Camorra. Then he was asked who killed his daughter, and he had the same answer,' says Alfonso, drawing an imaginary circle in the air with his finger.

I've invited Alfonso to dinner. Well, sort of. When I confessed that I only cook for myself as a general rule, my bland plates of roasted vegetables dressed up with cheese and pasta best kept for a private audience, he offered to cook. As a compromise, I demanded a shopping list of ingredients, which I brought home this afternoon, wine included.

Standing in my kitchen, Alfonso sticks his hand into his backpack on the benchtop and pulls out small bottles of *prosecco* and *Aperol.*

'For an *aperitivo,*' he winks, before reaching into the bag again to retrieve some smoked salmon, which I realise is the topping for the bread I bought.

Like a magician pulling rabbits from a hat, Alfonso scoops from his bag a bundle of fresh *vongole*, or clams (which he says he has already salted and washed), two *orate* fish (clean and ready for stuffing with the lemon, parsley and garlic I bought), a packet of spaghetti (who said there was a problem with mine?), small foil packages containing garlic and chilli (I don't hate cooking that much!) and a bottle of white wine (either he wants to impress me or seduce me, either way I'm not complaining).

The conversation flows as Alfonso mixes a *spritz* for our *aperitivo,* telling me that he once worked in a bar in London. He makes toast and dobs on butter before layering it with salmon for our entree. I watch as he sautés the clams in olive oil and garlic and adds a dash of white wine. Before he throws the spaghetti into the saucepan of boiling water, he places the pasta in with the clams for a few minutes so that the flavour, he explains, infuses into the pasta. It must be his secret weapon: minutes later I decide Alfonso's version of *spaghetti alle vongole* beats all the others I've tried in a string of local restaurants.

As we eat, Alfonso talks about 'A67, the first groups he played in as a teenager, and how music was a saving grace in his life. At a time when he wasn't seeing eye to eye with his parents, it gave him a freedom of expression that he was craving. In Rome, he studied music for three years and is now learning *solfeggio*, a technique for teaching singing which uses notes as syllables (Do, Re, Mi, Fa…), in order to sit an exam to qualify as a music teacher. I admire his dedication to his craft, and the pleasure he takes in it.

As I place the last fork of spaghetti in my mouth I glance at my watch. To my surprise it's midnight.

'Are you still hungry enough to eat that fish?' I ask my celebrity guest chef. To my relief, he shakes his head.

Three more hours pass before I walk across the terrace to see Alfonso off. Sober but drunk on great food and company, I glance at him and think how nice it is to meet a bloke who isn't afraid to wear his heart on his sleeve. I've known him for all of twenty-four hours, but tonight we've shared secrets like old friends and I have no fear that he'll break my confidence.

'Have you got plans on Sunday?' he asks.

I shake my head.

'Good, let's have lunch at a place I know near Pozzuoli. It's simple but with exceptional food…especially seafood.'

He gives me a lingering kiss and disappears down the stairwell.

Only a few hours later I zombie-shuffle to Paolo's newsstand. Unable to sleep in, I've just finished my morning walk and I'm delirious on four hours sleep. Upon Paolo's request, I take off my conspicuous sunglasses.

He raises his eyebrows and makes a friendly smirk. 'Ah, so you're seeing someone.'

I blush and motion to leave with my paper under arm, but Paolo urges me to wait as he serves some customers, then turns to me in a lull.

'When I start a relationship I keep all my flaws to myself,' he says, holding a fist to his heart. 'The beginning of any rapport is like being on a boat in a storm. There's wind and rain and confusion, and you don't understand anything. When the weather clears, only then can you see the rocks...'

Thanking my newsagent-cum-sailor for his earnest advice, I walk home and have a quick shower before grabbing some yoghurt for breakfast. In the small freezer section, the two fish Alfonso had stuffed ready for roasting rest on an oven tray.

Within half an hour they're swimming in the tide of plastic bags spilling over the sides of the rubbish bin nearest to my house. It's a waste of good food, but my freezer only functions at thirty per cent capacity, I have dinner plans for tonight, and Nicoletta is away.

I wonder if I'll have the nerve to tell Alfonso during our next culinary appointment. I question, too, how I'm going to distract myself for seventy-two hours, until Sunday dawns.

The hardest step is that taken to pass through the door

As November continues to whip Naples with fierce gales and sleet, dampening my enthusiasm for my morning walks along the sea promenade, I wake one morning at dawn to realise that a year has passed since I arrived in the city. Buried snug beneath a doona in the winter dark, I remember the arctic climes of my first home with Francesco and thank the Madonna for my cosy nest.

Hearing the pitter-patter of rain outside, I trip over my joggers (which I use to strategically block my bedroom doorway for self-motivation), and jump in the shower. I eat breakfast and watch the television news, sniggering at the army officer reading the weather report, perhaps the only corner of television not saturated with the *Veline* showgirls, who dress in less to tart up a string of variety programs.

So much has changed since I arrived. My colleagues have become friends, and my fear of Naples' dark side has faded to the degree my curiosity to understand the city's colourful and superstitious customs has grown. Once I was a tourist too scared to cross the Quartieri Spagnoli for fear of meeting trouble. Now it's rare to walk through my neighbourhood without saying hello to someone I know.

I send SMS messages to Francesco, Roberto, Manola and Massimo – my first reliably unreliable friends in Naples, and who remain my dearest companions – to say that it's my treat for dinner to celebrate my first anniversary. I wish Alfonso could come, but he's playing a gig somewhere up north near Milan.

Since our lunch date by the sea, we've barely spent a day apart in the past few weeks. We have so many shared views and interests, but it doesn't take much to realise how different our worlds are, especially our childhoods. One day Alfonso walked through my front door and jokingly gave me a 'present'.

'Shut your eyes,' he said, before placing in my outstretched palm a bullet he'd found near his house, to add to the bullet I thought I'd found the day before in my own neighbourhood.

'It's fake,' Alfonso had said when I gingerly picked up the gold object I'd seen lying on the ground metres from my front door.

'How would you know?' I asked.

It turned out that the father of one of Alfonso's best mates at school owned a Smith & Wesson. When the boy's father was away, he and Alfonso would swipe the gun and go shooting at cans in the country.

'How old were you?' I asked, realising about the scariest thing I'd faced in my youth in the bush was the occasional rampage of Simon the Angus bull, when he'd slip through the fence of a neighbouring property.

'About thirteen,' said Alfonso, whom I've finally – but still only occasionally – begun referring to as my *fidanzato*, after weeks of home practice saying the word without cringing. While it

informally means 'boyfriend', its precise translation is 'fiancé'.
I'm much better with *dolce metà*, or sweet half.

'Tell me you don't have a gun at home,' I joked, half wondering
if he'd tell me anyway, having seen my worried expression.

'Are you kidding? My mum would kill me!'

I put the bullet on my bookshelf beside the one I'd found, as
if adding a photo of our second newborn, and that night Alfonso
cooked me the umpteenth delicious meal and recounted high-
school anecdotes that made me laugh, and shudder. He had
arrived one day at school to find that rebel students had overnight
bricked up the main entrance door, and kids would regularly
start fires in classrooms to get out of school.

I often wonder how Alfonso coped when, at the age of eleven,
his family moved from respectable Vomero to Giuliano, not far
from Scampia, with its skyline of degraded, graffiti-scrawled
apartment buildings. Alfonso said his mother was mortified by
the move.

The more Alfonso talks about his misspent youth, the more
my imagination races to meeting his parents next week for
Christmas Eve dinner at their house and present-giving under
the tree. Perhaps I should give Alfonso's mum a special personal
alarm, upgrade his father's life-insurance policy, and buy my man
a gift voucher to have his car windows bullet-proofed.

My phone beeps with an SMS from Francesco saying he can
make dinner tonight. I grab my homemade lunch and an umbrella,
and head to the front door. Usually I'm in a hurry, but today
time is on my side. As I open the steel door Nicoletta and I share,
I can almost taste the *caffè macchiato* I'll order at a bar en route
to work.

As I go to place a foot on the first step, I stop short. The five
stairs leading down to the landing appear dark with moisture.

The janitor must have just cleaned them, I think, then realise it's not the right day.

I place my foot carefully on the first step and gently prod the sole of my shoe on the surface. It's soap-slippery, yet there is no smell of detergent. Easing my way down to the dry landing, I touch the last step and scrape a little onto my fingertip to smell.

My blood runs cold. It's oil.

In a blinding flash, I eye the front door of the middle-aged couple who live in the apartment to the immediate right of the steps and directly below our *terrazzo*. Sometimes I see the glum-faced husband with the couple's kindergarten-aged daughter in the elevator, but I've only glimpsed his wife once.

In recent days Nicoletta has been furious because her long-running feud with the family has escalated once again. The dispute hinges on the fact that the couple often park their car in the ground-floor courtyard of the palazzo, which would be fine if it didn't block off Nicoletta, who pays a reasonable sum to rent a garage at the back of the courtyard. Nicoletta has to harass them to move their car, which, she says with good reason, they have no right to park in the palazzo anyway.

Yesterday the feud worsened, with a finger-pointing Nicoletta threatening, not for the first time, to go to the police. And the husband dared her to do just that.

I stare at the oil and don't have to guess who slicked the stairwell only Nicoletta and I use. I can't remove the image of Nicoletta who, at fifty-five, isn't old but is no longer a spring chicken, slipping on the oil to suffer severe if not mortal injury. In the film *La Sconosciuta,* which I saw with Valerio, there is a scene where the female protagonist trips an elderly woman down a circular staircase. Like a cartoon, the pensioner does a sickening roll down dozens of steps before slumping on a landing. She winds up in a nursing home with brain damage.

As I stare at the oil my horror turns to anger. I, too, could have been hurt. I turn and consider hammering my fist on the family's door before a wave of fear stops me. I'm not sure I want to get involved. I call Nicoletta, expecting her to already be at work, but she's at home with the flu. She shrieks with fury before thanking me and vowing to call the police again.

At a nearby bar, I wait for my cup to cool so I can scull my espresso. I stare at the crowd filing in and out of the bar. Suddenly I see hostility everywhere.

At work I make a quick call to Alfonso, whom I've introduced briefly to Nicoletta. He makes me realise that the fight between my landlady and her neighbours reeks not only of the city's seething culture, but is symbolic of the historic battle between the *nobili*, nobles, and *poveri*, the poor. Nicoletta, a respected architect with an executive government job (who has an enormous heart but an air of snobbery about her), is pitched against a working-class family, who no doubt resent her wealth and status. The rich traditionally lived on the top floors of palazzos, while the poor servants stayed on the ground or lower levels.

'This incident might help you understand the dynamics of this city. It's built on contradictions, where good hearts can be aggressive,' he sighs.

Alfonso later sends me an email with a poem written by Neapolitan actor Toto, which describes the rage of the ghost of a marquis, who is buried in a grave beside that of a poor dustman. The ghost of the dustman scorns the marquis, saying that in death everyone is equal.

That night I meet my girlfriends Orfina, Anna and Claudia for an *aperitivo* at Superfly before heading to my favourite restaurant, Il Buon Gustaio, with Francesco, Manola, Roberto and Massimo. During dinner my belly aches with laughter as my friends try and convince me to leave town, saying my arrival has only triggered more episodes of violence and a deepening of the city's rubbish problem. Amid the good cheer I realise that I'll soon have to think about my future in Naples: my one-year contract with ANSA*med* expires in just under a month.

Buoyed by good company and vino, I accept Massimo's offer to walk me home, and ten minutes later find myself staring at the flight of steps to my apartment entrance. The oil is still there and I figure Nicoletta has been too ill to leave the house.

I tiptoe over it and slam the grate shut, cursing the neighbours under my breath. My first anniversary has passed like so many days in Naples: overflowing with colour and mirth, but tainted by darker forces.

Festive lights strung in the shapes of stars hang over via Toledo, and the approach of Christmas has put a spring in everyone's step. Regardless, walking anywhere in the city centre remains a chore. Until I moved to Naples, I considered myself a good street weaver, adept at walking swiftly in any crowd. But Neapolitans have an uncanny knack for blocking paths, zigzagging without rhyme or reason, oblivious to the passage of their fellow citizens. Unable to face the Christmas masses or the massive counter queues, I advise my family that I'll bring their gifts home in February, when I've planned a trip back to Australia.

When the ANSA*med* server crashes at work, my colleagues use the time to go shopping. I'm happy to peruse a few days of news in the local papers and magazines, which I never seem to have enough time to read properly.

On the cover of *L'Espresso* magazine, for the second time in as many weeks is author Roberto Saviano, the young Neapolitan whose laborious research into the ferocious *sistema* of the Camorra continues to spark debate. In a lengthy, impassioned feature, entitled 'Where Were You?', Saviano writes of the disastrous crime culture in Italy's entire south, and the homicides ignored with cynicism. He accuses politicians and institutions of failing to put a brake on the escalation of violence battering Naples, declaring that it's time to change the rules of the market, which currently favour the *sistema*.

I push aside *L'Espresso* to read the papers. The Naples-born Italian president, Giorgio Napolitano, has praised a recent initiative of the city's youth to traipse around the streets handing out small 'anti-Camorra' pegs, and has left his luxury digs in Rome to visit the Campania capital again. Official stops include a meeting with the city's leading scientists and researchers and a crowd shuffle in the struggling-class suburb of La Sanità.

The president was given a T-shirt that reads 'My Name is Giorgio and I'm Neapolitan' by the kids of Forcella, the inner-city parish of Father Merola and the *quartiere* where Annalisa Durante was gunned down. Merola recently lost scores of computers from his church in a robbery, and was placated by the portly Archbishop of Naples, Cardinal Crescenzio Sepe, who promised that the 'darkness' cloaking Naples would lift.

Forcella had something to smile about, however, when Italian football captain and local boy Fabio Cannavaro dropped by to show off his French *Ballon d'Oro*, or European Footballer of the Year award, which he won on the back of Italy's World Cup victory. 'Kids, you have to believe in your dreams…' said pin-up Cannavaro, before Forcella's good news ended the next day, when two masked killers gunned down thirty-two year old Giovanni Giuliano – son of *Nuova Famiglia* clan boss-turned-supergrass Luigi – as he played billiards in a club in the heart of the clan's turf.

Crime-scene photographs splashed across the dailies show the bloodied floor where Giuliano's body landed, directly beneath a huge poster of Diego Maradona, who was a friend of the victim's *camorrista* uncle Carmine. Amid the bloody newspaper coverage is a small feature on the curse of the Giuliano clan, and how Celeste Giuliano, Luigi's sister, tried to placate bitter infighting only to be arrested in her hide-out. The blue-eyed platinum-blonde had only one request before being put inside: a quick visit to her hairdresser.

The latest Camorra slaying provoked Father Merola to declare that he was leaving town, only to be convinced to stay by Cardinal Sepe and Annalisa Durante's father, Giovanni, who said Forcella would be condemned again if the priest fled: 'It would be as if my daughter was murdered for a second time.'

Pre-Christmas sales of the DVD of *'O Sistema*, a documentary about the ambush of a boss who tried to leave the Camorra, are booming at the illegal street stalls, selling for under two euro, almost a tenth of the retail copy.

And as Christmas looms Pope Benedict XVI has officially blessed Naples, saying that he is following the city's struggles; ditto Cardinal Sepe, who says the city's 'treasures' will remain despite the difficulties, but it's up to Neapolitans to 'touch them and make them shine'.

Or perhaps steal them: exactly one week before Christmas, thieves have stolen hundreds of antique figurines worth around one hundred million euro from the inner-city church of Saint Nicola of Carita. Dating back to the eighteenth century, and clad in three-hundred year old costumes, the figurines formed the church's nativity scene. 'These figurines are priceless,' said the parish priest, 'because their loss has ruined one of the greatest joys possible – that of children who flock here to see them.'

I shake my head in disbelief. I can understand Rolex-snatching robbers, but nativity figurines? The church thieves failed to take a lone donkey, several sheep and baby Jesus, as if they thought Naples needed some hope.

The ANSA*med* server is still out of action at five when I finish my shift. I snuggle into my favourite coat, a black and white check number I picked up for a song at a flea market, and wrap my scarf around my neck. I make my way to Piazza del Gesu before shuffling along the Spaccanapoli, teeming with harried shoppers and black-market stalls. Christmas lights hang from above and every few metres I pause, drawn in by some curiosity. I shake a snow-dome of the city and can't resist sampling the seasonal *mustaccioli*, diamond-shaped biscuits covered in chocolate.

At the intersection of via San Gregorio Armeno I look up the sloping street to see the usual tourist clot eyeballing the small *presepe* figurines. A few metres further on I take a sharp right turn to find the entrance to one of the campuses of Naples' Federico II University, where I have an appointment with Amato Lamberti, a professor in sociology and criminology. I walk into the square courtyard and take in the former convent buildings around me, with their white walls and metal-grated windows. I notice a man walking towards me from the far corner.

Lamberti set up the *Osservatorio sulla Camorra*, the Observatory on the Camorra, in 1981, a few months after the November 1980 earthquake. The Camorra, already an economic force, exploited the tragedy to win major building contracts and siphon off millions. Lamberti's observatory was the first centre of its type in Naples devoted to researching and promoting anti-Camorra initiatives, and building a social conscience against every form of organised crime.

Lamberti left the organisation when he entered politics – he was president of the province of Naples from 1995 to 2004 – and now concentrates on his university commitments, works with various community groups, and writes books to stimulate debate on Naples' social problems.

When I mentioned to Alfonso that I was reading the anti-crime crusader's latest offering, he gave me Lamberti's phone number. It turns out that Alfonso's band, 'A67, is collaborating with Lamberti on a social awareness project in schools. The professor raised his hand to rap on a song for 'A67's second album. As the silver-haired Lamberti, whom I estimate to be just shy of sixty, leads me into his office, I mentally swap his grey suit for a rapper's tracksuit and back-to-front baseball cap and stifle a giggle.

Born in Italy's northern Piedmont region, Lamberti learnt the Neapolitan dialect after studying in the city in his childhood, and transferred his degree to Federico II University when he won a study grant in 1971. This was the year after Raffaele Cutolo formed his formidable *Nuova Camorra Organizzata*, or New Organised Camorra.

'When I arrived,' says Lamberti, lighting a cigarette, 'I remember thinking that Naples was like the nineteenth or early twentieth century: the clean divide between the rich and poor, the intellectuals and plebs, hadn't disappeared. At the time, the idea was that the city needed development to stimulate a change for the better. But development really only involves one part of society – the rich – and then there was the problem of the Camorra, but people were oblivious to it.'

So much so that when Lamberti started his observatory, he faced a brick wall of denial.

'Everyone told me that the Camorra no longer existed, it was a thing of the past. And then the Camorra began to implode and the turf wars started, and suddenly everyone realised it was still in operation.'

The clan fighting was between Cutolo's *Nuova Camorra Organizzata* and the *Nuova Famiglia*, headed by Luigi Giuliano, whose son was recently gunned down in the billiard hall beneath the Maradona poster. With billions of earthquake funding coming from Rome, the two gangs fought for the biggest haul. A series of police 'maxi-blitzes' and a string of arrests in 1983 and 1984 helped bring down the warring clans, but it did little to kneecap the underworld. When Lamberti opened his observatory, there were around ten Camorra clans in the Campania region; today there are over one hundred in the province of Naples alone. It's no surprise, then, that not a day seems to pass without a newspaper photo of a blood-stained street.

Refreshingly, Lamberti says Naples has not stood still; there have been a string of cultural and building initiatives over the years. The problem is, he argues, that all the schemes have lacked a long-term vision and local clans have profited from the chaos. Worse, marginalised youth without job propects are becoming a type of reserve criminal army, whose baby-faced leaders' cold-blooded nerve knows no limits.

'The starting point to understanding Naples is accepting that it's built on illegal activity,' says Lamberti, ignoring a message beep on his mobile phone. He then asks me if I've seen the Christmas crowds at via San Gregorio Armeno, where the *presepe* figurines are sold.

'Naples is perhaps the only place, at least in Italy, where a grand artisan tradition like the *presepe* operates entirely in the black, from production to distribution to sale. In Naples, "absolute tolerance" rules.'

What annoys Lamberti is that Neapolitans prefer to complain about the rubbish emergency, about the violence and bag snatches, almost as if, he argues, delinquency and crime were not founded on poverty, but were hereditary illnesses. He says that urban development plans invariably centre on the wrong areas and marginalise the peripheries even further, while Naples' political leaders do nothing to genuinely reduce the class divide.

'The image that Goethe gives us of Naples is of aristocrats with the manners and sentiments of plebs. In fact it's worse, because they lack the imagination of true plebs, who live in the alleyways or in the *bassi*,' says Lamberti. 'The well-to-do have not changed. Everything outside their circle of friends and Borghese interests is ignored.'

From the safety of their homes in affluent areas like Vomero and Posillipo, asserts Lamberti, Naples' upper class views the rest of the city from the perspective of a tourist: loving it from afar, even drawing inspiration from it, but eschewing any responsibility for the social problems.

When I raise Interior Minister Giuliano Amato's security plan, Lamberti scoffs. 'In the painful history of Naples, politicians have never reduced the solution to the city's cultural problems to a so-called "security package",' he says, then reiterates that Naples' biggest problem is everyday illegal activity, with forty per cent of locals, or more than one in three, having had a run-in with the law. 'There is no need for a police state, we just need a state of rights,' he says, lighting another cigarette.

A well-researched plan to fight poverty, he argues, would cost one hundred times less than the security measures mooted by the government. And since Naples has ignored its problems for so long, Lamberti believes the Camorra has become a state in itself, a state which has no fear of the real state. He claims the majority of Neapolitans have no fear of crime and the Camorra, or at least those elements with which they have learnt to co-exist.

Naples has the will, pride and intelligence to change, he claims, but no development model should be put into action without an in-depth study of the social conditions at hand.

'In reality we don't know anything, or next to nothing, so we're not yet really capable of implementing, let alone developing projects that will meet society's demands,' he says, standing to make his way to his next class. 'But one thing is certain: we need to give dignity to the poor through honest work. Welfare in whatever form can't pull them out of the dependence they have on illegal markets run by the Camorra.'

As Lamberti accompanies me to the lift, I ask him where he lives in Naples.

'I live in Salerno,' he says, referring to the seaside town about an hour from Naples. 'I'd like to live here, but my wife would never agree, and my sons hate it.'

Lamberti's parting comment makes me think of Nicoletta, who has filed another complaint against her neighbours. Nicoletta was surprised when I confessed that the oil incident scared me; she agreed that it was a violent threat, but what upsets her more is that she's powerless to change the situation. Fed up, she has started looking at homes in Rome and is thinking of transferring there for work.

I think of my former Neapolitan flatmate in Rome, Adriano, who lived in the Quartieri Spagnoli in his university years and dreams of returning to help revamp the crumbling suburb. But Adriano has just bought a new house in Rome, far from the chaos of the South. He is part of the brain drain from a city that offers so few opportunities to its youth.

I still feel lucky to have come to Naples for work, but I wonder whether I should even be hoping for another year's contract, or how I'll feel if I don't get one. I have to pin down the man who hired me, Carlo, to find out what my future holds.

Catching up with my prosecutor friend Giovanni Corona for a pre-Christmas *aperitivo*, we agree that my hopes of tracing Pupetta Maresca are all but lost. I wrote a letter to the woman who avenged her *camorrista* husband's murder in 1955, eager to hear her views on Naples' criminal landscape. Alas, she is writing her memoirs and is bound by contract.

'If you want to talk to a woman who has fought the Camorra you should talk to Silvana Fucito,' says Corona, going on to explain that the Neapolitan mother attracted international headlines in 2004 when she became known as the first woman to go to the police to bring the Camorra to justice. Ranked among *Time* magazine's 'European Heroes in 2005', Silvana shares the same police protection service as Corona, who put Silvana's assailants behind bars.

I go to meet Silvana at one of Naples' anti-racket offices in the inner-city, housed in a beautiful historic palazzo, dirty-grey from pollution and age, on a wide street that leads up to the stazione Centrale. Rugged up in a coat and beanie, I dodge puddles and clutch my umbrella tightly in the rain. Like nothing else, this kind of weather seems to highlight the poverty in Naples: street sellers don cheap plastic raincoats, the wet no excuse to suspend trade, and gypsy women beg for coins from the shelter of doorways.

When the office door opens my gaze drops to rest upon a woman with streaked blonde hair, a broad face and steely eyes. I'm no giant at just over five foot seven, but Silvana Fucito barely reaches my shoulders despite her pair of retro wedge heels. Her chubby frame is wrapped in a black coat with fake fur collar trim, and as we sit down in an adjoining room she takes off a layer to reveal a black sweater with a Warhol image of Marilyn Monroe on the front.

As the fifty-six year old mother of three begins her tale, the horns of the frenetic traffic outside fade into nothing, her cigarette-husky voice commanding attention. I get the impression that she has learnt to tell a good tale after finding herself at the centre of a media circus.

Marrying in 1978, Silvana Fucito immediately went to work with her husband, Gennaro, at the paint business his parents opened a decade earlier. Side by side, the newlyweds toiled to build up clientele and expand the business, located in an industrial zone bordering San Giovanni and Barra in Naples' east, eventually doubling their staff when business started to boom.

'We saw our shop grow like a son – it was our pride and joy,' says Silvana, who was by then raising a young family.

By 1998 the family had bought various assets, including a seaside holiday cottage and a luxury yacht, when one day members of the Camorra clan from Barra paid them a visit and demanded a *pizzo,* which translates as a 'point' or 'peak', 'lace fabric', a 'goatee' or, in Silvana Fucito's case, 'protection money'.

For two stressful years, Gennaro endured constant visits from the *camorristi,* who either demanded money or asked to cash cheques for huge sums, threatening the businessman with a roughing up, and once, flashing a pistol. Each time, Gennaro held his nerve, insisting his company wasn't making a profit, or offering whatever other excuse he could think of.

'Why didn't you cave in like so many others?' I ask.

'Because once you pay you can't get out,' says Silvana, adding that she and her husband had decided without argument not to pay the *pizzo.* 'As soon as they see you are weak, you are gone.'

Besides, too much was at stake.

'My husband and I started work at 8 am and didn't get home until 8.30 pm, never going home for lunch. We worked six days a week, sometimes doing the accounting at home till 3 am. Our blood was in that shop – we passed our life there.'

Silvana pauses to light a cigarette. She takes a long, deliberate drag and leans across the table to grab a plastic cup to use as an ashtray. She turns her weary face to look at me again.

Penelope Green

'So when someone comes and flashes a gun and demands to cash a cheque for 25,000 euro, it makes your blood boil.'

The couple resisted until the situation worsened in 2000. Months earlier they had agreed to hire a young boy whose father, boss of the San Giovanni clan, was gunned down in a clan ambush. Fearing her son would suffer the same fate, the dead man's wife begged the Fucitos to give her son a future.

'We didn't want to hire this kid, he was about seventeen, but in the end his mum convinced us,' recalls Silvana. 'When he first started it was tough because he was used to living on his own terms. Playing the pinballs instead of working. But in the end he came good.'

Almost. When the boy saw his employers being threatened by the Barra clan, he approached them, says Silvana, 'in full, good faith' and offered to go and talk to his uncles – the brothers of his murdered father – about the situation.

Immediately after, the Barra clan stopped approaching the paint shop, but instead, the boy's immediate family started asking the Fucitos for a *pizzo* – for 'helping' them avoid paying a *pizzo* to the rival clan.

The young boy was mortified, says Silvana. In the years he had worked in the store he had 'completely changed...but obviously he still had links to his family'.

By now under pressure from two clans, Barra and San Giovanni, tension in the paint shop was escalating.

'Whenever someone with a suspicious face arrived we assumed it was a *camorrista*,' says Silvana. 'Then one day members of one of the clans arrived and said to my husband that he had to close the shop and go and talk to them.'

Gennaro returned unharmed, but after a few more visits to the clan boss' house – during which a knife was held to his throat, and a gun pointed at his temple – Silvana 'couldn't stand it any more'.

'I decided to go myself, thinking they wouldn't dare use the same "manners" on a woman.'

Having driven alone to the house, Silvana parked and walked past not one, but two pairs of *camorristi* guarding various entrances to the boss' hideaway.

'I had no fear, I wasn't thinking,' says Silvana, seeing my dumbfounded expression. 'When those men saw me I don't think they thought twice. As a woman, I was almost nothing, But instead I made them see that women are worth more than men.' A giggle brightens her face, but it somehow seems out of character.

Ushered into a spartan apartment within a housing commission block, Silvana was then seated at a table with a group of men, including the clan boss, all aged in their forties. They were 'simple' folk, Silvana says, and she guessed they were probably illiterate.

This only made things worse when she pulled out some accounting statements, which she had arranged with her local bank to fake, demonstrating that they had no money due to various loans and debts.

'When I told them we had no funds, the boss, to make a joke, said, "Why didn't you tell us earlier? We would have given you money!"' Silvana recalls with a bitter smile.

According to her, the men were intimidated, almost humiliated, by numbers and facts they couldn't quite grasp, and frustrated because they couldn't rough her up like they had with her husband.

Within minutes Silvana was walking down the stairs to freedom, her head 'completely empty'.

'It was a strange sensation, because I was embarrassed even to look at them. I was embarrassed *for* them, because I put myself in their shoes.'

For a few months the clans stopped passing by the Fucitos' shop, but then the routine began again, and lasted for almost another two years, with demands for a *pizzo* slowly getting higher.

'I know it sounds like a long time, but there were different clan members going in and out of jail, changes within the hierarchy, so the threats ebbed and flowed,' Silvana explains.

On 19 September 2002, on the San Gennaro public holiday, the Fucitos were relaxing at home having dinner when the phone rang. Their shop was on fire.

By the time they arrived it was engulfed by flames and firemen had already evacuated the twenty families living in the seven-storey apartment block above the ground-floor shop.

'Was the shop insured?' I ask.

'No, thank goodness.' Seeing my frown, Silvana continues. 'If it had been, some people would have thought that we had lit the fire to make money.'

'Okay, I understand, but why weren't you insured?'

'Look, sometimes reputation is more important than money. Just the idea that people might think we could be behind something like this made me feel sick. So we never had insurance. As it was, people accused us anyway... They were yelling at us, telling us that we'd have to pay for the damage to their homes...'

Before the Fucitos even had an idea of the total cost of the fire – in the end around three million euro – the family marched to the police, the stench of smoke still on their clothes.

'I didn't cry or yell, it's not in my nature,' she says. 'But that night we filed reports with the police on everything that had happened.'

Three days later, hours after police had sealed off the fire scene, Silvana woke to find her husband sitting on the edge of their bed, his hands cradling his head, tears streaming down his face.

'"What am I going to do with my life now?" he asked me. At that point I didn't have time to cry, I had to find something to restart our lives with, to distract him,' she says. 'I got on the phone and called my three children. We had a meeting in the kitchen.'

I smile despite myself, thinking about how the *cucina* is so central to the lives of Italians, in good times and bad.

United, the Fucitos decided to start from scratch. They put the business contact book, which was literally singed around the edges, on the kitchen table and wrote out each number. They called every client and asked for time to get back on their feet.

Seven months after the fire, police arrested fifteen members of the Camorra on charges ranging from extortion to possession of illegal weapons. Despite the fact that firemen found a petrol tank at the scene, arson was not on the charge list.

In November 2004, when Silvana and Gennaro went to the first court hearing of four of the fifteen *camorristi,* they were greeted by an international media frenzy and some of Naples' most important figures, including Mayor Rosa Russo Iervolino and Campania President Antonio Bassolino. Media interest was fanned by the fact that the Camorra was bitterly entrenched in the clan *faida* in Scampia and Secondigliano in Naples' north.

The heaviest sentence secured by the prosecutor in the Fucito case, Giovanni Corona, was eleven years.

'When the sentences were handed down it was a big victory, a moment of satisfaction. But the emptiness remains,' Silvana says, adding with certainty that she has no regrets in the entire affair.

The family sold their properties and boat, and mortgaged their home to open a new paint store in a different location. But it will take them years to pay off their debts.

Despite losing thirty-eight years of hard work and investment, Silvana remains proud of what she did, because she believes it encouraged others to speak out against the Camorra. She now volunteers her time to work on anti-racket campaigns to encourage other business owners to stand up to intimidation.

'They are rebelling because they've had enough,' says Silvana, who was once shunned by 'fearful' people when she walked into shops, but is now overwhelmed by their encouragement and open displays of affection. Aside from offering advice on how to address difficult situations, Silvana also visits schools.

'The first thing I tell children is that they can fight the Camorra, but they have to be honest – and not pretend to be oblivious to what's going on,' she says. 'Because the idea of the *omerta* [the Mafia term for not speaking out] starts so early. At home kids are taught to hide...'

Silvana admits that it won't be easy to reform Naples, but she believes the winds of change are blowing. More business owners are talking and more anti-racket offices are opening.

'Sometimes,' she says, 'I feel a wave of tiredness when I see that corruption exists in high places. That discourages you...But I'll stay put for as long as I know I can do something. Only when I've lost all hope, when I notice my voice is not being heard, will I leave Naples.'

Silvana pauses and looks at me. She lights another cigarette. 'We need a revolution, that's what we need. If a kid rides around without a helmet, if the rubbish rises up to your neck, if there are no traffic cops on the beat to lead by example...What's the Camorra got to do with it? We've blamed the criminal groups when in the end they don't figure in the equation.

'Naples is a population of *pulcinella* – that weak character who defended himself by either acting dumb or striking out with his baton. Neapolitans are undisciplined. They know how to cry but they do nothing to escape the situation.'

When I tell Silvana that I live in the Quartieri Spagnoli she almost shrieks in horror. 'I've never seen such degradation in the historic part of any other city. I feel bad when I see the suburb on television, how the people live in the *bassi*.'

I ask Silvana what she thinks of Naples' mayor, Rosa Russo Iervolino.

'She's not a bad person, rather she's a *grande donna*, but she doesn't have the grit to carry the city ahead, she's not respected. We need someone who faces the battle in front of everyone. Iervolino listens to the interests of the government first and is too cautious about saying or doing the wrong thing.'

There is a knock on the door. They're locking up and Silvana tells me that she must get to the shop before going home.

'I have to cook for more of my family at the moment,' she says. Her pregnant daughter lives in the same palazzo and usually joins her and Gennaro at the table. 'I have to cook hamburgers for my son, then my husband and his dad want fried cod... We'll be eight in total.' She sighs, but with joy on her face.

Out on the street, rugged up in coats and scarves, I remember a question that slipped my mind earlier.

'On the day of the fire, did the blood of San Gennaro liquefy?'

'No idea, I didn't go to church – I'm a very practical woman,' says Silvana before kissing my cheeks. 'Merry Christmas... If you ever feel like a family meal call me and come when you please.'

Una ce steva bona, e 'a facettero Madonna

Only one woman was honest, and they made her the Madonna

It's official – at least for the year 2005. According to a poll published two weeks before Christmas 2006, Italy's south registered almost fifty-eight per cent of the nation's six hundred plus murders in that year. With a death toll of eighty-eight, Naples has been branded the country's 'homicide capital'.

I digest the figures as I read the morning papers metres from the tobacco shop in the affluent *quartiere* of Vomero where, three days ago, the local media zoomed in on the fresh blood staining the tobacconist's steps. Fed up with being the victim of petty crime, the owner shot and killed a fleeing robber, who was also brandishing a firearm.

That's the thing about Naples: crime isn't reserved for notorious areas like Scampia and the city's periphery. Tourists in the old town are easy targets, while Camorra ambushes are often carried out amid packed street crowds, like the man assassinated near

Tania and Khalid's home. In my own neighbourhood, there have been two slayings in broad daylight in recent months.

I hear my name being called and swing around to see my boss, Carlo Gambalonga, vice director of ANSA. Carlo has asked me to speak to his journalism students at the local Suor Orsola Benincasa University. Public speaking is my least favourite pastime, but I could hardly say no.

He takes a final puff of one of his trademark cigars before throwing it on the ground and leading me through the tiny lanes of the university campus, which was once a monastery. To my relief, we walk into a room where only fifteen students sit around a table.

As I sit beside Carlo, the students ask me questions about journalism in general, but they seem more curious about what I think of Naples. I confess to them that I was excited about coming to the city for all the wrong reasons. But when it comes to what I like and don't like, I struggle to pinpoint themes without falling into clichés...before Carlo comes to my rescue.

'When I hired Penny, I knew she'd stay in Naples. I knew she'd fit in because it's a city built on sentiments.'

I feel my cheeks flush; I wonder how Carlo formed this opinion during my brief interview.

'In Naples, every sentiment is exaggerated,' he says. 'Mothers don't love their children – they consider them apart of themselves, like the Neapolitan proverb, "Children are pieces of heart". Women don't consider themselves "in love" with their partners, but linked to them like Siamese twins. And friendship is a pact of shared blood...'

'Let the teacher take over,' I say with a wink to the students, secretly relieved Carlo is on a roll.

Naples, according to Carlo, is a city of homicides and political confusion, all held together by strong emotions. And the warmth of the locals strikes the visitor first, before the historical beauty: no one is anonymous, or left feeling alone.

'Let me give you an example,' he says, his audience hanging on to his every word. 'Two weeks ago I left my home in Naples and caught a taxi to the station because I had to go to Rome, but when I arrived I realised I'd left my wallet at home.

'Mortified, I asked the taxi driver to give me his number so that when I returned I could track him down. He just turned to me and said, "Don't worry, I know where you live, but how are you going to get to Rome?" He gave me fifty euro and a smile and drove off. I can tell you now that that would never happen in Rome, Milan, or any other city in Italy. This is the Naples that wraps itself around you with the generosity of a mother… the Naples that I chose as my refuge, and where I return to from Rome every weekend.'

As we walk off campus, I seize the moment to ask Carlo about my contract, which expires in a little over two weeks. He tells me with a smile that it will be extended for another year, and that I can take almost a month off to return to Australia to see my family after Christmas. Relief mixes with confusion.

'*Grazie, sono contenta…Buon Natale!*' I wish Carlo a Merry Christmas and kiss his generous cheeks, then head for the funicular to get to work.

As I stand in the crowded railcar I weigh up the situation. I'd be a fool not to sign up for another year, because it's so hard to get a work contract in Italy without European citizenship. My early struggles in Rome are still fresh in my mind. Then, the ANSA*med* website has finally taken some steps forward, with images and more feature articles. And I've grown extremely fond of my colleagues, whose ambivalent relationship with Naples I can now relate to heartily. And I feel like I've only had an *assagino*, a small taste, of the city: its culture, its superstitions and traditions…its very soul.

I find Naples far more captivating than Rome: it has a vivacity I've never experienced in any other Italian city. The poverty is heart-wrenching, the chaos infuriating, but there's the glorious gulf, and the stickybeak locals, whose resignation to the state of their city can make you sigh, but whose good cheer is infectious. From whichever angle you look at it, I realise, Naples is all about sentiment, as Carlo says.

And now Alfonso is in the picture. Perhaps because I sense a real future with him, I've (so far) succeeded in not overanalysing things and ignoring the big and small question marks, like whether he's 'the one', what my wedding dress will be like, if he'll agree to an outdoor ceremony, if we want kids, and if so, when…because at thirty-three I'm not getting younger. For now, all I know is that I can't get enough of his company. Whether he's making me laugh or explaining something in Neapolitan, or enthusing about a particular song or book, I've never had so much fun, nor been so happy. The fact that he also happens to be *bellissimo*, doesn't hurt either.

Yet for as much as Neapolitans have taught me more than anyone else in Italy to live for the moment, I can't work out if I should stay. Something is calling me home. An Australian girl I met in Rome who had lived in Italy for years once told me that at the five-year mark expatriates in Italy hit crisis point. The New Year marks my fifth year. Cue drum roll.

I jump off the funicular and make a beeline to say a quick hello to my newsagent, Paolo. Christmas is less than three days away, and since I'm not sure if I'll be popping in as usual, I've bought my favourite newsagent in the entire world a handmade woollen beanie as a small festive gesture.

Paolo puts the crimson beanie on his head immediately and gives me a kiss. Caught off guard, he hands me a key ring with a gecko made of coloured beads.

A cheeky smile spreads across his face. 'Was that your *fidanzato* you introduced me to the other day?' he asks.

I smile back at him. 'Yes…Well, what did you think?'

'He seemed good, you know, made from good pasta,' says Paolo, pinching the air with his fingers as if kneading dough. I raise my eyebrows, but he's taking too much pleasure in having an audience to notice. 'You know, it's like when you're in the supermarket, and instead of buying a well-known pasta like Barilla, you choose a new pasta to try, which seems just as good…'

I wonder if there's a hidden meaning behind Paolo's remark: Alfonso's winter complexion is indeed white and soft like uncooked pasta. I think of the smorgasbord of Italian idioms I adore that have food as a metaphor, and in Naples they often revolve around *frutti di mare.* When a girl is less than pretty, for example, she is a *scorfano,* a type of particularly ugly fish that Alfonso once showed me at the market near home, or a *purpo*, Neapolitan for octopus.

I wish Paolo *Buon Natale* and give him a hug before turning on my heel. As I dash to work my mind moves at equal pace while I weigh up my future in Italy's murder capital.

Christmas Eve dawns and Alfonso stirs beside me. The best thing about my new squeeze is that he wakes at ungodly hours like I do, with just as much energy. We wander along the gulf as most of the city still sleeps. The sea is calm but grey clouds and mist cloak the islands offshore and Vesuvius in the far distance.

When I describe my recent trip to the volcano, where I walked along the crater but couldn't see the view because of fog, Alfonso pulls me up.

'Vesuvius is like a time bomb in the family lounge room,' he says with a seriousness I wasn't expecting. 'Naples lives in the shadow of one of the world's most dangerous volcanoes. It mirrors all the instability and unrest in this city.'

I'd never really thought of Vesuvius as a real threat, more like a dramatic backdrop. I encourage Alfonso to elaborate.

'Goethe, after visiting Vesuvius while it was erupting, said that Neapolitans would be different if they weren't stuck between God and Satan.

'And this is the key to understanding Naples and Neapolitans. It's as if this constant threat obliges you to live more intensely, because tomorrow it could all be over. Maybe your friend comes across money and invites you to eat out, to share his joy with you, but if the next day he finds himself without a penny, he might try and steal from you. Naples is divided between love and hate, just like Vesuvius: it makes the gulf unique and stupendous, yet it can destroy everything in an instant…'

As we skirt the sea promenade, I look at the specks of homes that rise almost to the summit of the volcano, over a kilometre high. Alfonso says there's a three-day evacuation plan for the seven hundred thousand residents whose homes sit below or upon the slopes, like the molluscs that cling to the sea walls. It's hard to imagine that such a plan would go like clockwork in a true emergency.

In the late afternoon I dress nervously before we head to Alfonso's for Christmas Eve dinner with his parents, Maria Rosaria and Enzo. Alfonso has told me it will be a casual affair, but I opt for smart-casual, just to be on the safe side: jeans, a simple but elegant black jumper, and a nice pair of black boots.

As if God knew I might have trouble remembering Alfonso's mother's name, we will be joined by another Maria Rosaria, a family friend the same age as Alfonso's parents, and her daughter Cinzia, Alfonso's first girlfriend, whom he now thinks of as a sister.

Before dinner we pay a visit to Alfonso's *nonna*, another Maria, who greets us at the front door in a dressing gown and fluffy slippers shaped like lion heads. As usual, like my own father refusing to go to church on 25 December, she is boycotting the Christmas Eve dinner, opting to save her energy for the main event.

She gives me a tour of her cosy apartment, the stand-out room being the dining area, full of beautiful art deco furniture, including a bar cabinet full of polished bottles of liqueur. Alfonso and I, both partial to a drop of grappa or *amaro,* catch each other's eye with a smile.

In the kitchen, Maria makes us a strong pot of espresso, which she sweetens without asking. In Naples, those who like their coffee without sugar, like me, often have to tell the barista to leave it out, otherwise a huge teaspoon is automatically added.

Alfonso points to a framed black and white photo on the wall of a handsome man with an elegant moustache. It's Alfonso's *nonno,* from whom he takes his name. He tells the tale of how his grandparents met: Alfonso Sr was walking along the sea promenade and looked up to see a young and comely Maria on the balcony of a palazzo. He walked into the building and knocked on doors until he found her. He proposed not long after, before he left at the outbreak of World War II.

I've already heard the romantic story, so I know Alfonso is repeating it for his grandmother. What he doesn't add, but what I know, is that when Alfonso Sr returned from the war he took a lover. When Maria found out she didn't kick up a fuss, but instead forced a compromise: she would use her husband's generous earnings to do as she pleased without him. And in the years that followed she travelled the world at his expense, luxury liners being her favourite mode of transport.

As Maria sits before us, her eyes roaming the room as she reminisces, I have a sudden yearning to see her as much as possible, missing my own grandparents in Sydney. When she says that she cooked *bacala* yesterday, I seize my chance. Giving Alfonso a wink, I tell Maria that *bacala alla casseruola*, with a sauce of capers, tomato and olives, is my favourite dish.

My ploy works.

'Well, you two must come over as soon as you can, perhaps next weekend,' Maria says, extinguishing her cigarette and standing to take our plates into the kitchen.

Night has already fallen by the time Alfonso and I begin the drive to his family home. He takes a detour as we near his suburb, Giugliano, and tells me the main road is best avoided after dark. Scores of people, including his friends, have been robbed by pairs of gun-toting ruffians on scooters.

We drive down the main shopping street of Giugliano; shops are closed but Christmas lights suspend across the street and the mood is quiet but festive. I feel guilty for thinking it would be a concrete jungle like nearby Scampia. Sure, it's a little desolate, but there are signs of life.

Alfonso clicks a remote control and the iron gates of a fence surrounding a cluster of apartments slide open. Before us a huge Christmas tree flickers with lights. We park and walk into a pale green, ten-storey apartment block.

A door swings open and I'm greeted by Alfonso's father, Enzo, who gives me a warm hug. A short, cuddly woman appears from the kitchen

'*Ciao*, I'm Maria Rosaria – but call me Rosie,' she says, kissing my cheeks.

I present her with a small handmade chocolate chest, a Christmas plant, with those distinctive red leaves, and two bottles of champagne, which she whisks away to open in the kitchen.

I scan my surroundings: a green upholstered couch covered in brightly coloured cushions decorates the living room, a porcelain bowl filled with lollies rests atop a glass coffee table. I peep through a doorway to the adjoining room where a table is set for dinner. In the corner I spy a fake green cactus as tall as me. 'Cool!' I exclaim, recalling my childhood Saturday morning Road Runner cartoon sessions. I giggle when Alfonso tells me the novelty rubber coat hanger, a wedding gift to his parents, is apparently worth quite a bit of money now.

Alfonso and I make small talk with his parents in the kitchen, where the heavy mix of scents makes my stomach rumble, and I wonder about their first impressions of their son's new flame. My nerves evaporate within minutes; Enzo and Maria Rosaria seem elated to see their son relaxed and happy with the first *fidanzata* he has invited to a family Christmas.

The doorbell rings again and the other Maria Rosaria and Cinzia arrive.

With his parents distracted, Alfonso leads me into his room and shuts the door. Books and CDs are crammed on shelves above a desk where a computer sits. A neatly made single bed lines another wall, with a television mounted at its foot for quality viewing. I know Alfonso's standing there, looking at his own room through my eyes, and I glance over and smile at him. I walk to a large window and look down on the dimly lit palazzo courtyard below, then turn back to casually inspect the photos and artwork hanging on the walls. One draws me in: Alfonso, aged eight, his dark eyes looking timid before the camera. He chuckles when I tell him about one of my own school photos for which I asked my mother to arrange my hair in the exact style of Princess Leia from *Star Wars*.

Finally he points to the large box on the floor wrapped in gift paper. We've agreed to exchange our presents privately, not wanting to face the scrutiny of his family. I open the box to find a DVD player and speaker set. Days earlier I mentioned my dismal computer stereo and how I'd grown tired of my self-imposed policy of not making sizeable purchases, in case I decide to return to Australia.

Alfonso's present speaks volumes.

I give him a hug and hand over his presents. Alfonso smiles when he unwraps a striped wool scarf and a grey cashmere jumper, and in the last, small package he finds a simple silver ring. I wanted him to have something that he could wear at all times when I'm in Australia for a month in the New Year. He wraps me in his arms.

At the dinner table we graze on antipasti, including fresh *mozzarella di bufala*, then on to *spaghetti alle vongole,* roasted fish, lobster, vegetables, salads and finally the traditional Italian *panettone* cake and the Neapolitan *struffoli*, small balls of biscuity dough sprinkled with hundreds and thousands and candied fruit. I field questions about what Australians do and eat at Christmas and struggle to understand Enzo, who speaks in thick dialect.

With a clap of her hands, Alfonso's mum announces that it's time to give out the presents. With a 'ho, ho, ho', I insist on playing Santa, and laughter rings out when Cinzia slides a gift from her mother – a sexy, red G-string – over her jeans for comic effect. I'm certain that similar silly antics are going on among my own family in Australia, where Christmas Day has just dawned.

After the present exchange, Alfonso and I read each other's minds in a glance. We had planned to drive out of town to spend a few days in Abruzzo, where Alfonso's grandfather left him a small apartment in the mountains. But with full bellies and growing tiredness, we opt to stay the night with his parents.

We say goodnight and retreat to Alfonso's room, where his mum somehow found time during the evening to make up a single bed beside her son's.

What is it with grown Italians sleeping in single beds? I decide to buck the system.

'All for one, one for all,' I say, squeezing myself beside Alfonso, who's not complaining.

Against all logic, I sleep without stirring.

After three days of clean mountain air, countryside road trips and delicious meals cooked by my personal chef, we return in time for my 9 am start at work. Today I also have an appointment with Naples' first female mayor, seventy-one year old Rosa Russo Iervolino.

A law graduate and widowed with three children, Iervolino's lengthy pre-mayor CV includes fifteen years as the vice president of the Women's Federation and Italy's first female minister of the interior. In 1999 she was also nominated as a candidate for the presidency of the republic.

A member of the centre-left Olive Tree Party, she was first elected mayor of Naples in 2001, but after her five-year term, Iervolino declared she would not run again because she was sick of the friendly fire from supposed allies. But she changed her tune and won a second term. Despite calling herself 'mayor of the people', with Naples continuing to wallow in crime, rubbish and poverty, Iervolino is still under siege, her critics saying she lacks the political will needed to transform the city.

I arrive at Palazzo San Giacomo in Piazza Municipio, a short walk from work, for my 5.15 pm appointment with the woman whose high-pitched voice is the butt of jokes in my office and, I suspect, throughout the city.

One of the mayor's press officers guides me into a small waiting room, where a white-haired man keeps me company. My nerves show when I comment on the beautiful antique furniture in the ornate room, pointing to the long oak table the man is standing behind.

'Yes, this type of furniture just doesn't exist any more,' he says, his face a study of seriousness as he strokes the table with his fingertips. 'When you get close up, you can almost hear it breathe.'

As my nerves begin to calm, the door swings open. I turn to see the woman with curly chestnut hair and two slits for eyes whom I see almost every day in the newspaper. Iervolino offers me a solid handshake.

As she leads me into her enormous office, with plush embroidered chairs, chandeliers and other regal trimmings, I make my standard apology that my poor Italian means I won't be able to use the formal *lei*, but instead the informal *tu*. She brushes off my apologies as we sit on a quaint lounge; a staffer sitting on a chair nearby smiles. Iervolino fits with the elegant decor that surrounds her: a pearl choker matches a conservative navy skirt suit, and her hair is perfectly styled. Sitting with one ankle crossing the other, she could be a queen posing for a portrait.

To break the ice, I ask the Naples-born mayor what she likes about the city, adding that it is, after all, too easy to point out its defects.

'Neapolitans,' she says, 'they have a very particular character, a vitality that you do not find in any other city in Italy, a capacity to relate to others.'

'How are they different from other Italians?' I ask, curious about how she views her constituency.

'I'll tell you a story…' she says, adopting a matronly tone. 'The other day, the minister of the interior, Giuliano Amato, visited here and we took him to a school where there was a discussion about good citizenship. The kids sang a few songs and Amato turned to me and said, "If I was at a school in the North, the children would have said to me, 'Mr Minister, we want to respect the law, we want to be obedient…' but these children immediately addressed me using *tu,* and they danced and sang with such enthusiasm and energy." Well, that's how I see the difference between a Neapolitan and an Italian.'

I ask Iervolino why she changed her mind to take on a second term in the face of ongoing criticism.

'At a certain point I realised that we had already travelled a long way. We had managed to make some progress and it would be dangerous for the city to turn back…So I decided to throw another five years of my life into it.'

'But at the time you said that leading Naples had been the most rewarding but most exhausting experience of your life. Why?'

Iervolino rubs the pearl choker and looks across the room. She looks back at me. 'When you are minister, it means facing a problem and focusing to resolve it,' she says. 'But to be mayor of Naples means that every single day I have to face a hundred problems. It's far more complex. And I have a smaller budget. So the breadth of our problems does not reflect the depth of our pockets.'

I suggest that it seems Naples hasn't changed for the better for decades – as my Neapolitan colleagues and friends often claim – and it needs the 'shock' recommended by the Italian prime minister, but Iervolino cuts in.

'First of all, Romano Prodi speaks of a city he doesn't know. Secondly, Naples has changed – for better and worse.'

For worse, she says, because a host of industries have closed over the years, exacerbating the employment drought. For better, because Naples now has some of the top universities and research institutions in the country.

I ask Iervolino what her priority is as 'mayor of the people' in what is probably her final term.

'The thirty-five thousand families in my province who live under the poverty threshold,' she insists, adding that the city's chronic rubbish problem is also high on her agenda.

Our discussion turns to the outcry over young author Roberto Saviano's book, *Gomorra*. Iervolino denies that she attacked Saviano for sensationalising the city's dark side, and insists that youth hold the key to reinventing Naples.

'We need to nurture a different set of values, and we're trying desperately to do just that,' she says, punching a fist in the air, a gesture which at first seems bizarrely out of character, but then somehow fits.

I tell the mayor that I've spoken to Giovanni Durante, and suggest that if it weren't for his daughter's death, he would probably still be working on the fringes, like so many other Neapolitans.

'How can things change,' I ask, 'if people can earn three times more than the average wage doing odd jobs for the Camorra?'

'If we had ten thousand new jobs the city would change, but this is the problem...People like Giovanni Durante, who lives near me and whom I consider a friend, are honest. But until now they've had to do the best they can. Maybe they don't sell drugs, but they flog fake CDs. People know what they are risking when they get involved with the Camorra – prison, even death – but if there is a positive alternative they won't take that risk.'

Broaching the controversy Iervolino sparked when Mario Merola died, the mayor denies that she ever described the famous

Neapolitan singer as a *guappo buono*, one of the so-called 'good-hearted' members of the Camorra, claiming it was a media beat-up.

'Look, I was born in a common *quartiere* near the port, where Merola worked, and he worked hard, and people loved him, certainly,' she says. 'At the funeral I saw that people needed someone…a Merola or a Maradona, a positive role model. I saw, too, the pain and, as always, the spectacle. I lost my husband when I had three small children but, notwithstanding I'm Neapolitan, I would never have dreamt of yelling like Merola's widow did. Pain in this city is always a bit of a show, but it is genuine. Nobody organised that enormous crowd at the funeral. That man represented hope.'

Pointing out that Iervolino once described herself as 'tough' because she commanded millions of police officers during her time as minister of the interior, I ask why Naples is viewed as ungovernable.

'Look, you can't categorise Naples like Rome or Florence. If I have the will to move ahead in Milan, I also have the means – I can find a job. In Naples it's the opposite. So it's very easy to be discouraged.'

When I tell the mayor of my impression of the city as being feminine, full of robust women with heart, she leans forward in her chair.

'*Attenzione.* Women here are extremely important,' she says, adding that her *nonna* didn't know how to read or write, but she raised eleven children whom she kept under tight rein. 'Neapolitan women have a grand capacity to suffer, but they protect the city, give it a humanity…'

The twenty minutes I've been promised with the mayor have expired. I fire random questions as fast as I can.

'What words come into your mind when you think of Naples?'

'Beautiful and fascinating. An aesthetic adventure, an inner adventure,' she says. 'Florence has art. But here we have art, panoramas, countryside, islands, poverty, riches…all together. Here you see a bit of everything.'

As Iervolino's staffer stands, I ask the mayor whether she intends to stay when her term expires, given she adores Naples so much.

'I don't know,' she says. 'I've always wanted to do more for refugees. If I have my health, perhaps in Cambodia, or somewhere else overseas. Then I've always dreamt of going to the closest possible point to the North Pole…'

'But is this your home?' I insist, determined to know if her heart really belongs to the city. I suddenly realise that I'm actually asking her the question I'm grappling with myself, just days before I have to sign my new work contract.

'It depends,' she says casually. 'I never had enough time with my children when they were young, and at the moment I have a daughter who lives between Naples and Rome and visits me once a week, another daughter in Brussels, and my son is also in Rome. So maybe that's why I have a gypsy spirit. But I still live in the house where I was born, and I'll never leave Naples in the sense of selling up my home. But I want to have other experiences before I'm useless to everyone.'

We are walking to the door as I ask Iervolino my final question: does she think she has made a difference in her time in office.

'I know just one thing,' she says, stopping at the door. 'I have done everything possible with great love, and this gives me a clean conscience. Naturally, I know one can always do more.'

It's New Year's Eve and it has been forty-eight hours since I saw Alfonso: he's had a temperature of forty degrees. Thankfully, he has made a comeback, so I'm in the heart of my suburb at the fruit shop I visit at least twice a week, to buy some supplies. We plan to have dinner at my house before going to a party.

As shop owner Angelo attends to the needs of an old lady with a grocery trolley, I glance at his wife, Tina, who is sitting in a chair inside the shop, her legs stretched out in front of a small heater.

'Are you tired?' I ask her.

'My dear, I was *born* tired,' she says with a grin before hauling herself to her feet and asking me if I've seen the day's papers.

Stuck to the wall of the fruit shop, alongside pieces of cardboard covered in photos from Halloween parties long ago, is a story from the local paper *Corriere della Sera*. The article says that the fruit shop I'm standing in, which has been run by the same family for forty years, recently distributed a questionnaire among its clientele in a bid to get feedback and improve its service.

Among the mostly positive and complimentary comments were a few unsavoury ones, including this from a woman who even signed her full name: 'The moment has arrived to put a massive stone around your wife's neck. Throw her in the sea. The world is full of women!'

Chuckling to herself, Tina, the wife in question, selects some fruit for me and throws in a bunch of basil and parsley for free, before returning to her chair and the small gas heater.

I walk down to via Toledo to meet Alfonso, who arrives carrying a beautiful bunch of flowers, mostly red roses.

'Hmmm, you should get sick more often,' I joke, before linking my arm through his to steer him home.

Along via Toledo, illegal market stands selling fireworks are doing a brisk trade. In fact, five hours before the clock will strike midnight to mark the New Year, the streets are already noisy with the whir and bang of fireworks, and smoke hangs in the street.

'How did your interview with the mayor go?' Alfonso asks, mimicking Iervolino's unfortunate voice and making me laugh.

With a shrug of my shoulders I say the meeting was neither a success nor a failure. It wasn't my intention to grill the mayor over policy nitty gritty, I just wanted a general discussion about the state of the city in her hands. Now I feel a bit lost, I tell Alfonso, as if I've taken just one more step in a countless number of steps in understanding Naples.

'Listen,' he says, kissing my forehead, 'things take time. And anyway, if Neapolitans can't work it out, how on earth can you? The first thing you need to work on is your dialect!'

At home, Alfonso takes out a CD he has been threatening to make me for weeks, with no less than 131 hits from the 1980s.

He puts it on and as he starts to sing a blast from the past, I smile, remembering that Saint Alfonso, from whom Alfonso naturally takes his name, was the protector of musicians. How can it be that Alfonso is *stonato*, or tone deaf? Whatever, the man more than makes up for it in the kitchen. Before too long we're enjoying his signature *spaghetti alle vongole* before a *secondo* of calamari rings stewed in a rich tomato sauce with peas and onions.

'How on earth did you survive before you met me?' Alfonso asks, pulling a face and leaning back in the chair he insists on taking at every meal, because it was the one he sat in on our first date.

Just as I'm about to make a witty riposte, I suddenly remember my only contribution to the meal – an apple crumble – in the oven. I race to the kitchen and am relieved to find I've just saved it from culinary hell.

As Alfonso compliments me on my baking prowess, he sticks a thermometer under one armpit and then teases me, saying the dessert has nonetheless propelled his temperature back to thirty-eight degrees. He swallows an antibiotic tablet as a massive boom comes from the street below, as if a house has been dynamited.

As we sip grappa, we suddenly realise that we have no hope of reaching Francesco's party in time for the midnight fireworks. It's at least a twenty minute walk and, more worryingly, Naples is starting to look like Beirut, with explosions ringing out practically every second.

'It's too dangerous, let's wait till twelve-thirty, then go,' Alfonso says.

We rug up and go outside to the terrace, where the air is thick with gunpowder. Another massive boom, strong enough to rock an office block, echoes around us and then, in the last ten seconds of 2006, there is a whir of crackers. On a terrace across the street I watch a young boy and a man lighting fireworks in empty wine bottles. The sparks are so close to the boy I can't watch.

'That's how my father lost part of his finger when he was a kid,' Alfonso says. 'How can a father let his child do that?'

A burst of colour sprays into the sky from Piazza del Plebiscito and the New Year is upon Naples and all its colour, noise and anarchy.

'*Ti amo*,' says Alfonso, his dark eyes glowing.

In truth, he has already told me these two important words. The first time I had a panic attack, before I realised the feeling was mutual.

Alfonso lipreads my response, drowned out by the exploding sky. Clown happy, we run inside to my bedroom to throw open the windows and watch the action on the street. From a terrace nearby a man throws a bag of rubbish from his balcony onto the street below. In Naples it's tradition, but the thought of bombing an innocent person below with leftover spaghetti and seafood juices just seems wrong.

My bedroom is suddenly as smoky as a night club. We shut the windows and go back to the terrace until around one o'clock. Inside we dance around the lounge room to Alfonso's CD, then finally collapse in a heap, while outside Naples continues to burn. So much for the party.

Amid the reports of New Year's Eve around Italy – with Naples recording over fifty fireworks injuries, the highest in the nation – is a curious story about the 'miracle' witnessed by a group of children. A statue of the Madonna apparently shed tears. Every so often in Naples, according to Alfonso, there are claims of such phenomena, as if the miracle of San Gennaro's blood isn't suitably outlandish.

I remember when I arrived in Naples how struck I was by the presence of the Madonna. The shrines are peppered throughout my neighbourhood and the historic centre.

Eager to understand their significance I make an appointment with Father Francesco Benincasa, director of the Study Centre of the Madonna dell'Arco, the city's most famous Virgin Mary. A serene figure, the Madonna dell'Arco generates a hysterical following, as do the a string of other Madonnas in the Campania region. On Easter Monday, she is the centre of a colourful celebration attended by thousands of pilgrims, who come to pay homage.

The cult of the Madonna dell'Arco harks back to Easter Monday in 1450, when one of two boys playing a ballgame with a mallet, botched a shot that knocked the trunk of tree shading a shrine of the Madonna. Angry about the shot, the youth hurled the ball at the Madonna. When it struck her left cheek, blood allegedly began to seep from her pale complexion.

Vesuvius dominates the skyline as Alfonso drives along the highway on a chilly January afternoon. We reach the church of the Madonna dell'Arco Sanctuary and walk to the reception to ask for Father Benincasa.

A short man with a Humpty Dumpty physique, Father Benincasa leads us to a small office. He takes off his beret and sits behind a desk gesturing for us to take the two chairs opposite him. I explain my interest in the Madonna, whose figure seems as iconic as the immigrant rose sellers in Rome. Father Benincasa nods and takes a moment before responding.

'The Madonna is appreciated in Naples because she represents family much more than the other saints.'

'She is a mother figure,' says Alfonso, echoing my thoughts.

'Yes, disposed to forgive,' says Father Benincasa. 'A saint can help you, but the Madonna is a *mamma*, with earthly sensibilities much more graspable for the everyman. She considers it important to not just save a person, but the whole environment which surrounds them.'

'It's fine to say the Madonna is like a mother who forgives,' says Alfonso, 'but how does that stop wrongdoers who think it's enough to ask forgiveness?'

Father Benincasa nods and smiles at Alfonso. He has no doubt heard the question before. 'Just as I try to reason with my flock, a mother who truly loves her child will find a way to make the child understand their error – even if she suffers in the process.'

It's not by chance, he points out, that devotion to the Madonna dell'Arco is often referred to as the devotion to the Mamma dell'Arco.

'Many people have her image in their homes, because she is part of their families, and they also come to visit her in church,' he says, adding that he knows a string of men with tattoos of the Madonna dell'Arco, including a man whose entire back is coloured with a portrait of her face.

'So, the Madonna is more powerful, in a sense, than God,' I suggest.

'Yes, maybe,' says Father Benincasa. 'Although He is everywhere, you can't touch God. In fact, when the pilgrims come to our church they don't have to search hard for the Madonna, she's not up high on a marble altar, she's physically close – you can stand in front of her portrait.'

I ask the priest why the Madonna dell'Arco, notwithstanding the many other festivals dedicated to the Madonna, seems to be the most prominent in Campania.

'It's not that the cult of the Madonna dell'Arco is more important, it simply offers a different way of expressing faith,' he says. 'The ceremony for the cult of the Madonna of Pompeii, for example, is very subdued.

'But when the pilgrims, or *fujenti,* arrive here on Easter Monday many of them are tired, nervous and full of contagious emotion. As they enter the church to give their thanks to the Madonna, various things can happen. Some feel sick, some pass out from the emotion, but some also fake fainting, and this is typically Neapolitan. I've seen groups of people sigh *ahhh* at the same time and faint in unison on their leader's cue.'

Father Benincasa chuckles and our eyes water with laughter. 'I tell them, "Listen, if you feel bad we can take you to the infirmary, but don't think we'll give you medicine. I'll give you a clip around the ears to wake you up!"'

'Perhaps the Madonna resonates more in Naples because women have a strong presence here,' I say.

'Yes, women have always saved the family in Naples, because grandmothers, mothers and sisters always defend the rights of their sons and brothers, even when they have done wrong.

'It's not that this doesn't happen in other cities, but they're more reserved, whereas here it creates headlines. Take any street in this city – if someone is ill, their suffering belongs to everyone around them. But in any other city it would be a private matter.'

Father Benincasa says the shrines to the Madonna, which are present in almost every street in his neighbourhood, are usually built by families who wish to thank her. If someone walks past one of the shrines, it's thought that their journey will be blessed.

Remembering the case reported in the papers a few days earlier of a nun who was arrested for being a 'messenger' for a Camorra clan, I ask the priest how many in his Easter Monday faithful are *camorristi*.

'Good and evil are present everywhere,' he says. 'But I don't think a mother makes distinctions between her children, she accepts them all. We just have to hope that a confession can bring about a real conversion.'

Naples has been compared to the sinning, biblical city of Gomorrah, making me wonder what on earth God must think of the city in its current state.

'God has much more sense than the Neapolitans, and I think sometimes He smiles when he sees that everyone speaks badly of Naples,' he says. 'I believe God suffers when He sees the iniquity that reigns in this city. But I also think there is a sense of solidarity that is re-awakening.

'It's useless if Neapolitans cry without responding constructively. There are so many people capable of bringing change to this city, and we need to encourage them, guide them.'

I smile wearily at the priest. 'Perhaps, if Neapolitans showed as much faith in Naples as the Madonna dell'Arco, change would come,' I suggest.

'Yes, but she continues to love her children, and in the same way we must love this city. If we truly love Naples, we will help her to be good.'

Father Benincasa accompanies us to the church museum, lined with hundreds of *ex voto*, or gifts, from the faithful to the Madonna dell'Arco. The first gift we see is a string of pearls with a note from a family giving their thanks to 'a grand mother' who is 'at the centre of our home'. There are framed sculptures of hands, legs, eyes, stomachs and even breasts – the healed body parts of people who remain indebted to the Madonna for performing a miracle for their health.

We move to a display of syringes and cigarette packets, with letters from people thanking the Madonna for having saved their loved ones from drug addiction.

When I reach a cabinet full of braids of human hair, Alfonso explains that they are symbols of vanity, and were probably offered to the Madonna by women who hope their gift will be seen as an act of selflessness. Appreciating the fixation many Italian women seem to have with their long manes, I suppress a giggle before moving along to a cabinet full of playing cards, witchcraft recipes and even voodoo dolls, relinquished by those who chose God over evil.

Spooked, I lead our group to some photos of the Easter Monday pilgrimage, with the faithful clad in white trousers and shirts. The images show people in tears and lying on the floor of the church, seemingly overcome by emotion. Beside the photos is a beautiful oil painting of the Madonna dell'Arco, with jewels adorning the canvas. Framed in a glass box, it's the portrait the faithful carry during the street procession on Easter Monday.

As we wind back through the museum, Father Benincasa recounts how he has lived in Switzerland, Germany and America. 'They all have fabulous cities, but they are cities without fantasy, and a city without fantasy has a population without hope,' he says.

'Fantasy is fine up to a point,' says Alfonso, ever the pragmatist. 'But I think Naples' problem is deeply cultural.'

'I agree,' Father Benincasa says. 'But historically it has always been like this. Don't forget that when a Neapolitan leaves his city, he uses all his intelligence and creativity, and he excels.'

'Yes, but here in Naples, he doesn't understand his capacity,' Alfonso says.

'That's because here a Neapolitan is stifled. He is only accused of being a *camorrista*, because the Camorra makes headlines, the garbage makes headlines…all these clichés!'

I relay *neomelodica* singer Sergio Donati's opinion that Naples makes headlines because it's the most loved city in the world.

'I think that's true,' says the priest, as we approach the church. 'Naples is a beautiful woman, a stupendous woman. She doesn't age, her beauty remains intact despite all those who want to ruin her. And she defends herself from attack, from those who want to destroy her. Naples will continue to live, to be beautiful, in spite of her enemies.'

I smile at Father Benincasa. 'Perhaps you, or the *signora,* can give me some advice,' I say with a wink, then explain that I've been doing some soul-searching to decide if I should stay in Naples for another year.

'You shouldn't ask God to resolve this problem, but you must ask God for the capacity to know how to look around you, to evaluate, and then choose,' says Father Benincasa, pulling at his beret. 'But I believe that at the point you are, it would be worth staying another year, because I think this year something will happen, something will be realised.'

'And after a year?'

'You will have had an experience that many others will never have, and you will be able to speak favourably of this city.'

We exchange warm handshakes and enter the church to sneak a look at the painting of the Madonna dell'Arco. Our timing is off – mass is on and we can only glimpse the beautiful portrait from afar.

Outside, the sun emerges from behind clouds for the first time all morning. As I reach for Alfonso's hand a ray of light catches the ruby and diamond setting of my late grandmother Oriel's ring. I've finally taken it from safekeeping and have restored it to my right ring finger. I no longer feel scared to wear something so precious.

I say a little *grazie* to the Madonna for all my fortunes. God may be present everywhere, as Father Benincasa says, but it's the Madonna I've felt watching over me since I arrived in Naples.

See Naples and learn how to live.

Acknowledgments

In Australia, enormous thanks to my parents and sisters and their families – I miss you all so much. Special thanks also to Deb Callaghan and to the energetic team at Hachette, in particular Bernadette Foley, Rebecca Roberts and Emma Rusher. To Nic Parkhill, Rob Kelly, Erin Kenneally, Mandy Roberts, Evie Gelastopoulous and Andrew White, Madeleine Coorey, Trudy Harris, Rebecca Aduckiewicz, James Waller and Kirsten Lathwell, for your constant cheer and support. To Iain Shedden, Bryce Corbett and Vivienne Stanton, for your advice and encouragement. Thanks also to Chris Maund and Julie Hodges at Mushroom.

In Italy, *grazie infinite a* Adriano Piccone, Massi Baccanico, Francesco Minicci and the extended Minicci family, Massimo Ricciuti, Federico and Novella Ricciuti, Manola Scalfari, Roberto Valentini, Paolo and Francesca Piccone, Carlo Giordano, Emiliano di Cupo, Mario Spada, Suzy and Delfo, Francesco Forni, Enzo Correale, Gigi Calvino, Nicoletta Ricciardelli, Anna and Claudia Caruso, Orfina and Sabrina, Giovanni Corona, Giovanni Durante, Father Luigi Merola, Amato Lamberti, Enrico Russo, Daniela Lepore, Eleanora Albanese and Jacobo Fo, Nicola Oddati, Gianni Maddaloni, Ricardo Dalisi, Rosa Russo Iervolino, Vincenzo Pagano, Corrado Catenacci, Father Francesco Benincasa, Silvana Fulcito, *quei bravi ragazzi di* 'A67, Valerio Iossa, Julian Bees and *un abbraccione a* Paolo Lista, Naples' cheeriest newsagent.

To Carmen Micillo at publisher Tullio Pironti and Charlotte Humphrey at IB Tauris.

Special thanks also to Daniela Andreoli, Vivianna Famulari and Charlotte Owen, for your support from afar.

At ANSA, my enormous gratitude to Carlo Gambalonga, Anna Maria Miele, Stefano Polli, Mario Zaccheria, Rosaria Caramiello and Enzo La Penna; and to past and present colleagues at ANSA*med*: Francesco Tedesco (for answering all my questions), Nando Piantadosi (your generosity knows no bounds), Benedetta Guerrera, Annalisa Rapana and Tania D'Amico (for helping me write all those letters), Marco Cesario, Alfonso Abagnale, Mario Zaccaria, Enrico Tibuzzi and Antonella Tarquini. Thanks for putting up with my deadline stress.

Heartfelt thanks to my Neapolitan family, Enzo and Maria Rosaria Muras, for your affection and generosity, and to the warm and welcoming Procidani, in particular Enzo and Gilda, Glorianna and those who work or loiter at Bar Capriccio.

Last but not least, to Alfonso, for your *amore* and infinite patience.

Sources

Books

Allum, Felia, *Camorristi, Politicians and Businessmen: The Transformation of Organised Crime in Post-war Naples*, Northern Universities Press, Leeds, 2003

Andolfo, Matilde, *Il Diario di Annalisa*, Tullio Pironti Editore, Naples, 2005

Behan, Tom, *See Naples and Die: The Camorra and Organised Crime*, IB Tauris & Co. Ltd, London, 2002

Bocca, Giorgio, *Napoli Siamo Noi*, Giangiacomo Feltrinelli Editore, Milan, 2006

Hazzard, Shirley, *The Bay of Noon*, Picador, New York, 2003

Lamberti, Amato, *Lazzaroni, Napoli sono anche loro*, Graus Editore, Naples, 2006

Lewis, Norman, *Naples '44*, Eland, London, 2002

Saviano, Roberto, *Gomorra*, Feltrinelli Editore, Milan, 2006

Serao, Matilde, *Il Ventre di Napoli*, Avagliano Editore, Rome, 2002

Striano, Enzo, *Il Resto Di Niente*, Arnoldo Mondadori Editore, Milan, 2005

Films

Cosi' Parlo' Bellavista (Italy, 1980), directed by Luciano De Crescenzo

Ieri, Oggi e Domani (Italy, 1963), directed by Vittorio de Sica

Il Camorrista (Italy, 1986), directed by Giuseppe Tornatore

Il Sindaco del Rione Sanità (Italy, 1960), directed by Eduardo de Filippo

L'oro di Napoli (Italy, 1954), directed by Vittorio de Sica

Miseria e Nobiltà (Italy, 1954), directed by Mario Mattoli

Napoli Milionaria (Italy, 1950), directed by Eduardo de Filippo

No Grazie il Caffè Mi Rende Nervoso (Italy, 1982), directed by Lodovico Gasparini

Operazione San Gennaro (Italy, 1966), directed by Dino Risi

Ricomincio da Tre (Italy, 1980), directed by Massimo Troisi

Scusate il Ritardo (Italy, 1982), directed by Massimo Troisi

New from Penelope Green
Coming in 2009

GIRL BY SEA

As a hapless single woman with a tired-looking pantry and barely there cooking prowess, the only thing I knew with certainty was that a male who knew his way about the kitchen won sizeable brownie points. And so it was that after a string of unsatisfying flirtations in Naples a comely local suddenly wooed me with his *cucina*. Don't get me wrong. Alfonso has many winning qualities, but he is at his best in the kitchen.

While my accent will always brand me a foreigner in Italy, I have become one hundred per cent Italian in at least one sense: I am food *obsessed*. And I was soon fully committed to Alfonso's meatballs – spiced with garlic and pine nuts and drowning in a rich tomato *ragu* – not to mention his signature *spaghetti alle vongole*. After my salad-heavy single days, every meal lovingly prepared by my Neapolitan squeeze was a gastronomic affair.

Not surprisingly, I was more than willing to move in with Alfonso, and keen for a dose of the quiet life after spending two years in chaotic Naples, I was happy to go with his suggestion and check out rental options on Procida, an island off the Campania coast, an hour or so by ferry from Naples.

Swept away by a luminous and sprawling apartment with a terrace rivalling the size of a rugby pitch and a lounge-room window offering views to our island neighbour, Capri, we signed a year-long lease and piled our belongings into Alfonso's butter-box car.

It wasn't until the ferry began to ease into Procida's port that I was suddenly gripped by panic. *Am I, are we, barking mad?*

We'd barely been together two months, were still in that blissful honeymoon phase and convinced that we could start a new life on a speck in the Tyrrhenian Sea.

I suppressed the small pangs of fear and squeezed Alfonso's hand as we watched the ramp being slowly winched down. The desire to test our relationship was too strong. The idea of discovering our new island home simply too appetising…